MONEY ENOUGH

Everyday Practices for Living Faithfully in the Global Economy

Douglas A. Hicks

 JOSSEY-BASS
A Wiley Imprint
www.josseybass.com

Published by Jossey-Bass
A Wiley Imprint
989 Market Street, San Francisco, CA 94103-1741—www.josseybass.com

Jossey-Bass books and products are available through most bookstores. To contact Jossey-Bass directly call our Customer Care Department within the U.S. at 800-956-7739, outside the U.S. at 317-572-3986, or fax 317-572-4002.

Jossey-Bass also publishes its books in a variety of electronic formats. Some content that appears in print may not be available in electronic books.

Library of Congress Cataloging-in-Publication Data
Hicks, Douglas A.
Money enough : everyday practices for living faithfully in the global economy / Douglas Hicks.
    p. cm. — (The practices of faith series)
    Includes bibliographical references and index.
    ISBN 978-0-7879-9775-5 (pbk.)
 1. Finance, Personal—Religious aspects. 2. Money—Religious aspects.
    3. Quality of life. I. Title.
    HG179.H458 2010
    332.024—dc22
    2009041096

Printed in the United States of America
FIRST EDITION
PB Printing   10 9 8 7 6 5 4 3 2 1

THE PRACTICES OF FAITH SERIES

Dorothy C. Bass, Series Editor

Practicing Our Faith:
A Way of Life for a Searching People
Dorothy C. Bass, Editor

Receiving the Day: Christian Practices
for Opening the Gift of Time
Dorothy C. Bass

Money Enough: Everyday Practices
for Living Faithfully in the Global Economy
Douglas A. Hicks

Testimony: Talking Ourselves into Being Christian
Thomas G. Long

In the Midst of Chaos:
Caring for Children as Spiritual Practice
Bonnie Miller-McLemore

Honoring the Body: Meditations on a Christian Practice
Stephanie Paulsell

A Song to Sing, A Life to Live:
Reflections on Music as Spiritual Practice
Donald Saliers and Emily Saliers

Lord, Have Mercy:
Praying for Justice with Conviction and Humility
Claire E. Wolfteich

Contents

For my teachers

Editor's Foreword

Not long ago, the global economy was shaken by the worst financial crisis since the Great Depression. I did not realize what was happening until spectacular stories of failure and fraud on Wall Street began to appear on the front page of my daily newspaper, but soon everyone I knew was experiencing the impact in one way or another. As jobs disappeared, retirement savings shrank, and house values took a nosedive, Jesus' admonition not to store up for ourselves treasures on earth seemed remarkably relevant, even if it was not especially comforting.

Today many people have relinquished careless assumptions about the economy and their place in it. In a volatile economy with a minimal safety net, massive unemployment, and widespread hunger, concern about earthly well-being is justified; after all, human flourishing is a concern Scripture places close to the heart of God, a generous creator who intends that everyone be safe and fed. At the same time, a new mood of thoughtfulness has taken hold. What is it that we truly need and desire? many are asking. Have we pursued lifestyles of abundance when what we really long for is abundant life? And how do our economic desires and pursuits affect others, especially those who suffer most in the global economy in both "good" times and "bad"?

These are not questions to be asked in a time of crisis and then put away until the next downturn. These are enduring questions, and how we answer them orders our way of living in the world. How we answer shapes our sense of who we are as human beings. How we answer—not just in words but also through our actions—shapes our relationships with God and with our neighbors near and far.

In this exciting and challenging book, Douglas A. Hicks speaks directly to such questions and concerns. As a scholar with training in both economics and theology, and also as a Christian minister, husband, father, and friend, he brings a unique mix of helpful and engaging insights to this study of everyday economic life. Those who seek a life-giving way of life in the midst of today's complex economy will find him a wonderfully helpful teacher. He is honest about the difficulties entailed in pursuing a life-giving way of life in today's economy, but he does not allow these difficulties to paralyze our search for a way of life that is abundant in the things that matter most—justice, mercy, right relations with others, and God's love for each of us and for the world as a whole.

I am delighted to add *Money Enough: Everyday Practices for Living Faithfully in the Global Economy* to the Practices of Faith Series, which offers resources drawn from the deep wells of Christian belief and experience to those who long to live with integrity in the rapidly changing world of the twenty-first century. Like other books in the series, it is addressed both to committed Christians searching for ways to practice their faith more fully and to people of every faith who are concerned about human flourishing. Hicks's title—like his book as a whole—reflects the combination of wide vision and down-to-earth detail that shapes the entire series. Here we set our daily concerns in the encompassing context of God's love for the entire world, across time and around the globe. And here we ask how our everyday practices can be shaped in ways that reflect and respond to this great love.

As you explore these pages and consider how you may live more faithfully in the midst of global economic change, I encourage you to find companions with whom to discuss, pray about, and live your economic life. To assist you in this endeavor, a *Guide for Learning, Conversation, and Growth* based on this book is available at www.practicingourfaith.org.

Dorothy C. Bass
Editor, Practices of Faith Series
November, 2009

Preface

W e long for a rest from the hustle and bustle of demanding work. We hunger for more time with family. We thirst for economic security. We await the day when we and our neighbors can afford health care. We hope for a world without pollution and poverty.

Those of us who are people of faith believe, or want to believe, that our faith has something important to say about economic life. Jesus spoke of the sparrows and told us not to worry about our food and clothing. He said that worrying could not add an hour to a life—wisdom confirmed today by medical experts, who say that the stress of modern consumer culture tends to shorten our lives. Jesus taught us to pray that our debts would be forgiven and that we would forgive the debts of our neighbor. Meanwhile, we know that credit-card and educational indebtedness is devastating millions of Americans, and national debt plagues not only the United States but many of the countries of the developing or "two-thirds" world. Jesus spoke of economic issues more often than any other "worldly" topic.

Many biblical texts offer counsel for working and spending—and recreating and sharing. Yet, although we might not want to admit this thought, it is easy to discount biblical wisdom as too quaint, archaic, or simplistic. After all, we are living in fast-paced, complicated times. Jesus told his disciples to take only the sandals and tunics they were wearing, and to expect the hospitality of strangers. He talked far more about giving stuff away than about earning income or investing it. Are these texts to be taken literally—and if so, what would it mean to wear tunics and sandals in Columbus, Ohio, or Hartford, Connecticut? It would be easy to write off Jesus' specific economic practices as nice but not hard-edged enough for modern commercial life.

The challenge, in a nutshell, is that the Christian economic ethic that we find in the Bible is focused primarily on an economy based on person-to-person relationships. Although ancient Jews and Christians were situated in imperial economies, carpenters knew their clients, and buyers and sellers interacted in markets that were located in neighborhoods or village centers. Alms were meant to support local people in need, although communities sometimes took offerings for needy people and groups far away. Even in those cases, though, there was some personal connection across the miles.

In today's global economy, we do not usually have personal relationships with people who shape our economic lives. Some might know the local baker, but most people buy bread from the grocery store. We are still less likely to know who made our clothes, or even where they were made. Even if the tag is marked with a particular country's name, odds are good that the garment was made in a variety of steps around the world. The scale of the global financial system means that our investments and financial transactions are rarely personal. In fact, given the functionality and ubiquity of ATMs and online banking, it is possible to do our banking without ever interacting with a human being at all. We need to update an economic ethic designed for personal relations in order to frame our decisions and actions in an impersonal, global market.

What are people trying to live out faith commitments to do? At present, there appear to be two leading options. On one hand, we can "baptize" current economic practices, perhaps through prosperity theology or the gospel of self-help. On the other hand, we can reject the world and retreat into the so-called simple life, with a wholesale rejection of television, restaurants, and the like. The first option is too easy a way out. The second is nearly impossible. And, even to the extent that it is doable, it is an individualistic opt-out approach to what is a society-wide problem.

A colleague put the dilemma this way: "We need a middle way; I am not able to make my own clothes, as in the opt-out approach, even if I had the time. On the other hand, I can do more than still driving my SUV but being a little nicer at Starbucks."[1]

We can do better than either of these choices. The Christian story offers a saner and truer way of living than unbridled consumerism. It calls us not to renounce the market but to humanize it. In our everyday practices—how we work and rest, want and need, spend and save, serve and engage public life—our faith provides us rich resources for thinking and acting. Our everyday economic activities can become practices within a well-lived Christian life.

Some see the solution in fleeing from the material world into the natural world. We must surely acknowledge the beauty and wonder of God's creation, but we mustn't think that the answer to our economic anxiety is to renounce material practices altogether. Rather, we need to understand all of life, from the bread we break in communion to the bread we buy, bake, or eat at home, as part of the same embodied life we are called to live in this good creation. Our life requires bread, even if we require much more than that. Our economic goods and economic relationships should be, and can be, an inextricable part of a faithful, joyful life. Economics can be about how we manage our personal and collective practices within God's household, which is all of creation.

This book offers reflections for people of faith and other thoughtful readers who want to shape everyday lives, Monday through Saturday, that connect to the things they declare and pray for in worship on Sunday. Even to put the problem in terms of Sunday-versus-Monday, however, overlooks the pressures that many of us face to work on Sundays, too. Or, after laboring long hours throughout the week, it often seems that the most worshipful thing we can do on Sunday is to sleep in, relax, or go for a walk in God's creation. This book takes up the task of weaving work and worship, God and Mammon, Sunday and Monday into an integrated Christian life.

"Money enough" is shorthand for a vision of everyday economic practices in which money is a necessary but not a sufficient part. The Gospel promises abundant life, but the money part of abundance has more to do with achieving adequate economic conditions than with getting rich. Abundance entails an overall quality of life, and thus so much more than material goods. Each chapter of the book takes up a different economic practice, including laboring, providing, doing justice, and so on. In all, there are nine such topics that together touch on the very mundane but also very perplexing aspects of our economic life. Considering these topics will also allow us to fit our individual and local practices into the wider challenges of a global economy. The introductory chapter begins with "surviving" in this economy—but we do not lose sight of hope for an economy in which we and our neighbors, near and far, have money enough not merely to survive but to flourish.

Douglas A. Hicks
Richmond, Virginia
November, 2009

Acknowledgments

I dedicate this book to my teachers and could not have written it without them. Indeed, I became a college professor because of the ways they have lived out their own vocations. These teachers—from school, church, and higher education—have modeled not only excellence but also integrity. From their respective vantage points they have helped me grapple with fundamental questions of economics, ethics, and faith. They have communicated their commitments by teaching them and by putting them into practice.

The book includes stories of three of these—the economist Charles Ratliff Jr., the religious ethicist Thomas E. McCollough Jr., and the philosopher-economist Amartya Sen. But many others deserve mention as well. Teachers at Park Tudor School, including Joanne and Tom Black, William L. Browning Sr., and David A. Kivela, taught me to think critically and appreciatively about the world. I will long remember James D. Miller, a youthful youth minister, leading a group of privileged high schoolers to Mexico in order to work with people suffering abject poverty. William G. Enright, as senior pastor at Second Presbyterian Church in Indianapolis, encouraged people of means to nurture their philanthropy; he continues this good work at the Lake Institute on Faith and Giving.

In addition to Charles Ratliff, his colleagues in Davidson College's Economics Department—Clark G. Ross, Peter N. Hess, David W. Martin, and Dennis R. Appleyard—helped me learn that theirs is a discipline with a moral purpose: improving the human condition. They have been valuable teachers. Professors in the Religion Department at Davidson helped me discover the fundamental ways that faith intersects with the practices of economics and society. In particular, I have learned much from R. David Kaylor and Trent Foley. The late Lois A. "Sandy" Kemp led my college semester in Spain program and also taught me to appreciate the cultures of Latin America. She enjoyed being called *tacaña*—"stingy" is the colloquial translation, but I prefer to think of her as financially prudent.

Mary McClintock Fulkerson, Teresa Berger, and the late Frederick Herzog guided me at Duke Divinity School to understand the integration of faith and social practices, including work for a more just economic order. At Harvard, Ronald F. Thiemann, Diana L. Eck, Harvey Cox, the late John Rawls, Stephen A. Marglin, J. Bryan Hehir, and Cornel West—as well as David Hollenbach at Boston College—challenged me to understand the myriad connections of religion and society.

I am also grateful to generous colleagues who agreed to read this manuscript: Alexander Evans, Juliette Jeanfreau, Rebecca Todd Peters, Mark Valeri, Jonathan Wight, and Thad Williamson. The research skills of librarian Lucretia McCulley are unparalleled. I also thank others who provided me assistance on specific issues or topics: Samuel L. Adams, Robert D. Austin, David D. Burhans, R. Charles Grant, Sandra J. Peart, Terry L. Price, and Marianne Vermeer. Their insights made this a more readable and integrated book (though any errors or inconsistencies that remain are my own).

It is also fitting to recognize the communities of faith to which I have belonged. I have profound respect for the leaders and parishioners of these congregations for the ways in which they have grappled with issues of faith and economic life: Second Presbyterian Church in Indianapolis; Davidson College Presbyterian Church in Davidson, North Carolina; St. John's Presbyterian Church and Northgate Presbyterian Church in Durham, North Carolina; Clarendon Hill

Presbyterian Church in Somerville, Massachusetts; and Bon Air Presbyterian Church in Richmond, Virginia.

I want to thank Dorothy C. Bass for her invitation to write this book as part of the Practices of Faith Series. She has the gift of making insightful criticisms with genuine grace. I am honored to be a colleague with the authors in this series and with participants in a number of initiatives of the Valparaiso Project on the Education and Formation of People in Faith and the Lilly Endowment, Inc. I also wish to thank Sheryl Fullerton at Jossey-Bass for believing in this project and supporting my writing. I also acknowledge Sheryl's fine publishing colleagues who helped move this book from manuscript to reality, including Joanne Clapp Fullagar, Alison Knowles, Hilary Powers, and Carrie Wright.

The ideas in this book draw upon and, I hope, bring together work I have done in various academic and church settings. I have presented some of these ideas at Vanderbilt University, through the sponsorship of its Religion and Economy faculty research group, and at the Maryville Symposium on Faith and the Liberal Arts at Maryville College. I appreciate the generous hospitality of the faculty and staff at both institutions. This book includes some material from the latter presentation, which is published in the *Maryville Symposium Proceedings* (Maryville, TN: Maryville College, 2007). I have also adapted for this book some of the material from two previously published chapters and an essay: "Making a Good Living," in Susan R. Briehl, ed., *On Our Way* (Nashville, TN: Upper Room Books, 2010); "Global Inequality," in *Christian Reflection: A Series in Faith and Ethics* 24 (Waco, TX: Center of Christian Ethics, Baylor University: summer 2007); and "Global Poverty and Bono's Celebrity Activism: An Analysis of Moral Imagination and Motivation," in Douglas A. Hicks and Mark Valeri, eds., *Global Neighbors: Christian Faith and Moral Obligation in Today's Economy* (Grand Rapids, MI: Eerdmans, 2008).

I thank the students in a course on Christianity and the market economy, which I offered at Harvard Divinity School in 2003, and at Union Theological Seminary and Presbyterian School of Christian Education in 2007, for engaging these questions in a sustained way over a semester. And I acknowledge my wonderful colleagues at the Jepson School of Leadership Studies at the University of Richmond.

My wife, Catherine L. Bagwell, read the entire manuscript, chapter by chapter. She commented with particular interest upon the sections related to sharing within the household. I reflect in the book about the personal nature of the challenges of living with integrity in the global economy. Catherine is a true companion in this shared enterprise, especially as we seek, however imperfectly, to convey our values to our children, Noah and Ada. More than once, I have recalled the title of fellow series author Bonnie J. Miller-McLemore's book, *In the Midst of Chaos: Caring for Children as Spiritual Practice.*

I hope that, out of the hustle and bustle of my own efforts to integrate work, family, church, and community, this book offers readers some insights for responding in their own way to the particular economic challenges that they face.

Chapter 1

SURVIVING

❧

Give me neither poverty nor riches;
feed me with the food that I need.
—Proverbs 30:8b

Where did our money go? In less than eighteen months, the 60 percent of Americans who have money in the stock market saw the value of their holdings cut in half, as the Dow Jones Industrial Average dove from a high of over 14,000 to a low below 7,000. People with 401(k) retirement accounts watched their nest eggs shrivel. To make matters worse, Bernard Madoff made off with close to $65 billion through his global Ponzi scheme. That investment opportunity was really a house of cards, and the cards were human beings and charitable organizations whose entire fortunes toppled over.

MAKING ENDS MEET

Many people have lost not only their money but their homes, too. In the postwar period, owning a home became a symbol of economic prosperity and the American dream itself. The tax system and other government programs created strong incentives for people to become owners and not to remain renters. But too many people got in over their heads with sub-prime loans or excessive mortgage payments. They have lost their houses, or they are struggling to make their mortgage payments. Most other homeowners have experienced a significant decline in the value of their real estate.

In this tough economic climate, how much is enough to survive? Retirees and those ready to retire want to know. With our market culture placing such high value on economic productivity, they fear that they will be disdained as burdens on society. And they worry that they might become actual burdens on their loved ones. Worse yet, some see the possibility that no one will be there to take care of them if their money runs out. Given the short-term turmoil and the more permanent culture of productivity, retirement today can seem like a huge risk.

For parents working to make ends meet, how much is enough? Kids need clothes, and shoes, and food. Are summer camps a luxury or a necessity? What about cell phones—are they a needless expense or are they a necessary ingredient of social participation for today's young people? And don't mention the word *college*. Tuition has increased faster in the past three decades than almost any other good or service in the American economy. It's now $80,000 for four years of a public university or $200,000 for a private one—can you be serious?

Young adults are graduating from high school and college with grim job prospects. Compounding the effects of a shrunken economy, which supports fewer jobs, is the reality that potential retirees have not exited the workforce. Elders who choose to keep working—or do so because they cannot afford to retire in this economy—thus delay the domino effect that opens up entry-level positions for young adults. As a result, many twenty-somethings have extended their education, which brings them face to face with the higher costs of higher education.

In official terms, how much do people need to survive? The U.S. Census Bureau's poverty threshold is about $17,000 for a family of three and about $22,000 for a family of four.[1] These figures are based on an old budget formula that doesn't take account of the disproportionately large rises, over recent decades, in the costs of housing, health care, and child care. Yet, even when the poverty line stands this low, an adult working a minimum-wage job for forty hours a week, fifty-two weeks a year, cannot lift a family of three to that level—at least not without additional help from the government. Shouldn't working a full-time job pay enough to keep a small family out of poverty?

Even those whose earnings place them far above the poverty line say they have difficulty making ends meet. People earning $200,000 per year talk about how they can't afford to live near their work because housing costs in many urban and suburban areas remain so high. Others who make much less lament the pressures they feel as part of a squeezed middle class. Even before the recent recession, the average wage of the American worker had not risen in thirty years, once the figure is adjusted for inflation. Meanwhile, the cost of many goods has been skyrocketing. These are issues far more enduring than any single economic up or down cycle. Recent American economic prosperity does not appear to have made the "average American" much better off in financial terms. We wonder if we can leave economic conditions for the next generation that are at least as good as what we have experienced.

Economic pressures add another source of worry as well: difficulties in balancing work and the rest of life. Fifty years ago, experts predicted that technology would reduce work hours and increase leisure—but these projections have proven false. Women's rate of participation in the labor force nearly doubled from 1950 to 2000, and the average number of hours worked by each woman in the workforce increased significantly. Women have taken jobs outside the home in record numbers not merely because of heightened public consciousness of women's equal humanity but also as a matter of economic necessity. For their part, men in the labor force have also increased their working hours. Average vacation time per year has decreased. In short, more people are working, and they are working longer hours with shorter vacations, than was the case three or four decades ago.[2]

Runaway consumerism exacerbates the resulting problems. Put pressures on money and pressures on time together and add strong desires for consumer goods, and you get what the economist Juliet Schor has called the "work and spend" cycle. When people want consumer goods more than they want additional free time, they work longer to pay the bills, and the work-and-spend cycle spins faster and faster. The technological goods that seemed once to promise leisure—appliances, computers, smart phones, and the like—instead become desires that lead to more work.

Of course, our work-and-spend society has an underside as well: many people are unemployed. While those who have jobs are toiling long hours (with fewer coworkers to bear the load) and trying to keep up with work, family, and leisure, people without jobs strive merely to make ends meet. It takes a huge investment of time to do a job search, and it can all seem to be wasted in a tough job market.

These economic realities raise the decibel level on a question that has long existed just beneath the surface of this highly productive consumer economy: How much is enough?

GLOBALIZING OUR VIEW

For some three billion people on the planet, all this talk of wealth and money's rise and fall is merely fantasy. In global terms, everyone reading this book is rich. The median income in the world, once it is adjusted to account for different purchasing power in different countries, is less than $2,000 a year. The average income in the United States is in the top 10 percent of world incomes—and probably in the top 5 percent.[3] At the other end of the distribution, the figures are staggering. Roughly a billion people earn less than $1 per day. According to the World Bank, 1.4 billion people live below $1.25 per day, adjusted for purchasing power: This is the world standard for absolute, or extreme, poverty. Nearly half of the world's population earns less than $2 a day. In a globalizing economy, $730 a year does not go a long way. According to the Food and Agriculture Organization of the United Nations, nearly one billion people were undernourished in 2007, with the economic crisis of 2008 pushing countless others into this condition. And the World Health Organization and UNICEF estimate that about 1.1 billion people lack access to safe drinking water.[4] *Surviving* has a different sound, a different degree of severity, for people living on the margins of the global economy.

The largest Wall Street bailout, which became law in October 2008, carried a staggering price tag: $700 billion. As the bill worked its way through the U.S. Congress and was signed by President George W. Bush, I kept coming back to one thought. This whole process seemed to be going so fast—and at the end, it had taken less than two weeks. By contrast, for a decade, I have been reading about how much it would cost to provide basic education, clean drinking water, safe sewage, basic health care, and adequate nutrition for all people in the world. The best estimates for meeting *all* of the basic needs for everyone are on the order of $200 billion per year. To be sure, analysts debate this number—especially the "transaction costs" to get basic goods and services into the hands of those who need them. But this figure gives a sense of the magnitude of the challenge. The cost would be shared by the industrialized countries of the world until the poorest countries were to reach a point of development—as early as 2025—at which time they could provide a sufficient safety net for their citizens without further foreign assistance.[5] United Nations officials, economists, and celebrities have urged world leaders to find the means to fund these basic services. But all along, naysayers and critics have called the amount of money "unrealistic." They have said that it is "naive" to think that we could make significant headway on these problems.

Are we left to believe that it is unrealistic to find $200 billion a year to fight poverty, while in our country alone we can fund, in a matter of weeks, $700 billion to rescue our financial institutions? It is all a matter of priorities. It is a matter of our imagination—of what we are willing to believe is possible. And it will require collective action.

Addressing such questions is never simple or straightforward. In fact, some have argued that if Wall Street had been allowed to fail, all would have been worse off, and more poverty, in the United States and internationally, would have ensued. There is a legitimate argument to be made that the bailout was necessary precisely because the failure of the financial system hit the most vulnerable people the hardest. But if poverty were a chief concern, would it not have been a good idea to dedicate at least a share of the $700 billion to direct poverty alleviation, in the United States and around the world?

Practicing the Economics of "Enough"

It is easy to become disheartened, or at least perplexed and frustrated, amid these financial realities. According to the standard definition of the field (introduced by Lionel Robbins in 1932), *economics* concerns the allocation of scarce goods for competing uses.[6] Scarcity and competition are the key concepts. This view assumes that there is no way to satisfy all needs and wants. Human beings are seen always to prefer more of a good to less of it, always trying to maximize their self-interest while everyone else is doing likewise. Hence, the starting place is a competitive marketplace in which it is impossible to satisfy everyone—or even anyone—completely. This understanding of economics affirms the view that there is never enough.

In this book, while acknowledging the valuable insights that economics can offer, I develop a different approach by shifting our thinking about economic life in theological directions. We will view our economic decision making as one of our most important attempts to live a good and faithful life. We will place our own well-being, and that of our loved ones, within the context of six and a half billion other people also seeking to make ends meet on God's green earth. Thinking about money in our individual or family life is difficult enough. To connect our personal-finance questions with U.S. society or the global economy is an even more daunting challenge. Yet that is precisely the aim of these chapters. As we think about where our money goes, what the ends are that we are trying to meet with money, and how much money is enough, we are called to connect our own economic realities with the global economy.

My college economics professor, Charles Ratliff Jr., would begin his courses with an exercise in etymology. He would break down the word *economics* into its components, the Greek words *oikos* (household) and *nomos* (law), that is, the law of the household. He meant to convey to all his young economists that economics is chiefly about managing the household. And the scale of household could range from the personal level to the global one. This idea also makes it possible to see the relationship between economic concerns and ecological ones—*oikos* is the root word for both. Theologically speaking, when we talk about the global household, we are talking about God's creation.

As I got to know Dr. Ratliff during my time as an economics major, I learned that this perspective on the discipline was integrally tied to his own faith as a Methodist. I discovered that he practiced in his life what he professed in the classroom. Dr. Ratliff had spent three years teaching at the Forman Christian College in Lahore, Pakistan, sharing his insights into economics even as he learned a great deal about human and economic development from his hosts. Just as significant, when he returned from Pakistan to teach for three more decades at Davidson College, Dr. Ratliff quietly lived out his faith commitments. He helped lead his church into local and international missions, he worked on antipoverty campaigns in Davidson and neighboring Charlotte, North Carolina, and he helped establish a vibrant Habitat for Humanity chapter in town. Most of all, his students experienced his passion for justice and peace—*God's shalom,* he would call it—through his vocation of teaching.

Dr. Ratliff's faith-based view of managing the global household so as to provide enough for all people is certainly consistent with many voices in economics. Indeed, many economists see their discipline and their craft as aligned with the high goal of improving the lives of people around the world. Adam Smith, the eighteenth-century founder of classical economics, advocated for subsidized public education and viewed free trade as a means by which impoverished workers could better their lot as the national standard of living went up. Alfred Marshall, the greatest economist at the beginning of the twentieth century, stated it very well: "The question of whether it is really impossible that all should start in the world with a fair chance of leading a cultured life, free from the pains of poverty . . . [gives] to economic studies their chief and their highest interest."[7]

Viewing economics as managing God's household redefines our thinking about money in terms beyond the mere pursuit of our individual self-interest. It requires us to think carefully about doing justice, sharing burdens and bounty, and meeting needs of people we care about deeply and people we do not even know or like. This framework faces head-on the realities of scarcity of many economic goods—some as vital as safe drinking water and nutritious food. Yet it also entails the fundamental conviction that there is enough for all people to live decent lives worthy of their human dignity.

A great tension pervades any attempt to think morally and theologically about economic life in our time. On one hand, financial questions are fundamental to our very survival, and thus they deserve close attention. On the other hand, we need a critical perspective on our own tendency to confuse survival with comfort. *Survival* can denote an absolute condition, but it can also become a relative term that shifts upwards with prosperity. We must learn to recognize and often resist our propensity always to want more—no easy task when the commercial messages we receive every day appeal to our deepest longings. If we do not learn to discern and even limit our desires for material goods, we will never have enough.

SPENDING OR SAVING?

"The world is too much with us," the poet William Wordsworth wrote in 1807; "late and soon, /Getting and spending, we lay waste our powers."[8] In Wordsworth's native England, the Industrial Revolution was transforming cities and lives. Wordsworth, who had been born in the beauty and relative tranquility of northwest England's Lake District, became disillusioned in his adult years by what he saw as the emptiness of modern urban life. After earning his degree at Trinity College of Cambridge University, he traveled to France and Germany, experiencing a more cosmopolitan lifestyle. But Wordsworth ultimately preferred the pastoral life, and he returned to the Lake District, where he could be closer to nature and avoid the excesses and bustle of commercial England.

Today, the work-spend pressures of consumerism tempt some people to long for this kind of quieter, more pastoral lifestyle. We always seem to be chasing our tails, working more and spending more, just to keep up. Ads for every product under the sun bombard us at each turn—the billboards, the pop-up ads, the junk mail. There appears to be little escape from anxiety and the hectic pace of our economy. But without a special calling to be a Romantic poet or to live off the land, most of us will remain in our urban and suburban contexts. The task is not to escape those places but to discover and develop practices that allow us to reject the excesses of consumerism.

Americans seem to have responded to the economic slowdown precisely by saving more and spending less. (At least some of this trend results from tighter restrictions limiting consumers' access to credit.) The personal savings rate in the country increased during the recession, to 3 or 4 percent, the highest rates seen this decade. This is the advice that many analysts had given Americans for years—spend less and save more. Ironically, in the face of a recession, policymakers appeared befuddled, and they offered confusing if not contradictory advice. Some said that Americans should spend more in order to stimulate the economy. The marketers and communications departments of major corporations joined the chorus of politicians, deftly turning toward selling the act of spending as the patriotic thing to do. The struggling car companies have called "all of us" to pull together and weather this storm. Why not buy a GM or Chrysler car and show the can-do American spirit? A construction industry representative encourages people to renovate their homes, calling it their patriotic contribution to stimulating the economy.[9] After all, when the rates of return on saving and investing appear to be small (or negative), an alternative use of money—buying consumer goods—has increased appeal. Being told it is also a way to love your country may boost such spending even more.

INTERPRETING THE CRISIS

Where is our moral compass to make sense of this economic situation? How little public voice there has been from religious leaders to help us understand the spiritual or ethical dimensions of the crisis. At one level, this makes sense. It is hard enough to think carefully about economic life from a theological perspective. It is even more difficult when complex, unprecedented shocks hit the financial system. Still, this is a time at which moral and theological insights can be of real value.

Christian views on the recession belong under the category of *theodicy*—understanding God's role in the face of suffering. Why do bad things happen to good people? Why do bad things happen at all? Does God allow them, or does God even cause them? Does God punish evildoers? And so on. Whether we are focusing on struggles within our personal lives, American society, or the global economy, we should be asking them in terms of theodicy.

Christian thinkers have been all over the map on the recession, what it means, and how to escape it. Some preachers and theologians have seen the economic crisis as a lesson for people who have become so dependent on earthly things that they have forgotten God. So the crisis is a blessing in disguise, a call back to faithfulness—and dependence—on God.[10] It is not a big leap to suggest from this view that God caused the crisis. The more common approach is to blame the crisis on greedy and deceptive actions by bankers, mortgage companies, and captains of industry. Those who take this view call the crisis a condemnation—the chickens coming home to roost—of these morally repugnant actors.

I read the breakdown of the financial system as a disastrous event that God did not cause. It was, instead, a result of human failures. God allows an economic collapse to take place as a result of the freedoms that God grants people to pursue their ends. But the human abuses of that freedom were both individual and systemic. That is, the human sin present in the economy is not a matter of a few bad apples who took advantage, though there surely are people who bear particular culpability due to the egregiousness of their actions. But that is not the key point. The Archbishop of Canterbury, Rowan Williams, stated: "It is not for believers to join in the search for scapegoats, because there will always be, for the religious self, an awareness of complicity in social evil."[11]

All of us who invested without asking questions about where our money was going have some complicity—and even culpability. I don't mean only those who got caught up in the too-good-to-be-true Ponzi schemes. How many of us with 401(k) plans thought long or hard about how our accounts were showing steady, strong growth? Which of us who took out mortgages wondered whether we should be buying a house as nice as the one we were purchasing? For my part, I remember well—when my wife and I bought our first house—the sense of intimidation and awe at the number of zeros in the loan amount and the fact that we were committing to make mortgage payments almost reaching to our projected retirement years. Those feelings should probably still be with us every month when our mortgage payment is due. But instead, the payments have become a routine practice—even more so with the automatic deduction coming from our bank account.

How many people did not focus first upon the recession's impacts on our own families? Even though we knew, or should have known, that the widespread effects would be most severe upon the most economically vulnerable, our reactions largely remained self-interested. We have all been participants in a tangled web of human temptation and even sin that has contributed to the economic fall.

This is a messier interpretation than saying either that God caused the crisis or that a few bad apples did. Archbishop Williams named the crisis as the shared human "complicity in social evil." God gives humans freedom, but it is we humans ourselves who produce the systems that can go haywire.

God is also present in the crisis through human acts of compassion and justice to alleviate suffering. We are also implicated in the crisis—in a quite different way this time—through those actions by which we ease others' suffering. Churches, mosques, and synagogues around the country and beyond have opened their doors to support the hungry and provide job retraining and employment referral services for the jobless. While some congregations have given more and others less to mission and social-service outreach, many ministers report that their parishioners have stretched themselves, in faith, beyond their normal giving levels in the effort to comfort the suffering. Faith-based charities, which have seen their budgets cut even as the need for their services has never been greater, have streamlined their missions. They have made special appeals for additional donations so that they could fill food pantries and deliver health care to the newly (and already) uninsured. In these practices, they are doing God's work. Beyond these acts of compassionate service, we also see God's presence in the motivated and dedicated efforts of citizens, analysts, and lawmakers who have strived to fix broken systems. As the renowned economist Rebecca Blank reminds us, in our complex political and economic system, the Christian obligation to neighbor-love is fulfilled not through personal acts of charity alone but also by better aligning our complicated political and economic policies with justice. God's own compassion and justice are reflected through these efforts.[12]

What are we to do from here? Surely this is a time for thrift and caution. These are the same virtues of Christian life that thinkers have cited for centuries. Indeed, a cautious approach to economic life, so familiar to previous generations of American and European Christians, likely had religious roots. The notion of a "Protestant ethic" as a key factor in capitalism's rise came from the great German sociologist Max Weber, writing at the beginning of the twentieth century. Weber emphasized the importance of austerity. He asserted that the spirit of industry arose within Christians who were anxious to demonstrate that they were among God's elect. This industriousness earned money for workers and capital investors, but their Christian morals forbade them from displaying any ostentation. Thriftiness was to be their lifestyle. So they saved, and their savings fueled further investment. Their way of life was conducive to the emergence of capitalism.[13]

In our own time, some analysts suggest that practicing Christian thriftiness would damage the economy. The economy, they say, requires money to circulate quickly so as to keep itself going and to keep people employed. The economist Deirdre McCloskey has called this view an absurdity, suggesting provocatively that only non-economists could hold it. McCloskey asserts that the economic system will adjust itself and will reward efficiency for whatever goods people value—including leisure. If Christian values had more influence, "The economy would encourage specialization to satisfy human desires in much the same way as it does now. People would buy Bibles and spirit-enhancing trips to Yosemite instead of *The Monica Story* and trips to Disney World, but we would still value high-speed presses for the books and airplanes for the trips. The desires would be different, but that doesn't change how the system works best." Greed is not good, she maintains. Prudence is.[14]

Yet what are we to make of the advocates of public and personal stimulus who tell us to spend, spend, spend? Contrariwise, many people of faith simultaneously making a conversion to a simpler lifestyle could actually sink the economy into a deeper hole. After all, McCloskey's view of thrift is for the long term—she even wrote presciently, in 2004, "No doubt such a conversion would be a shock to General Motors."[15] As unlikely as it may be, if everyone stopped buying goods at exactly the same moment, this change in consumer behavior would, in fact, jolt the system.

At a time when the economy needs anything but a further slowdown, should we conclude that it is a Christian duty—as well as a patriotic duty—to spend more money? There is no straightforward way to read the Christian story as calling people to forgo thrift in times of crisis in order to boost the economy. In fact, advocates of market stimulus have generally not even attempted to frame their argument in theological terms. Rather, we see what is often the case: Christian theology and ethics are largely silent when it comes to specifics, leaving the domain of policy recommendation to the logic and language of economists and merchants.

So what exactly are we to do? Is Christian faith supposed to make a difference in our economic decisions? If we answer yes, we still must figure out just how. Should it be to save more than the national average, or less? To spend more, or less? To give more, or less? To work more, or less? To choose a career that pays more, or one that pays less? To possess more, or less? The chapters to follow tackle these questions and raise others.

SIMPLIFYING WITHOUT EXITING

Many thoughtful people have sought to reject altogether the predominant practices of consumerism. They have pursued the simple life, slowing down the pace of their lives. In the process, they have been able to be friendlier toward, and commune with, nature. Wordsworth, for his part, would approve. Jesus' own ministry, in which he wandered from village to village and depended upon the hospitality of strangers, also seems consistent with this approach.

Yet if we commit to simplify our lives and engage more attentively with the environment, we only increase the number of practical and ethical questions we confront. That is, unless we live on a self-sufficient farm (and probably even if we do), we still will face hundreds of economic and ecological decisions every day. Paper or plastic? Cloth diapers or disposable ones? Is a new car with hybrid technology really better for the environment than an older, smaller car that gets good gas mileage? If we own a clunker, should we drive it until it wears out since producing any new car requires energy to produce it? Should we drive to the store to buy something, or order it on the Internet and have it shipped? Shall we pay to live in a more expensive neighborhood that is close to work and school so we can have a shorter commute? If we are going to own a computer, what do we do about the fact that most are designed to be nearly obsolete in three or four years and probably contain toxic chemicals that could end up in a landfill?

Consider the public effort by some Christians to ask, "What would Jesus drive?" They wanted to suggest, by alluding to the now-popular question "What would Jesus do?" (WWJD), that Christians should express strong concern about the environment. They declared that Christians had no business driving gas-guzzling luxury vehicles. Automobiles play a large part in making the United States the largest greenhouse gas emitter in the world. Theirs was a witty campaign that aimed to get people to think theologically about their transportation routines.

These Christians were ridiculed for their naïveté, however. One national columnist, George Will, even retorted with his own attempt at humor. Will wrote that Jesus rode into Jerusalem upon a donkey—"a fuel-guzzling and high-pollution conveyance"![16] Will's indictment of these Christian leaders was not merely meant to poke fun at those who were combining their faith and their concern for the earth. Rather, he expressed disdain for the campaigners for implying that "Christianity is not just good news, it is also good scientific and economic policy analysis."

Will is correct that Christian activists can be quick—and mistaken—to oversimplify biblical or theological messages for economic living. Yet Will errs by not allowing for the possibility that Christian faith can help us think about the economy and the environment in our everyday lives. Even so, his criticism is a helpful reminder that we will need an approach based on more than a catchy question.

Like our own personal decisions, our public and civic spaces seem inundated by the market. Amid shrinking budgets, public schools take contributions from local businesses to fund arts and athletics, and they sign exclusive vendor contracts with soda companies. Our formerly religious and other nonprofit hospitals now bear corporate names. Even our public sports arenas are now owned—or at least named—by companies. The football arena in Indianapolis used to be called the Hoosier Dome, a label that meant something to us "Hoosiers" from Indiana. Then it was the RCA Dome. Lacking the latest skyboxes and other luxuries, it was replaced in 2008 by Lucas Oil Stadium, which bears the name of a California-based company that few in Indianapolis had ever heard of. The residents of Houston had to rename their baseball stadium when "Enron" no longer evoked civic pride (to say the least). The corporation in which so many in Houston and elsewhere had placed their trust cheated its employees and stockholders out of their financial security. More recently, the New York Mets opened their new stadium in Queens bearing the name Citi Field, named after Citigroup. The financial institution had agreed to pay $20 million per year for naming rights before it had to go begging to the U.S. government in 2008, receiving $45 billion in bailout money. That prompted two New York City politicians to propose that the stadium be named "Citi/Taxpayer Field."[17] The entanglements that come with corporate sponsorships are anything but simple. Churches, other nonprofits, and governments can no more protect themselves from the market than they can operate without money.

At the collective as well as the personal level, we must ask not how to opt out of the market but how to harness the market to achieve ends that are consistent with our values. Through coordinated action, we can also help shape the market in ways that promote human dignity and respect for God's creation. This work of harnessing and shaping the economy is essential not only for surviving in a tough economy but for promoting human well-being.

Chapter 2

VALUING

Where your treasure is, there your heart will be also.
—Matthew 6:21

What is the value of a human life? It's almost an offensive question. Surely life is priceless—beyond any number we could place on it. Human life, like all life, is a gift from God. Yet that theological statement can come into conflict with necessary economic calculations.

CALCULATING OUR VALUES

Kenneth Feinberg had the unenviable job of placing a monetary value on the lives lost in the tragedy of September 11, 2001. He was appointed by Congress as the "Special Master" of the federal government's victim compensation fund. The rules gave no one recourse or appeal from Feinberg's decisions. For months, as the public face of Washington's response, Feinberg was yelled at and insulted in open and private meetings by families of the victims. How would the surviving families be compensated for the death of their loved one? What price would the U.S. government put on the loss of each of these victims? And who gave this "Special Master" the godlike powers of naming the value of life?

Feinberg determined the compensation that the government would provide in terms of each victim's salary and other financial returns that were forgone because of a life cut short. This was standard legal and economic practice. The family of the food server at the Windows on the World restaurant received far less compensation than that of the financial analyst at the high-powered Cantor Fitzgerald investment firm. Among the victims' families and in the wider public, criticism mounted against this practice.

In his book *What Is Life Worth?* Feinberg grapples with the moral significance of operating as if one life is worth more than another life. Of course, some people disagreed over the amount of any given victim's lost income, but this kind of objection accepted the premise that the economic value of the life was to be determined by financial factors. The deeper moral question is whether it was fair in the first place to determine public compensation for victims according to each one's earning power. Could this practice be squared with the democratic ideal of moral equality? That question haunted Feinberg for the months and years following the commission's work.[1]

When another tragedy happened in 2007—the massacre of thirty-two faculty and students on the Virginia Tech campus—Feinberg was called in again as an expert in victim compensation. This time, as he puts it, "I realized that Feinberg the citizen should trump Feinberg the lawyer." He helped the administrators of Virginia Tech decide that payment should be meted out according to the principle of equal moral worth. The "Hokie Spirit Memorial Fund" compensated the victims' families on equal financial terms.[2]

Feinberg used the term *citizen* to describe his intuitive commitment to equality. He contrasted this with the economic method used in legal determinations of lost income. He named this tension well. The democratic political system is based on the doctrine of moral equality, and this ideal is instituted in practice through the principle of "one person, one vote." Surrounding that commitment are laws that help us limit, at least, the inequalities in political and civic voice that are created by other forms of influence. The potential sway of money is the key concern. Citizens enjoy approximate equality in their common interactions in the public arena.

In contrast, the guarantees of equality within the market are much narrower. Consumers, laborers, and other market participants are to be treated equally in the sense that each person should be free to participate in the market. Race, gender, and other demographic attributes should have no bearing on their economic actions. (In reality, of course, studies show that such attributes do continue to provoke unequal treatment.) But there is one important difference. The market economy does not provide equal voice or influence to each participant. On the contrary, the market allocates economic returns to economic inputs: land, labor, and capital. Those people with command over larger inputs, including education, skills, and talents, will receive more back than those with smaller inputs.

Some defenders of the market declare that almost everyone has labor power to contribute as an input. This is true. And the idea that everyone can participate seems to be egalitarian. But tremendous disparities exist in terms of the specific inputs that individuals bring to the market. Someone who is dependable and able-bodied but without a basic education will start at or near the minimum wage; minimal labor qualifications will yield a minimal return. In stark contrast, at the other end of the labor-market spectrum, Bill Gates's time, according to one estimate, is worth about $650,000 per hour. He earns so much from his labor that, the joke goes, it would not be worth his time to lean down and pick up a $100 bill. He would earn more to work for those additional three seconds.[3]

The rules of the market, then, do not treat each person as equally influential. Rather, every dollar is equal. That is, each dollar has equivalent power, and people with more money have more economic power. Those with more money are "more equal" than those who have less. If democracy is built around the principle of one person, one vote, then in capitalism, the concept is one dollar, one vote.

If money did not have a powerful influence in politics, the judicial system, and a host of other spheres, we would have less reason to care about great inequalities of income or wealth. That is because, the political philosopher Michael Walzer has suggested, the other important goods of life—political participation, basic security, and so on—would not be affected by economic disparities. But, unfortunately, money does play a vital part in exacerbating inequalities in many parts of life.

Take, for instance, health care. In the United States, about 45 million people, or 15 percent of the population, lack health insurance, and another 20 million don't have adequate coverage. Should basic medical coverage be something that any person, by virtue of being human, deserves? If so, who should pay for it? With every right comes a corresponding obligation of someone or some institution to provide it. On one hand, it makes sense that having medical procedures and treatment is a private economic good with a cost to be borne by each consumer, and by that reasoning the price of health care can be determined by the interaction of supply and demand. On the other hand, some of the economic benefits accruing from good health have positive external effects beyond individuals. In many ways health is a public good, with the benefits of any individual's good health extending to many other people in the workplace and community. Further, being in good health has value beyond any monetary figure we assign to it. Even if it could not be shown that improved health would have benefits for other people, the opportunity to live in good health should not be limited by economic status.

So too with education. How do we put a price tag on learning, understanding, and knowledge? Many people, especially those of us who have committed our careers to teaching, believe that education has intrinsic benefits. Even if knowledge and critical-thinking skills acquired through educational experience had no economic benefits (or negative ones), we would still fight for them to be provided to all citizens. But that is nice to say . . . until the next sentence is, "Come to my university, where tuition, room, and board is $50,000 a year." All of a sudden, it makes sense for parents and other would-be contributors to ask, "What do we get in return for this expense?" Indeed, the public is justified in asking this question, too, as even private educational institutions receive direct and indirect public contributions—ranging from the Federal Work-Study Program's support of students to grants and tax benefits.

And so it is all the rage in higher education, in particular, to talk about our students as "customers" and to assess our programs in terms of what instrumental benefits students attain from them. Recently, a member of my university's board of trustees asked me how we could assess the impact that one of the school's programs, community-based learning, was having on our graduates. This is a key question, but it is not simple to answer concretely. The answers lie in students' awareness of social issues and public policy, specific knowledge of local agencies, cross-cultural understanding, and the ability to connect theory to practice. The board member went on to specify further what he meant. How do we know, he wondered, that students doing community-based courses get selected for more job interviews and are hired more frequently by top-paying firms?

Not only do I believe that this question would be hard to answer empirically, I am not at all certain that it is the proper measure of the success of this educational initiative. I do not believe we can fully capture the benefits of learning in the community—or in the classroom, for that matter—in a monetary figure. Stated differently, it is not necessary to show that an educational program has financial benefits to regard it as valuable or successful. The achievements for which the program is designed may or may not have financial benefits.

Thus, when we talk about value, we must be certain to avoid the assumption that goods can be reduced to their financial price tag. Or that monetary terms encapsulate the full value of any good. It remains true, certainly, that calculating costs and benefits of certain goods—including health, education, and even life itself—is a necessity in economic life. Even within economic figuring, though, it is not the case that we should set price tags for goods according to the "market-clearing" point at which supply and demand meet. Sometimes the bottom line is not. Sometimes business is not just business. Intrinsic values cannot be monetized.

ORDERING LIFE THEOCENTRICALLY

Conflicts over values pervade human life. We can't serve two masters, but competing demands apply in and across every sphere of life. The question isn't "Do we serve?" but rather "What or whom shall we serve?" What difference does faith make for this question?

We always determine value in relation to some center, the ethicist H. Richard Niebuhr wrote—a center that, in some way or another, we serve. Niebuhr spoke of Christian distinctiveness not as "election to special status" but as "election to service." If Christians are special in some way, it is only in being especially called to serve God in and through serving others.

The challenge is that each of us has not just one center of value but many. For example, many people balance value commitments to family, political community, and the workplace. For parents, "family values" might lead them to do almost anything to protect their children. The political center of value is the nation-state, and patriotism makes many demands—to the point of asking citizens and soldiers, in cases of war, to give their lives to defend the country. In fact, this is why the great political philosopher Jean-Jacques Rousseau was suspicious of Christians—he didn't believe they would care enough about death to fight hard for their country. And so they might make lousy soldiers unless the state could create sufficient national loyalty.[4]

The center of value in the market is economic productivity. From this center derives the respective worth of inputs such as land, capital, and labor. Within this model, people are valued for the economic contribution they make to production. Without the checks of other values beyond the market, such as the basic rights due to citizens, employee health and safety might not be guaranteed in the workplace.[5] At the same time, compensation packages for premature death get settled in terms of lost income.

Niebuhr argues that we should understand all centers of value except one to be relative—that is, to have meaning only within their context or sphere of life. Family members are precious, but beyond the household, your loved one is like everyone else's. Political equality is important, but it only provides political guarantees within one's own nation-state. Economic productivity is significant, but it leaves unanswered political and cultural questions.

There is one absolute or ultimate center of value, Niebuhr emphasizes. That is God. All relative centers of value should align with the absolute center. Put differently, human centers of value are only "penultimate," and they must give way, when inconsistency arises, to the ultimate value, God.

To state that people should place their ultimate value in the absolute (God) is not to deny that they also have genuine responsibilities within many spheres and to many different communities. In fact, Niebuhr states, many domains such as economics, art, politics, and science appropriately have values that provide order and purpose for those activities. But determinations of value in any part of life should always be "made in mindfulness of absolute value-relations."[6]

Another way of naming this perspective is *theocentrism*. As the name suggests, theocentrism places God in the middle of all human activities. This moral frame stands as a guard against human propensities for *idolatry,* the tendency to make other beings or activities the end-all and be-all of life. *Anthropocentrism* places humans at the center, as if all of creation revolves around us. *Egocentrism* makes each person the axis of a private universe.

Econocentrism, then, can be understood as a worldview that places a monetary value on all goods and activities. It reduces people and things to their financial worth. It places money, or financial security, or economic status at the center of life without qualification. This frame, as H. Richard Niebuhr helps us to see, is idolatrous. It makes a god out of things that are important but not ultimate.

Where do we see econocentrism today? In practices that confuse financial influence for (im)moral influence, such as when the affluent are able to get away with behavior that lands ordinary people in jail. In vocational decisions that value salary over other aspects of quality of life, such as when individuals choose career paths based on economic status alone. And in public policies that favor short-term economic benefits over careful attention to social and climate concerns, such as when governments waive environmental standards so that companies can quickly boost output.

Theocentrism, in contrast to econocentrism, acknowledges the importance of economic well-being without making it ultimate. For people who wish to align their lives, as best they know how, around practicing faith in God, economic decisions should always be made with a view to a relative center, such as financial security, but also with a focus on more enduring values that reflect God's purposes. The old saying is instructive: Show me your checkbook, and I will show you your values.

The minister M. Craig Barnes writes about his recent visit with an elderly parishioner: "Jack's small Spartan room makes it painfully clear that in the end we all die stripped of most of the things we spent a lifetime collecting."[7] Barnes is describing the loneliness of the nursing home setting. It doesn't matter if those institutions are dressed up to look like nice hotels: "No one is all that interested in dying at the Marriott." But Barnes is also making a key theological point about the meaninglessness, in any ultimate sense, of amassing material goods over a lifetime.

The Gospel of Luke also has something to say about this. A rich man with a productive farm keeps building bigger barns just to store his "grain and goods." He can hardly build storage quickly enough to keep up with his accumulating bounty. But, we read, he finally begins to relax—or to try to do so. "Soul, you have ample goods laid up for many years; relax, eat, drink, be merry." In response, God has one word for him: *Fool.* "This very night your life is being demanded of you. And the things you have prepared, whose will they be?" (Luke 12:15–21).

Practicing Theocentrism

So what should we do with the stuff we have collected? One of my faculty mentors, Dr. Thomas E. McCollough Jr., taught in the Religion Department at Duke University. He had encouraged me to become passionate about teaching and he had helped me gain admission to a doctoral program at Harvard in religion, ethics, and economics. A few years later he decided to retire to care for his beloved wife, Mary Lee, who was experiencing Alzheimer's disease. As Tom's retirement date approached he summoned me to Durham to see him. When I got to town, he gave me one of the most generous gifts I have been privileged to receive. Tom offered me any books from his office that I would find to be of value. These were the volumes he had gathered together over a forty-year career in Europe and the United States. He requested just one thing: that I take only those books that I thought I would use. He would offer the remaining volumes to other friends and a local university.

College professors often become *bibliocentric,* collecting books for the sake of possessing them. An administrative colleague once surmised that professors store so many books in their offices so that they might feel secure in their own world. And others have suggested that we fill shelf after shelf with volumes in order to impress our students with tomes and treatises that we appear to have read and to understand. Many professors—and I may be one of them—express our materialism through books.

But not Tom McCollough. As a professor in the best sense of that word, he cherished his books, but not because they were commodities or signs of status. Tom placed a high value on his collection, but it was always in relation to his teaching and writing. It was part of the educational enterprise and the life of the mind. He bought and kept books because they were full of ideas that could change people's lives. His generous act of giving away his prized books certainly changed me.

Every time I pull one of those volumes from my shelf, I experience a sense of connection to my mentors, especially Tom. Often when I teach about a classic text, like one by Aristotle or Kierkegaard, I will reach for Tom's edition to learn from his own underlining and notes in the margin. In this way, if I manage to do my part in teaching, Tom's insights continue to be communicated to college students through his books.

Tom McCollough's generous gift stands as a witness against econocentrism and for more enduring and faithful purposes. He did not renounce books as commercial commodities. Nor did he treat them like fetishes or museum objects to be observed but not defaced. He used them toward the ends of good thinking and good teaching. He read them. He marked them up. He piled them all over his office. When it came time to retire, Tom was not devastated by clearing out his office. Instead, he passed on his books with the expectation of their continued good use.

Keeping Money in Its Proper Place

Even as we live in a consumer economy in which material things such as books and food and clothing are important, we know that life is more than that (Matthew 6:25). Tom McCollough's books were "priceless" to me: I could not have bought them or the sense of continuity and tradition that came with them. Although he could have found a market for them, he would not have accepted money for them. The books are worth more than money.

We cannot eat actual dollars and we cannot build a house with them—at least not easily. Dollars are only means that help us to accomplish some kinds of ends. During the Jim Crow era in the U.S. South, some African Americans had wealth, but they still could not sit at the lunch counters of the department stores. Their money was no good for that. And no matter how much money they had, they could not sit in the whites-only section of the movie theaters or restaurants. To this day, there are societies in which a woman, no matter how wealthy, cannot own property. Indeed, she may be treated as property.

Consider money in a little different way. Greater personal income does not make us as happy as we had believed that it would prior to acquiring it. Why not? As I discuss further in the next chapter, the main reason is that we cannot keep up with our own desires. We cannot distinguish well enough between our needs and our wants. For impoverished persons, this is especially debilitating, when social pressures to own certain goods as status symbols lead to credit-card and payday-loan debts. For all of us, as long as we try to keep up with the consumer messages we get from our neighbors and from advertising campaigns, we will perpetuate the economic race. It is high time that we stop thinking about money as the goal of our material lives. Don't get me wrong. Money remains a vital means. All people need money enough to buy basic goods and services that allow them to pursue their other priorities. Having financial wherewithal opens many doors. Money can't buy love, but it can enable people to pay for online subscriptions to Match.com and pay for gas and parking to drive to a restaurant for a date. Thus people need enough money, but money is not enough. Money is just one part of a social system that helps us meet our needs. If we shift our thinking about money from being an end in itself to a means alone, we can view economic life in a new way.

UNDERSTANDING CAPABILITIES

A Nobel Prize winner in economics, Amartya Sen gives us a bigger and better vocabulary than income for thinking about economic goods. Sen grew up on the Indian subcontinent, and although he was from a privileged family, poor people were ever-present. He attributes his intellectual interest in poverty, inequality, and economic development to his childhood experiences. During the Bengal famine of 1943, Sen says he encountered thousands of people who begged for food. His grandfather allowed him to share one small tin of rice with those who asked—but only one per family. This and similar experiences shaped Sen's view of economics as a tool for understanding the most basic elements of human well-being.

Sen asserts that economists, and the rest of us, should focus not on what currency is easiest to measure but instead on what people truly value. Sen suggests that that is not money, or even happiness understood in a subjective way. We should value those *capabilities* that are part of well-being and that allow people to have agency, or the ability to have influence, in their own lives.

Human capabilities are those truly important things that we are able to do and be. For example, are we nourished and healthy? Do we have decent housing? Are we able to participate in the cultural life of our community? Are we political participants? Are we well educated? Can we practice our religion? Do we have friends? Affirmative answers to these questions mean that we have attained important capabilities.[8]

What capabilities are necessary to allow people to live faithfully in the global economy? What practices can help in that enterprise? Sen does not identify a definitive set of capabilities that all humans value or should value (and he does not write from a faith-based perspective). Martha Nussbaum, a philosopher who works on capabilities from an Aristotelian framework, does offer a list of capabilities that she suggests all people value.[9] Without settling the question of whether capabilities are indeed universal, here is a list of important capabilities:

Human Capabilities: Examples
- Being well nourished
- Being in good health
- Having decent shelter
- Being literate

- Being well educated
- Having meaningful work
- Recreating and communing with nature
- Having supportive relationships
- Appearing in public without shame
- Participating in political, cultural, and economic life
- Belonging to familial, communal, and social groups
- Contributing to one's family, groups, and society
- Expressing religious commitments and worshiping God

For securing decent nutrition, health care, and housing, for instance, money is an important input. But even for these capabilities, being literate about food, exercise, and the housing market are at least as vital as having money to spend. Just think of the people who fall into large sums of money but do not have the ability to convert that money into capabilities such as health or financial security. Think of lottery winners and teenage superstar celebrities who squander their money. And remember the parable of the prodigal son—about which I have more to say in Chapter Seven. The younger, "prodigal" son managed—with remarkable efficiency!—to squander his entire inheritance and become dependent once again on his parents (Luke 15:11–32). Without the pure grace of his father, the son would have suffered tremendously from his most efficient squandering.

A focus on capabilities allows us to talk about values within any context, because the capabilities approach emphasizes the ends we are trying to serve. In examining politics, being a full and equal participant is a key capability that we care about. In looking at health, we can focus not on dollars spent on care but on outcomes such as being in good health. In analyzing a new job, for example, we no longer ask (or only ask), How much money does it pay? Instead, we ask, What does this job allow me to be, or to do, that I otherwise would not be able to attain?

The capabilities approach is compatible with a theocentric view of the world. Human capabilities allow people to express their human dignity. The most fundamental conviction about human beings in Christian faith is that all people are created in the image of God. Because of this priceless gift that God has conferred on humans, they have dignity. Some philosophers will debate whether that dignity is inherent and inalienable (as I am stating) or whether, instead, it can actually be taken away when people are treated inhumanely.[10] In either view, human dignity demands that people be able to attain well-being and to pursue their own ends. Human capability offers a constructive way to talk about such well-being and purposes.[11]

In a theocentric perspective, the ends that humans have been created to pursue begin with God and God's purposes. The Westminster Catechism puts it well (though in the language of its time): "Question. 1. What is the chief end of man? Answer. Man's chief end is to glorify God, and to enjoy him forever."[12] The capabilities approach allows us to be specific about this fundamental but general theological conviction. Being able to worship God is one such capability. So too are the ones related to economic goods, political participation, education, and so on.

It should now be clear that, in comparison to capabilities, focusing on money alone does not allow us to attend as readily or consistently to all aspects of a well-lived life. No one would deny that in overall terms, all other things being equal, having more money tends to have some net positive effect on well-being. Yet in specific cases, money's impact is lower than expected or even of no significance. For instance, Sen has shown that there is no consistent relationship between income and life expectancy, a most basic indicator of well-being. States and regions like Sri Lanka and Kerala (in southwest India) have very low incomes but boast life expectancies approaching those in the most industrialized nations. In contrast, other countries, like Brazil, Gabon, and South Africa, are quite "inefficient" at converting their relatively high incomes into adequate life expectancies. In the higher-income context, the United States stands second in the world rankings (after Luxembourg) in terms of income per capita, but as of 2005, the U.S. figure for life expectancy at birth, 77.9 years, was tied for twenty-ninth place.[13] Income leaves much to be desired if we want to protect human dignity and promote overall well-being.

Indeed, at the personal level, earning income may even have a negative relationship to at least a few capabilities. I have a few friends with high-powered jobs, truly exciting jobs, who are so busy that they have lost their capacity to connect with other people. They do not have the time. Or when they do have time, they cannot slow down from the "let's move" or "let's win" mentality. They cannot appreciate, on their own terms, the complexity and nuance of a good novel, or the laughter of children. So much for having friends or participating in community life. These economically successful people may have gained the whole world but lost their souls.

H. Richard Niebuhr would say that, in this example and more broadly, the relative value of economic success has, unfortunately, become an ultimate value. Remember the elderly man Jack in the nursing home: Having the economic means to support yourself is a very good thing, but it does not take away the loneliness.

There is a more hopeful path. It has to do with an understanding of joy-filled life as different from one centered on material prosperity. As Jesus said succinctly, "One's life does not consist in the abundance of possessions" (Luke 12:15b). We should leave behind the familiar way of thinking that assesses how "well-off" people are in dollar terms. We can determine, individually and together, what capabilities do matter to us, why they matter, and what we can do with them.

PRACTICING VALUES

I opened this chapter by asking what value we place on life; let us come full circle. The ultimate capability is life itself. It may well be true, in theological terms, that it would be better to die than to live under certain conditions—for instance, if living meant having to go against one's fundamental values, or if dying resulted from protecting an innocent person. But in everyday circumstances, life is a necessary condition for achieving well-being and pursuing worthy ends.

The single most striking calculation I have encountered in my career bears directly on this point. It is Amartya Sen's determination that at least 100 million women are "missing." Missing from where? They are not hiding and they have not been kidnapped. Instead, as Sen and other scholars have estimated, more than 100 million females should be alive who are simply not alive. There are more females than males in the world today—mostly because of the fact that, when the life cycle has a chance to run its full course, women tend to outlive men. (More boys are born than girls, but males are less resilient than females at every age.) But given the levels of development around the world, there should be a much greater number of females alive than are actually alive. The math is somewhat complicated, but Sen and a few other scholars have shown that given even roughly equal conditions for girls and boys, and for women and men, there would be 100 million more females alive today. The "missing women" problem disproportionately occurs in East and South Asia and North Africa. In China alone we would expect 50 million more females, and 40 million more in India.[14]

A part of the female-to-male gap is attributable, and increasingly so, to sex-selective abortions. For this reason India has outlawed informing the parents of the sex of a fetus—but the practice is still carried out. Selective abortions, in turn, arise from economic and cultural realities—such as the fact that in many communities, women have lower moral status, fewer opportunities for public life, and less earning power than men do.

But the reality of 100 million missing females also has to do with everyday practices once babies are born—practices at the dinner table, in household chores, in educational decisions. In some regions of India, for example, girls tend to get less food than boys. When it is time for seconds, the parents dole them out to the boys. Researchers have also demonstrated that an injury must be more serious for a girl than for a boy before parents decide to take their child to the hospital for medical treatment.

Will kids stay in school, or will their parents tell them to drop out in order to help around the house or in the fields? Around the world, girls are still more likely than boys to drop out of primary or secondary schooling. So boys have higher educational levels and more earning power, and the cycle of differential treatment of males and females continues to the next generation.

Thus everyday economic practices by parents and others—such as what and how much children eat and when they receive medical care—make a world of difference in how a child's life turns out. Differential treatment in such everyday practices, then, effectively values some lives over others. In the case of missing women, it is the relative devaluing of female lives. It's not as blatant as the compensation formula the 9/11 "Special Master" applied, but it is massively more widespread in practice.

On a more hopeful note, studies show that when mothers are educated, they tend to have more agency within the household, and their decisions promote the well-being of their family members at a higher proportion than decisions by fathers. Both boys and girls benefit from their mothers' increased decision making—though girls, starting in a lower position, benefit relatively more than boys, bringing the capability of girls closer to that of boys.[15]

These household studies from South Asia and elsewhere may seem to be a world away from U.S. economic and social realities. They are not. A recent study showed that there are significant issues of differential birth rates (negatively affecting females) among some U.S. demographic subgroups corresponding to the regions and cultures that tend to value boys over girls. This is not a regional issue—it is now a global issue, including in the United States.[16]

These household studies also illuminate an insight applicable universally: Parents' everyday practices can begin a positive cycle toward increasing the capabilities of their children.[17] As a parent, I often think about how best to treat my two kids, Noah and Ada, on equal terms without treating them the same. They are developing their own interests and talents—and, of course, some of these are partially or significantly framed by gender roles in our society. My spouse and I have struggled with this question, and we find it to be just a small consolation to realize that there are only so many things under our own control. And we realize that we too have internalized and frequently enact gender stereotypes, whether we mean to do so or not. For us to treat our children as moral equals is to help them both, each individually, to develop their distinctive capabilities. They each need good health care and nutrition, but their needs on this front are not identical. In very daily practices, it means pushing both of them to eat their vegetables, but each child's list of tolerable veggies is, unfortunately, different. With other capabilities, such as participating in social circles and having friends, the differences between and among children are even greater. Parents, and society as a whole, value the life of every child by attending to each one's particular needs and capabilities.

Living faithfully in the global economy begins when we shift our values and our practices from acquiring goods and financial security to developing our own capabilities and the capabilities of our neighbors. We will still need to make, at least in de facto terms, calculations about the economic value of life—for purposes such as cost-benefit analysis at the policy level and in certain legal cases. But much more pervasive are the decisions we make within our typical routine, such as caring for and educating children, participating in our neighborhood and political system, and buying, selling, and working. In those practices we must honor the dignity equally bestowed on each person. Whatever their economic situation, all have been created in the image of God, who is the center of our values. Valuing human life connects closely to the array of other economic practices that we undertake every day.

Chapter 3

DISCERNING
DESIRES

❧

Why do you spend your money for that which is not bread?
—Isaiah 55:2a

The advertisers had taught my son to recognize brands before he reached his third birthday. He did not yet know how to read or even name letters. But one day, as I was pushing him around town in his stroller, he spotted a vehicle rounding the corner. He shouted, jubilantly: "Big—red—Coke truck!"

How did Noah know what this truck was advertising? His mother and I had not, to our recollection, shown him a Coke product, and we rarely had Coca-Cola in our house. We watched some television but had tried not to do so when he was awake, and although newspapers were often scattered on our kitchen table, he hadn't paid attention to them. Yet this question remains a mystery: How had our two-year-old become able to recognize the ubiquitous, iconic red symbol of global capitalism?

And he was gleeful about it. He liked the truck. This, too, would probably please the purveyors of the Coke brand. At the "World of Coca-Cola," a museum and shrine to the beverage in Atlanta, Georgia, the theme is HAPPINESS. The Coca-Cola Theater shows, every seven to ten minutes, a film titled "Inside the Happiness Factory:

A Documentary." It is an animated world of agreeable workers producing Coke in a fanciful jungle-meets-factory setting. All of the film's imaginary activity is meant to occur within a Coke machine. It is quite entertaining, and even a bit irreverent toward the global corporation and its employees.

After the film, the Coca-Cola Theater's screen lifts and visitors are invited to walk right into the Happiness Factory. Here, kids and adults can have their picture taken with the cuddly Coke Polar Bear and sample varieties of Coke products from around the world. During my visit, I kept wondering if I would encounter the Oompa-Loompas or the chocolate river from Willy Wonka's factory.

The "Coca-Cola Experience" portrays the famous beverage as just an ordinary part of life. In one gallery, you can view old postcards from across America that have the famous Coke image—the one my two-year-old son recognized—dotting the landscape and skyline. A few feet away, you can read letters written by customers describing how important Coke has been to them. "Over the years, hundreds of people have sent us stories about how Coca-Cola has affected their lives. Whether it is a childhood memory, a reminder of family gatherings, or a recollection of good times with friends, Coca-Cola has impacted the lives of people all over the world."[1]

PURSUING HAPPINESS

What's the problem with branding that weaves Coke into the very fabric of our world? After all, as I would be the first to admit, it can be sort of fun. The slogans through the years have staying power. "Have a Coke and a smile!" Isn't it "the real thing"? "You can't beat the feeling." Indelibly written on my own childhood memory is the 1971 commercial of diverse people standing together on a hilltop, singing, "I'd like to teach the world to sing in perfect harmony . . . I'd like to buy the world a Coke . . ."

Theologically speaking, the trouble is that Coke is not the real thing. It does not—no product could—live up to the promises for how it can change your life. So, why do many people prefer Coca-Cola to water? In this case, people believe they can't be happy without it. That is the unabashed goal of the marketing campaigns of Coca-Cola—and of its competitors for that matter. Coke is not just sugary water; it is part of a "happy" lifestyle. It adds life. Just ask my son.

But then ask nutritionists whether sodas are healthy for children (or adults). Kids do not need the sugar; water is far better for them. In fact, in 2006 Coca-Cola and two other beverage companies agreed to remove some high-calorie drinks and to limit others from public schools because of their relationship to the severe increase in child obesity in the United States over the past three decades. Tougher governmental nutrition guidelines led many school systems to want to replace sodas with healthier options, such as water, milk, or juice.

Ironically, schools had trouble completing this removal because they had already bound themselves through exclusive licensing and product contracts with Coke or Pepsi that they could not afford to break. That is, the local school systems had become dependent upon their contracts with soda companies to help meet their budgets. In hard economic times (even before the recession), educational systems had turned to commercial sources of funding to supplement their limited revenues from government sources. It is easy to see the appeal to cash-strapped principals and superintendents of lucrative contracts from beverage companies. Nonetheless, once schools were drawn in, maintaining the contracts could become, like soda drinking itself, an addictive habit.[2]

So, again, what is the problem with imprinting kids and adults to like Coke or Pepsi? It creates a desire within us for a product that is not healthy and that draws us into a world of other products and other desires. It infiltrates the world of children, and adults, and convinces us that happiness derives from drinking a drink or living a certain lifestyle. Before children form their understanding of what they need in this world, they learn to want Coca-Cola. There is no simple line between wants and needs, and producers of goods across the spectrum want to convince potential customers that they both want and need their product.

THIRSTING GLOBALLY

Coca-Cola has a global presence, reaching almost every country in the world—and every corner of those nations. When I was traveling

Discerning Desires

in Mexico in the 1980s, I learned that more villages received regular Coke deliveries than had potable water. Put differently, there were—and still are—children around the world who recognize the Coke truck but do not enjoy access to clean drinking water. They want Coke but they need water.

Perhaps, you might say, there is very little relationship between the presence of Coke and the lack of potable drinking water. Who could blame Coca-Cola for trying to make global inroads to sell its products? It is good business to reach new markets. In India, however, the Coca-Cola Company has found itself in a battle with local residents surrounding some of its forty-nine production plants, particularly in the water-starved region of Rajasthan. Small farmers have claimed that the presence of the soda giant has lowered their water table some 50 percent, and that the farmers now need more powerful pumps and irrigation equipment just to keep up with their farming. As one resident stated: "Every day, a thousand vehicles come out of that factory taking away our water. What is left for our kids?"[3] Even with advanced technology, it still takes significantly more than a gallon of potable water to make a gallon of soda. Coca-Cola boasts that it is relatively efficient, but it uses 2.7 gallons of water to make 1 gallon of soda.

Thus a number of social-action alliances and watchdog groups make the connection between Coca-Cola production and the shortage of healthy water. In response to this criticism, perhaps, Coca-Cola has become a founding partner in the Global Water Challenge, touting its work such as "Kenya Water for Schools" to make water available to schoolchildren. It has formed a partnership with the WWF (formerly the World Wildlife Fund) to promote water conservation. Each of these, and various other local programs in which Coke participates, sounds like a noble initiative. But even taken together, they are dwarfed by the worldwide production and marketing of Coca-Cola. They probably increase the positive brand recognition of the soda manufacturer and hence increase the demand for its product.

In the bigger picture, of course, the problem extends beyond any single corporation or product. Coca-Cola serves as a high-profile example that could be multiplied by the impact of hundreds of other companies marketing their products around the world. Why are some people's desires valued over other people's needs? This is a question that firms do not try to answer. Firms (like the market as a whole) make no distinction between wants and needs. Rather, they pursue those with the purchasing power to buy their products.

The global availability of Coca-Cola also reveals how much is possible if we were to seek to reach all people with drinking water. If Coke can get its products to every corner of the world, why can't we get clean, affordable water there, too? This will require moral imagination and individual and collective practices to follow.

SHAPING NEEDS

Wants and needs. In my introductory economics course in college, I learned that the standard economic model assumes that, by definition, more of a good is always preferred to less, and that tastes and preferences are unchanging. These assumptions come with important caveats—caveats acknowledging that they necessarily simplify actual human behavior. Models are not really meant to describe a real person's actions; rather, they help us describe and predict behavior "as if" people acted in this way.[4]

Once we accept the standard framework, then advertising has only the function of sharing information about products—not of actually changing consumers' desires. No real-life economist maintains that people's preferences or perceived needs and wants are unchanging, but the model perpetuates that assumption in basic economics courses. Economists must add further assumptions and do second-order analysis if they want to focus on the role that advertising plays in shaping those desires.

Economic studies, then, are very different from economic reality. In our market system, a starting point for firms is to supply a product to meet some demand that consumers express. It is not important whether this demand is actually a want or a need—what is important is that for one reason or another, people buy the product. In practice, companies do what they can, not only to share information about their products but also to make people desire their products. They set out to tell potential purchasers that their lives will be better with this soda, or that car, or this cell phone.

Have you noticed that the newest ads sometimes never make a pitch at all? Gone are the days of a smiling spokesmodel telling us why we need a certain brand of toothpaste. Now we get commercials designed "merely" to increase brand identity. There are mini-narratives of athletes going the extra mile—with a Nike swoosh briefly appearing on screen. Cavemen repeatedly get angry at Geico for using the slogan "So easy a caveman can do it," with no mention that Geico is an insurance company. Perhaps the ultimate in brand-recognition advertising is the series of ads promoting the Dutch financial company ING: A person sits on a park bench, apparently blocking the letters that would precede "ing" in an English word. But when he stands up and reveals nothing in front of the letters, the audience learns that ING is a brand name.

On television, consumer goods have moved from commercials to product placements within programs. One prime-time show, *Friday Night Lights,* made a placement deal with Applebee's. By the third season, two of the lead characters were servers at the restaurant, and almost every week team celebrations or other meet-ups were happening at Applebee's. There is no longer separation between commercials and programs.

The point is to place brands and goods within our consciousness. Can you still imagine schools without advertising? Highways without billboards? Web sites without ads? Commercialism has so infiltrated our social lives that we accept it as normal. It seems impossible to cordon off some part of our lives as "commercial-free."

In fact, people are willing to sell themselves for commercial purposes. Witness the college students who offer to sell their bodies as billboards in exchange for tuition. Last week, my children and I drove past a man standing in the median. "Daddy," my son asked, "why is that man dressed up like a banana?" Surprised by the question (it's not one I frequently hear), I looked over to see a man dressed in a banana costume, jumping up and down. He was waving a sign advertising a home for sale in the neighborhood. Was it his home? I wondered how desperate a person would have to be in order to don an outrageous costume and dance in traffic. It seems that everything is for sale—even our dignity. The larger irony is that even more degrading than dressing up like a banana is losing one's home.

Consumer messages are so prevalent that it would be impossible to separate the times when our desires are being shaped from when they are not. It is better to acknowledge—as ethicists have done at least from Aristotle—that our desires are always being shaped. The question is not if we should have desires, but how we will shape them faithfully. Which desires will we cultivate, and which will we try to shape into more healthy ways of living?

Much ink has been spilled trying to separate wants from needs. The latter are to be more highly prioritized. We may want many things, but our needs are those things that are genuinely essential for living. One school of thought in economic development focuses on the "basic needs" approach—valuing above all those goods and services that help people first to survive and then to reach some basic standard of living. The problem that this approach has faced, not surprisingly, is how to adequately define what basic needs are. It is easy enough, of course, to distinguish potable drinking water from fine port wine, decent shelter from posh mansions, and basic medical services from optional cosmetic surgery.

In actuality, the lines between wants and needs are blurry. What is required for basic transportation—a bike, a reliable car, or a public transport system? Which "food basket" is considered adequate for healthy living? Do people need free basic health care, or is that just what they want? We can separate basic from luxury, but where is the line between basic and decent, or decent and middle-class? If basic becomes the middle, or average—and perhaps it should be—then the goalpost for what we label as basic is always moving with society's norms.

So wants and needs are complicated. Beyond subsistence levels of nutrition and shelter, they are shaped by relative as much as by absolute factors. Adam Smith wrote this about human needs:

> By necessaries I understand not only the commodities which
> are indispensably necessary for the support of life, but
> what ever the custom of the country renders it indecent for
> creditable people, even of the lowest order, to be without.
> A linen shirt, for example, is, strictly speaking, not a neces-
> sary of life. The Greeks and Romans lived, I suppose, very
> comfortably though they had no linen. But in the present

41

times, through the greater part of Europe, a creditable day-labourer would be ashamed to appear in public without a linen shirt, the want of which would be supposed to denote that disgraceful degree of poverty which, it is presumed, nobody can fall into without extreme bad conduct.[5]

Smith suggests that needs are always defined by the culture in which we live. That means that as our society changes, our own sense of what we need changes, too. Sure, we could attempt to make the distinction between what we think we need and what we really need. A shirt, whether linen as in Smith's example or cotton-poly as in most of our closets, is not something we really need—not to survive, at least. But the understanding of ourselves and our place in the world is not just our perception. It is real to us.

Let's put this in the language of capabilities. Being able to appear in public life (by fitting into the basic or customary dress code) is an important capability within a well-lived life, but the material means by which to attain it vary by culture and context. We affirm the value of social inclusion and participation without determining which kind of shirt, jeans, or shoes a person needs to achieve that.

So we return to the reality noted throughout this chapter that making a distinction between wants and needs, in some definitive way, is difficult if not impossible. There are many gray areas. Both derive from our desires, which are objective and subjective at the same time. Rather than resolve these dichotomies, we must ask fuller questions about what we should properly desire within a well-lived life. We need to practice discernment in what we desire, asking, Is this want or need consistent with expanding my capability and that of others? Or is it a fleeting feeling that compels me to chase happiness without much promise of helping me reach it?

RUNNING TO STAND STILL

Meanwhile, the human imagination seems to have nearly limitless capacity to want (or to be enticed to want) new consumer goods. This desire drives the consumer marketplace. It is what keeps us on a gerbil wheel. Or a better analogy is the original carrot and stick—the carrot that carriage drivers dangle enticingly in front of their horses. No matter how fast the horses charge toward the carrot, it always stays a fixed distance out ahead. Most of us, that is, can imagine new wants at least as fast as we can increase our income to keep up.

Indeed, happiness studies have helped shed light on a complicated relationship between money and happiness. Affluent people report higher levels of happiness than do poor people in that same society. But beyond basic subsistence levels, or an amount adequate to escape poverty, the effects of additional dollars on increasing happiness are small. (In some cases, they are even negative. For instance, studies suggest that affluent teenagers have higher levels of depression, anxiety, and substance abuse than children from impoverished families do.)

In fact, the economic and sociological experts suggest that absolute increases in income do not play nearly as important a role in our happiness as we might think. What does have a powerful influence on behavior, according to economic studies, is our relative status within peer groups that we consider important.[6] Six decades ago, James Duesenberry gave a classic example of this phenomenon, which has come to be known as "keeping up with the Joneses." Duesenberry suggested that we look at our next-door neighbors' driveways. "What kind of reaction is produced by looking at a friend's new car or looking at houses or apartments better than one's own? The response is likely to be a feeling of dissatisfaction with one's own house or car."[7] Today, commercials based on people checking out their neighbor's car still resonate with American consumers. "Thou shalt not covet thy neighbor's BMW" may be scriptural, but we are almost all backsliders.

People report that they would be happier to live in a situation in which they had lesser goods—a smaller house, a simpler car, and so on—as long as their neighbors had even less than they did. The average person would prefer a house of 3,000 square feet when the neighbors' houses are 2,500 square feet to having, instead, a house of 4,000 square feet if the neighbors lived in mansions of 5,000 square feet. That is, people are not made happier by some absolute number of square feet of their house or fancier tires on their car.

How much income do people need to say they have enough? Twenty percent more. Whatever income they have now (beyond poverty levels), people tend to report that they need an additional

20 percent. This finding holds true for the working class, middle class, and the affluent. We all think we need just a little bit more to be satisfied. No matter how much we currently have.[8] One of my friends says that teaching is like Boyle's Law, the chemistry formula that relates pressure and volume of a gas: Professors can expand the amount of material we have to fit any amount of time we have to present it. (This is not just because professors can be full of hot air.) Human desire is like that, too. Our desires—our sense of what we want and need—can fill whatever space we have in our disposable income. And there will always be pressure to expand that income by 20 percent. We will never be satiated unless we can find ways to hold our material desires in check.

DEALING WITH STUFF

Sometimes our materialism can literally weigh us down. One summer when I was in divinity school, I set out to travel across Europe, from Spain to Russia. I had a second-class train pass, a few hundred bucks, and a backpack. My friend Ken, a fellow graduate student, agreed to travel with me. His backpack was a lot smaller and lighter than mine. Before the trip I had found a bargain—so I thought— on the extra-large pack with a host of expandable compartments. I would be happy (I figured) to have space for extra stuff, such as an additional pair of shoes and a second camera lens. Here was Boyle's Law again: My desire for stuff created pressure to find a bigger backpack, and then I expanded my supplies to fit the available space.

I quickly came to regret the excess baggage. For six weeks Ken and I carried our possessions on our backs, from train station to youth hostel and often to museum and restaurant. My back was sore every time we had to transfer from one place to the next—which was almost every day. Whenever we sat in a small café, a commonplace in Europe, I had to share my allotted space with my big pack. Meanwhile, Ken was always there with a more modest-sized pack to remind me of how I should have packed. He never gloated, and indeed, he would sometimes trade off gear with me on long treks, to share the load.

I thought I needed everything that was in my pack, but I did not. Ken always had enough in his lighter one. He packed well, but he also was willing to go without the extra sweater, the extra hat, the extra camera lens. He was a freer traveler because he was able to realize that he had enough.

Traveling by backpack, of course, is not how most of us live our everyday lives. The burden of our stuff is not literally on our backs. Yet it remains a burden. At my college, every August I see new students arrive in their parents' mini-vans, SUVs, and rental vans, with more and more loads of electronics and clothes to squeeze into the small residence-hall rooms. I glance at exhausted parents, siblings, significant others, and college staff helping people carry this stuff. How much of it is necessary?

And, for those who move into a house or apartment, or get married, these moments provide an occasion for friends and family to give more stuff. Most gifts, of course, are well intentioned and of some use. But cumulatively, the stuff requires more closet space—and psychic space—to keep up with it. Where do we put the Christmas china from Aunt Roberta for eleven months a year? What do I do with a bread-maker (and will I ever take it out of the box)? How often will I use this power tool?

In a figurative sense, the goods that we possess create a giant backpack that we must carry. In some ways, at least, goods can possess us.

I may have overstated the negative aspects of material goods. I mean to highlight what we tend to underestimate: their less tangible and often nonfinancial costs. We have to move stuff, store it, protect it, and repair it. And we worry about it. And being anxious about our material goods is just what Jesus implored us not to do—right after, according to Matthew's Gospel, he declared, "No one can serve two masters. . . . You cannot serve God and wealth" (Matthew 6:24). Thinking again of the backpack, these passages help make sense of another saying of Jesus: "Come to me, all you that are weary and are carrying heavy burdens, and I will give you rest. Take my yoke upon you, and learn from me" (Matthew 11:28–29a). Could it be that Jesus' way calls people with possessions, like those disciples who set down their nets to follow him, to travel with lighter backpacks?

This is not a call for an ascetic lifestyle, in which the denial of basic necessities somehow makes us more pious or holy. There are, indeed, appropriate uses of the spiritual disciplines—such as fasting during Lent—that help us become aware of our bodily needs and dependence upon God and others for our material well-being. But ascetic practices make sense because they are departures from the norm of meeting basic needs.

As we look around our contemporary culture, of course, asceticism is certainly not the word that comes to mind. The billboard for Aquos televisions towered over the interstate: "Change your TV, change your life." This was a promise for a better way, a better life. It was a call to improve our human condition. Such ads are a constant reminder to would-be consumers of what they do not have. They are a promise of salvation (from unhappiness) even as they are subtle criticisms of the lives that people lead without those products. They tempt us to buy things in the hope of a more satisfied life, and yet the studies of happiness strongly suggest that, for most products, the thrill will soon wear off and our lives will be little improved— and much complicated—by more and more consumer goods.

Yet there is no escape from these messages of consumerism. We can pursue the simple life. We can go TV-free. We can spend less on Christmas gifts. But unless we retreat into sectarian enclaves or into the Amazon, we are going to see ads on our screen and in our mailbox. Long ago, Jonah learned that he could not flee from God. Unfortunately, perhaps, no one can flee the messages of the market.

Thus it will be no simple task to live with less stuff. Our own sense of what we need, and what we desire, is shaped by the culture around us. The air we breathe is that of a consumer economy. So in many ways, asking individuals simply to desire less is to attempt to address a collective, culture-wide problem with a personal solution. A major part of the response to consumerism must be personal, to be sure. But we must also attend to the society- and community-level dimensions. (This task comprises a good part of the book's final three chapters.)

SHOPPING AS MORAL ACTIVITY

Even as we must critically identify the ways in which consumerism cannot possibly deliver what it promises, we should also name the aspects of market participation that do contribute to a well-lived life.

In the language of capabilities, being a social and economic participant is an important aspect of our agency and an intrinsic component of human well-being.

Before "the market" took on the sense of an impersonal, global
mechanism by which supply meets demand at some equilibrium
price, the market was a physical place where buyers and sellers meet
face-to-face to exchange goods. Shopping is, at its best, both an end
and a means. It is a means for people to acquire the goods needed
(or wanted) for living. Unless we were in a society where people
produced everything for themselves, some form of specialization
and trading is necessary. Shopping in some form is thus a necessary
activity.

We can say more than that, however. Meeting in the marketplace to exchange goods can be a healthy and humane activity that
is valuable for its own sake. That is, shopping is not just a means
toward meeting needs. Instead, it is a social activity, whereby people
meet and interact. Shopping can help meet the need for human socia-
bility. "Market day" is a civic event—usually filling a central public
square with booths and people. When I travel abroad, I have learned
to consult guidebooks and ask my local friends, When is market day?
It is usually a spectacle and a way to learn about the local customs
of a place. The growth of farmers markets in the United States has
helped revive the practice of "going to market" in American cities.

In a suburban area notable for its state-of-the-art shopping
mall and its heavy traffic, a billboard was posted above a new con-
dominium complex: "Live where you shop." The phrasing seemed
exactly backwards to me. The problem is one of priorities. Contrary
to this slogan and the popular bumper sticker, we don't live to shop.
Or, at least, we should not. But neither do we shop merely to live.
Shopping can properly be an enjoyable form of human interaction.

It is a laudable goal to integrate our lives so that our common economic activities—working, shopping, eating out—would
fit well and easily with our other activities. Some forms of city and
neighborhood planning, such as the "new urbanism," aim to re-
capture the benefits of sidewalks, street grids, and local storefronts.
These approaches tout sustainable local communities that are walk-
able and also accessible by public transportation as well as private
automobiles.

Yet the vision of the marketplace as a site of neighbors meeting neighbors sounds a little nostalgic in the age of Walmart and Costco. Our market is far more impersonal today than it has ever been. Products are made around the world and sold around the world. From the time of Adam Smith to Karl Marx to the present, economists have praised the virtues of specialization, while also noting the pitfalls of that process for laborers. Marx's writings on the alienation of labor provide an enduring caution against dehumanizing factory labor. By the time a factory worker's product comes to market, it has likely changed hands a half-dozen times.

Less noted has been the near impossibility in a global economy of knowing who the producers of your goods are. This is a kind of depersonalization, if not alienation, of consumers from their products. Even in earlier times and simpler economies, of course, the idea that the sellers were the makers of products was often incorrect. There have always been middlemen and merchants. Yet this does not undercut the point that today's market is depersonalized like never before. If we care about a humane economy, then this two-way loss of personal connection between buyers and sellers is a drawback.

My colleague in the Economics Department at Richmond, Jonathan Wight, begins his economic development course with an exercise. He simply asks students if they know where their clothes and other goods—cell phones, watches, backpacks, and so on—were produced. He divides the students into small groups, and for a moment in the class, the learning becomes tangible. Students are reading each other's labels, and laughing awkwardly on occasion at the bodily nature of the exercise. When the class of twenty or thirty students reconvenes, Professor Wight can always be sure of one thing: The class is the United Nations of stuff. Dozens and dozens of countries are represented, including the United States. But some labels are ambiguous or simply omit where the products are made. Professor Wight and his in-class exercise make the point well: There is almost no way to know the producers of the goods you possess.

In response to this impersonal marketplace, some local consumers have sought to add the human connection back into their daily or weekly practices. At the local level, thriving farmers markets have arisen across the country; the number of these almost tripled between 1994 and 2008.[9] Farmers markets combine a number of benefits—especially fresh food and lower transportation costs. Usually, unless excessive technology is used to grow products locally, they also realize a reduced environmental impact. Knowing the farmers who grow the crops and having a sense of place where your food is produced are added benefits that humanize the shopping and cooking.

A different strategy, especially for goods that cannot be readily made locally, is to link up and deal directly with a group or organization that makes products abroad. Nonprofit organizations have developed niche markets for international goods that come with stories of their producers and the commitment to ethical exchanges. Buyers do not meet the sellers in person, but liaison organizations establish a sustained and dependable relationship that connects buyer and seller. In Chapter Eight I profile the ways that the organizations SERRV and Ten Thousand Villages put these ideas into practice.

For all its potential to fulfill the capability of social participation, shopping can be the reflection of desire gone wild. There is even a clinical word for uncontrollable shopping—*oniomania*—which is classified as an impulse-control disorder. Shopping too easily loses its proper place within a well-lived life. Excessive shopping leads to a loss of time for other activities, especially when people add extra work hours to their routines in order to pay for their purchases. It also takes away money from other priorities, including economic ends such as saving, investing, and giving. And it contributes significantly to indebtedness, which is a national disease. It becomes the tail that wags the dog—recall the slogan "Live where you shop." Other parts of life can be subordinated to a lifestyle of shopping.

Consuming and Polluting

Shopping has an environmental footprint. But individual consumers cannot easily decide to make shopping a more eco-friendly practice. In my city of Richmond, there are very few grocery stores, discount stores, or movie theaters located in pedestrian-friendly neighborhoods. You have to drive. Last summer I took my kids to run Saturday errands, which included a trip to the pet store and to Target. The

Discerning Desires

two stores are less than two blocks apart, though they are separated by a large parking lot. I must have been feeling eco-friendly, because I thought I would hold hands with the kids and walk between the stores—instead of parking a second time. (Moving the car becomes twice the work when it involves buckling and unbuckling car seats.) So we stepped out from the pet store's sidewalk toward Target.

That was the first and the last time. It turns out that pedestrians traversing the Target parking lot embody the word *target*. It was a two-block walk, but crossing the Red Sea would have been easier. SUVs and cars whiz by, not seeing the young kids until they round the corner or have them in their direct path. How easy it would have been to have created a pedestrian walkway through the middle of that lot, or around its perimeter. Moreover, huge parking lots such as this one are environmentally unfriendly, not only because of the heavy car use and need to park at each store, but also because of the effects of water runoff, temperature retention, and a host of other factors. Yet consumers have not asked for significant changes to the shopping set-ups that assume the routine of park-as-you-shop. After all, it is convenient enough to drive from store to store as long as they have large enough parking lots.

The energy expended in the actual practice of shopping is just a slice of consumerism's environmental impact. The production, use, and disposal of products are more detrimental. U.S. citizens make up less than 5 percent of the global population, but we consume between a fourth and a fifth of its energy.[10] We have an increasing landfill and waste disposal problem, and we are net exporters of garbage. If the Chinese drove cars at the same rate as U.S. consumers, we would not be able to breathe on the planet.[11]

China and the rest of the developing world are moving in that direction. Latin Americans, Africans, and Asians are moving, some more rapidly than others, toward the material lifestyle of the industrialized nations, that fifth of the world's population living in high-income countries. The United Nations Development Programme has estimated that this high-income 20 percent of the world population makes 86 percent of all private consumption expenditures.[12] These are the spending patterns, replete with images of the happy consumer lifestyle promoted in global advertising, that people around the world are emulating.

It is daunting to think of tackling a global economic and environmental crisis. And yet it seems too meager to focus on our own individual use and reuse patterns. At the University of Richmond, we took a modest approach last year. A planning team of faculty and staff decided to launch an educational effort addressing people's consumption patterns and helping them think of ways to recycle or repurpose discarded items. Drawing on the school's unique mascot, the spider, the University announced the Eco-Spider Challenge. The contest was for groups of students to produce a University of Richmond spider by using only recycled materials. The idea came from cities that host art celebrations and commission local artists to decorate their city with public art. For example, a few years ago Chicago displayed more than two hundred cows across the Windy City.

The University of Richmond took this idea and made it green. About twenty spiders, from table-top size to human size, appeared around campus on a spring weekend. Each spider was accompanied by a short essay on the environmental significance of the spider. Eventually, the momentum created by the Eco-Spider helped make possible a campus-wide staff position of sustainability coordinator and a series of programming events on energy conservation and waste disposal on campus.

As I discuss in Chapter Nine, caring for creation is a vital linkage between spiritual and economic practices. Understanding the environmental impact of our consumer choices is an essential part of our spending and consuming habits. And these ecological questions remind us that our own desires and goods belong within a wider context, and that we can play a part in managing God's creation.

PURSUING CAPABILITIES, NOT HAPPINESS

"Why do you spend your money for that which is not bread and your labor for that which does not satisfy?" So the author of Isaiah asked the people. This is part of Isaiah's wider theological perspective on what a restored Israelite community would look like. The hopeful vision is cast in economic (and ecological) terms: "Ho, everyone who thirsts, come to the waters; and you that have no money, come, buy and eat! Come, buy wine and milk without money and without price" (Isaiah 55:1). The biblical narrative declares that genuine satisfaction is more than instant gratification. It is more than happiness as an emotional feeling or as a fluctuating subjective state dependent on material goods. Why do we spend our money on stuff that doesn't satisfy? Economists have reminded us that the endless pursuit of consumer goods will more likely place us in competition with our neighbors than provide any sense of enduring satisfaction. For we can be sure that our neighbors will also seek the same goods that we do, and we will be off to the races. We will be chasing consumer happiness that remains just beyond our reach.

We should be concerned about well-being and not about happiness alone. People can be happily ignorant about suffering in the world, and the poor can be pacified or mollified with their lot. Marx called religion the opium of the people because the faith he saw seemed to justify the vast inequalities of power and income in the industrial capitalism of mid-nineteenth-century England and Europe. Using a different image, religion was one of the flowers that decorated the chains of oppression that the poor suffered.[13] You do not have to be a Marxist to worry about the ways that poverty can corrode the hope of young people to improve their lot. People adjust their expectations of what is possible. When eighth-graders decide to blow off school and play hooky with their friends, for example, they are wrongly choosing happiness over well-being. When parents take a big share of their paychecks to splurge on piles of Christmas presents to please their kids, they have shown good intentions but squandered resources for happiness over well-being.

Jesus asks people why they choose material pleasures over more enduring goods. "Do not store up for yourselves treasures on earth, where moth and rust consume and where thieves break in and steal; but store up for yourselves treasures in heaven, where neither moth nor rust consumes and where thieves do not break in and steal. For where your treasure is, there your heart will be also" (Matthew 6:19–21). It is easy to "spiritualize" this passage to see Jesus as saying that material goods are bad. It is true that stuff breaks, rusts, and gets stolen—and all of this is a source of anxiety. (Happiness studies show that we are more troubled by what might happen than by bad events that actually happen.[14]) But I have a different reading. Jesus is calling us to pursue those goods—in our very earthly, everyday practices—that are consistent with a theocentric view of the world. These are the goods that will endure. These goods help expand our own capabilities and those of our neighbors. These treasures are more communal and relational than most of the things that we buy and store.

Jesus challenged his followers to choose treasures that would put their heart in heavenly matters. Put differently: How do we discern our desires and then align them with our theocentric values? This is where the language of capabilities can help in our everyday decisions about spending. We should shift our focus from promoting happiness to developing human capabilities—our own and those of others. *Does this purchase allow me to be better nourished? Will this expenditure allow someone to participate in the life of the community? Does it promote better public health?* These are goods that will not be destroyed by rust or moth. And nutritious food, civic engagement, and health care are more difficult than consumer goods to steal. They are consistent with valuing human life as created in God's image.

It is not easy, of course, to shape our desires in any particular direction—and we cannot do it alone. Indeed, the very act of discerning what our real desires are is a complicated task that requires boring through layers of self-understanding and even, for many of us, some self-deception. Advertisers appeal to our desires for a reason—instant gratification and the promise of happiness, however fleeting, beckon to us. We do not have to be ascetics to live faithfully in the global economy, but we need to be willing to ask the critical questions about our own consumerism. Shopping will remain an everyday practice, but it will be shopping in the context of human capabilities and treasures that endure.

Chapter 4

PROVIDING

❧

You open your hand, satisfying the desire of every living thing.
—Psalm 145:16

None of us is God, and none of us can claim certainty about God's plans or purposes. Even as we affirm the value of human agency, we also acknowledge that our finite or limited ability to make change is a good thing. It reminds us that we are not fully in control of our own life or the lives of others. And that is okay. The quest for economic affluence can stem from the mistaken belief that we can buy our own, or our family's, happiness. We cannot. It requires faith every day to engage in economic life, especially because people can and do violate our trust in the marketplace (and elsewhere). We need faith, along with good common sense, to believe we can make ends meet. Amid the uncertainties of real life, we implicitly have to trust, every day, that something beyond our own control will get us through, or else we remain paralyzed. For Christians, that "something" is God. God is a God of providence, we affirm. God provides. God will provide.

John Calvin, the great French figure in the Protestant Reformation, offers the fullest account of providence. For Calvin, at the root of this doctrine is a message of comfort. When Calvin published his masterwork, *The Institutes of the Christian Religion,* in 1536, he was an exile writing from Switzerland to his Huguenot brothers and sisters who were being persecuted in France. He framed providence as the ultimate conviction that God is in charge of the world and of each life, despite the adversities and tribulations that people are suffering.

In this social context, believers were to hold fast to the faith that God would provide what they truly needed. In matters of economic "prosperity," as Calvin put it, God's followers had much reason for comfort. "Gratitude of mind for the favorable outcome of things, patience in adversity, and also incredible freedom from worry about the future all necessarily follow upon this knowledge" that the world is under the providence of God.[1] Calvin helps us see, then, that providence gives us faith that God's activity in the world will provide— including materially—for all people.

Does this mean, since God is going to do the providing, that we human beings should not work, that we should not give of our possessions, or that we should not persevere in our calling to serve our neighbors and work for justice? By no means. Calvin directly rejects any such dichotomy between divine and human agency. But it does mean that worrying excessively about job or economic security can be a futile, and an unhealthy, exercise. It calls us to respond gratefully to the opportunities set before us and then to have faith that God will be with us in that good work.

We can easily forget to thank God for the blessings of provision that we enjoy every day. One tangible practice is giving thanks through prayer at mealtime for the food that we eat. This has become an awkward practice for many of us who share meals at restaurants with friends, colleagues, and clients. It is not always customary in America today to pray in this public setting. The respect for religious diversity is an understandable reason for this hesitancy—we cannot and should not assume that all our acquaintances believe as we do. So the food arrives at lunch with a new colleague or friend. There is the uncomfortable pause. *Should I pray? Will he pray?* For my part, I always play it by ear. Often, if I am unsure how to proceed, I will say, "We are grateful for this food," or, "I am grateful to have a chance to get together." Sometimes, my companion will say, "Yes, indeed," or even, "Amen." (Other times, all I get is a blank stare.) All of this is to say that we should find ways to express our gratitude in our daily routines.

Another part of this awkwardness is simply our desire to be in control and our desire not to thank any outside party for our provisions. Perhaps this is not just a modern problem, however. Moses warns the Israelites that, when they reach the land of promise, "a land where you may eat bread without scarcity, where you will lack nothing" (Deuteronomy 8:9a), they might become complacent in their material comfort, and hence forget God. They might also forget their communal requirements to remember the poor and treat the vulnerable with respect. The dangers of economic prosperity include selfishness, injustice, and a loss of faithfulness. Often, our lack of gratitude is hard to pinpoint in specific sinful acts of commission (what we do) or omission (what we fail to do). It results from immersing ourselves in a fast-paced culture that operates as if we can all be self-sustaining. It is a generalized failure to live in a spirit of gratitude.

The good news is that, whether or not we appropriately express thankfulness, God does provide. Like God's provision of manna in the wilderness, when the community sticks together and cares for one another, there is enough for everyone.

FEEDING THE 6.5 BILLION

The claim that God provides runs counter to the stark contemporary reality in which about a billion human beings do not have enough food to escape malnutrition.[2] For many people, the poor and others, the statement that God provides may seem to be a smug dismissal of the reality of hunger and malnutrition—as though these blights are either temporary or less significant than spiritual well-being.

According to the experts, the issue of malnutrition is not one of the overall availability of food—it is one of distribution. It is not a supply problem—it is a sharing problem. The Food and Agriculture Organization of the United Nations reports that there are approximately 2,800 kilocalories of daily food supply available for every man, woman, and child on the planet.[3] This means that there is more than enough food to feed everyone in the world at a nutritionally adequate standard. The challenge is for people to enjoy the economic, techno-logical, and infrastructural access to obtain the food and other sources of nutrition that they need.

We thus must make our claims that God provides within the context of widespread malnutrition while also understanding that there is sufficient supply to meet nutrition standards for all people. We will come to view this theological claim as a call for people to help alleviate such deprivation. This perspective is reflected in the feeding of the five thousand, a story that appears in all four Gospels (Mark 6:3–44; Matthew 14:13–21; Luke 9:10–17; John 6:1–13).

After hearing that his friend John the Baptist had been killed, Jesus had had enough of human community for a while. So he set out on his own trek, as he had done on various occasions, to gath-er himself and pray. There is no indication in the biblical story of whether Jesus had taken enough provisions for himself. We simply read that crowds from multiple towns in the area followed him out into the countryside. He was overrun with people.

Jesus' disciples, his inner circle, suddenly appear in the story and suggest that he send these followers away. But Jesus had already shown compassion for the needy in the crowd; he had healed the sick who found him. Now he told his disciples not to shun the masses but to feed them. They were spiritual travelers, but they were also bodily travelers who needed food and water to survive.

The presenting problem of the followers is that they had not come prepared with food. Maybe they were like the disciples them-selves who, when Jesus said, "Follow me," had immediately dropped their daily routine to join in (Mark 1:16–20). Unlike Simon, Andrew, James, and John, these followers didn't even need a direct invitation from Jesus to come.

And there were a lot of them. The Gospel writer Matthew is most direct in saying that there were not just five thousand people to feed. There were five thousand *men,* with women and children in addition to that number.

How did they locate enough food for everybody? There is no account of a giant celestial loaf of bread that fell from heaven. There is no mention of a rescue helicopter that delivered to a drop zone. Rather, somebody came up with five loaves and two fish. The Gos-pel of John says that this food came from a boy (John 6:9). John thus emphasizes the unpreparedness of the adults in the crowd and highlights the grace-filled nature of the miracle. Only a boy had thought to bring food—or perhaps only he was willing to share what he had. Jesus told the disciples to pass the supplies around, and the loaves and fish miraculously multiplied. The text says that everyone was filled.

Was this a "supernatural" miracle by which Jesus made bread and fish appear from thin air? Or was it a "social" miracle? Is it possible, in other words, that some people in the crowd were so moved by Jesus' call to eat together that they pulled food from their satchels to throw into the common supply? Perhaps some people had been guarding a half-loaf of bread for their family, and others had a little wine in their wineskins that they had been saving for themselves.

The truth is, of course, that we don't know what kind of miracle happened when Jesus fed those thousands of people. Miracles are signs that God is acting in a special way—in a way that remains mysterious to human understanding. But however he did it, Jesus created a community out of that crowd. In Jesus' day or in our own, to create a community who will share their food and share themselves is nothing short of miraculous.

In not-so-subtle language, the Gospel writers present this story as a model for the Lord's Supper. Matthew puts it this way: "Taking the five loaves and the two fish, he looked up to heaven, and blessed and broke the loaves, and gave them to the disciples, and the disciples gave them to the crowds" (Matthew 14:19b). These phrases closely track the words of institution for Holy Communion. In both the feeding story and the Lord's Supper, bread is not just some spiritual good; on the contrary, bread is the ordinary, material product that is made holy by the way that it is used to give and sustain life.

When I read of the five thousand hungry men and the untold thousands of women and children in that rural place, I also hear echoes of the one billion hungry men, women, and children in our world who also hunger and thirst for adequate sustenance. An almost incomprehensible number—it is over three times the entire population of the United States. What kind of miracle will it take to provide bread and fish and enough to drink?

We already know the basic answer to that question, but we have to live it out. It will require sharing—massive sharing—by individuals and communities, and through just and efficient social systems of distribution. It has everything in the world to do with the faith that God, acting through and beyond people, will perform miracles of provision.

Providing a Healthy Home

Neville Selhore told me that miracles occur in his community every day. After seeing it for myself, I believe him. Neville leads the Sahara House in New Delhi, India, where he and a small staff provide a therapeutic, transitional community for former drug addicts and HIV-positive persons. Without Sahara House, these clients would likely be homeless on the streets of India's teeming capital city.

Sahara House is home to eighty or ninety people and sometimes more, a quarter of whom are living with HIV. Some of the girls and women in Sahara House's care are former workers in the sex industry who either escaped or were rescued from that life. Many people suffering drug addictions enter Sahara House for six months, often coming off the street. Once they recover their health and break their addiction, the Sahara House staff encourages them to find work in order to regain regularity and a sense of structure in their lives. They then move to a transitional or halfway house where they can progress toward independent living.

Neville and his colleagues have trouble explaining the wide range of services they provide—from basic health services and rehabilitation to counseling and vocational training. In addition to the clinic, there is a transitional home next door, a small shop for making crafts for income nearby, a women's and children's shelter down the street, and a day care center in the basement.

When I visited Sahara House along with a colleague from my university, two aspects of this place immediately struck me. First, the depth of need and the degree of compassionate response made it clear that this was a community practicing Christian hospitality. We experienced that hospitality ourselves. As Neville emphasizes, Sahara House makes no effort to convert anyone; yet he and his colleagues are visibly inspired by their faith to put into practice the Gospel call to care for society's forgotten neighbors. They even welcome people who have been rejected by other clinics and hospitals because of addictions or, in at least a few cases, a criminal record.

The second remarkable hallmark of Sahara House is its staff members' utter dependence on God and other people to allow them to function. Neville told me that in all of its years of existence, Sahara House has had no budget. It has received small grants from a host of international sources, including nongovernmental organizations, but he and his colleagues largely depend upon individual donors to support their work. Neville stated that some observers, visitors, and potential funders have wanted Sahara House to be more structured, just as others want the staff to be more evangelistic in their appeals to Christian faith as they serve their clients. Neville insists on "going on faith."

Not that Sahara House's loose structure and trust in God's providing has been easy. Neville told us about having to cancel or postpone an HIV+ nutrition program that his staff had wanted to offer. The money did not come.

Neville described his costs to us: At the time we met, rent was 40,000 rupees a month, and his staff could feed the whole community for just over 1,000 rupees a day. Together, the basic food and housing for the entire community was thus under $100 per day. When we visited him on a Tuesday, he told us that he had enough money in hand to run the community until Friday.

I confess that when I heard Neville's story, I wanted to join the chorus of constructive critics who recommend a greater structure. He needs a plan, I wanted to shout out. Stated more pointedly: Is it irresponsible to lead a community delivering vital services to a vulnerable population without a plan extending, literally, into next week? I was skeptical (and still am) of the view that trusting God means waiting for miracles to happen before the food and medical supplies run out.

Neville anticipated my questions, with a smile, even before I could ask them. Theirs was a community of practice that witnesses to God, and they were living out their faith that God would provide the means for them to serve their mission. It had worked thus far, and the quality of faith required by this approach was a fundamental part of what made the community work.

Neville also told me that he has known times when he had money, and now he does not have money. You can't compare the two situations, he said. I think he was suggesting, given the joy he communicates about his current role at Sahara House, that he is better off in overall terms now than when he lived on his own with more financial security. Neville told me that in his current vocation, he gets to see God working at close quarters. He said that he works with those "who've been given up and looked over—people who should be dead by now." With a smile he added that he and his wife Elizabeth had lived downstairs since 1985, and they raised their three children in the community.

My American colleague and I each made a contribution to the work of Sahara House—we gave all of the cash that we were carrying, and I can't remember exactly how much it was. But we both knew when we gave it that it was very little money. We figured we had helped support the community's operating costs for two days. That would get them through the weekend. Was that enough?

Sahara House offers a counterweight, a form of witness to all of us who feel an obsessive need to figure out exactly how we are going to make ends meet and have cash left over. We allow financial concerns, usually trivial ones by comparison to the realities the residents and staff of Sahara House face, to steal our attention from other matters. It would be possible, of course, to apply the Sahara community's approach and (lack of) planning in a literal way. Most of us are not called to live in an intentional community or to live hand-to-mouth from the generosity of neighbors and strangers. Here we are back at the same conundrum we have faced before: If we are not willing or able to copy the practices of the biblical saints—or, in this case, of a current-day saint—then what are we left with? What should we take away from the example of a community that is living the Gospel in extraordinary ways when we go back to our ordinary lives?

PROVIDING FOR ONE ANOTHER

In my own experience, the answers to some of these questions might be found in another community—this one in Burgundy, France. At the Taizé monastery, about a hundred monks lead a common life of worship, work, and hospitality, welcoming thousands of visitors every week. Taizé is one of the most spiritually vibrant Christian communities in the world. It has become a spiritual pilgrimage site of sorts for the churched and unchurched alike.[4]

The logistics of Taizé's hospitality—providing food and shelter to the masses—is a marvel. And it serves as a model.

Brother Roger founded the monastery of Taizé, in the village of that name, in 1940 as a witness to God's peaceable vision amid the violence of World War II. From its earliest days, the community's daily practices have been shaped by that vision, including providing a safe haven to Jews fleeing occupied France for Switzerland. In an impoverished postwar France, it served workers and the indigent in the agricultural lands of Burgundy and in some of France's industrial cities. These practices of justice and outreach went hand in hand with the prayer, contemplation, and music that are now the hallmarks of Taizé.

The village of Taizé is a lovely place, but it is in the middle of the countryside. The medieval monastery of Cluny is only about a dozen miles away, but otherwise, Taizé is no geographical crossroads. Yet it has become a cultural and religious crossroads; the monks themselves have come from Catholic, Protestant, and Orthodox traditions around the world.

In the sixties, young people from around France and across Europe began traveling to Taizé as pilgrims. The steady stream of visitors must have seemed peculiar to the brothers of Taizé, at first. As at other monasteries, the Rule of Taizé included a call to hospitality: "In each guest it is Christ himself whom we have to receive; so let us learn to be welcoming and be ready to offer our free time. Our hospitality should be generous and discerning."[5]

On a given weekend in the summer, at least three thousand young adults and families arrive at Taizé. They must each find a place to stay, a way to eat, and information about the daily activities and worship services. Dozens of languages are spoken by the visitors, most of whom have arrived at Taizé for the first time. Many have transferred from a train to a local bus to get here, while others arrive by charter bus or private automobile. There is no supermarket or hotel in the community—only common kitchens, guest houses, and tents.

How do people get acclimated and integrated, then, into the community? How do the hosts provide for the needs of the visitors? The answer, in short, is *organized hospitality.* Over the decades the brothers of Taizé have developed a routine that enables them to welcome numbers far beyond what the brothers acting alone could handle. They empower volunteers to do most of the work. Longer-term guests soon become hosts. Those who are spiritual seekers are also workers.

With the advent of the Internet, the Taizé community has now shifted to e-mail much of its practice of welcoming its would-be visitors preparing to arrive. (When I first made inquiry about traveling to Taizé, in 1987, I received a hand-written note from the brother in charge of hospitality.) Upon arrival at the community on Sunday afternoons, people and groups are sorted out, in the welcome area, by language and type of program. Families with children move to a house a few hundred yards away. People bringing their own tents are directed to certain areas; people staying in guest houses or the large tentlike building are guided to those places. Food and lodging at Taizé is a segmented market. People pay, in general terms, according to their ability to contribute. The brothers have set up a rate structure according to two criteria—age group and country of residence. Young people under thirty from the industrializing countries in Africa and Asia, for instance, are asked to pay about 5 euros a day. Adults over thirty from Western Europe and North America are asked to contribute between 15 and 25 euros daily. No one, however, is turned away for lack of money to pay.

Food distribution is on a massive scale. As someone who has eaten many cold meals—meals intended to be hot ones—at camps, conferences, and conventions, I am amazed by the efficiency with which food is served at Taizé. And after each breakfast, lunch, and dinner, volunteers collect and clean the thousands of bowls, cups, and utensils in time for the next feeding of the thousands.

Those expecting a gourmet meal will be disappointed. But those content with well-prepared, simple, and nourishing food will be satisfied. Taizé calls itself a "parable of community." Every time I participate in a meal there, I experience the feeding of the five thousand.

When I first visited Taizé, I spent two weeks in the community. What appeared to me on my first day to be a mysterious and perhaps miraculous occurrence—moving people to where they needed to be—became, at the start of the second week, a loosely organized system based upon veteran guests welcoming new guests. Considering that most of these so-called veterans had been there for only a week, this well-functioning social system seemed even more miraculous than I had thought on arrival.

Thus the Taizé example helps answer the questions I have for saints like Neville Selhore and others who expect miracles to happen every day. The brothers of Taizé—and also the staff at Sahara House—believe deeply that God provides. But they do not wait for God to bake the bread, or set up the tents, or clean the dishes. They and their colleagues get to work on these practices. They firmly believe that they are striving to achieve God's purposes. God is acting through them and their organizations, and so they set about to accomplish their tasks as efficiently and humanely as possible.

This engaged or active faith is even more evident for me at Taizé than at Sahara House, but partly that is my own bias. Whereas I was only a visitor at Sahara House, I became an active participant in the spiritual and practical life at Taizé. Neville Selhore will tell you that most of the activities and programs of Sahara House are run by former participants, including ex–drug addicts who have come to believe deeply in redemption and second chances. And they work to make those things possible for others.

It is surprising, perhaps, to look to two deeply and intentionally spiritual communities in order to discover the ways in which God provides for very practical human needs in the so-called real world. But the lessons of Sahara House and Taizé also hold in our more ordinary lives: God provides, but God usually provides through our own caring and committed actions done for and with each other.

BREADWINNING

The *breadwinner*. It's a common term to describe a person who provides bread for a group of dependents. The reference to bread, as we have already seen, evokes the provision and sustenance of life itself. *Are you the breadwinner in your family?* This question was traditionally aimed at men alone—or it was not even posed at all, because people assumed it was the man. The term comes from middle English words for *loaf ward,* or guardian or provider of the bread. Loaf ward was condensed to form the word *lord* in medieval times. The social superior—presumed to be male—was the one who would provide the bread, or the necessaries of life, for those in the household. *Lady,* a word deriving from the term *loaf kneader,* designated the one who prepares the food within the household, who was one of those depending upon the breadwinner to provide.

The "male breadwinner family" came to predominate in Western societies during the period of industrialization as a common model of organizing the household. The husband and father leaves the private or domestic sphere to enter the public workplace so he can earn enough money to support his dependents, which include the wife and mother and their children. The wife and mother in this model stays at home, within the domestic sphere, performing the domestic work of household chores and child rearing. The man is part of the formal labor market, receiving income for his effort, while the woman's labor is informal; that is, it receives no market compensation.

The practice and ideology of the male breadwinner family resulted from a number of factors. Some scholars emphasize the relatively higher wage rates that men could receive, vis-à-vis women, in the formal labor market. This explanation, of course, raises other questions about why a gender-based pay differential existed in the first place. Much industrial work was manual labor, requiring physical strength, which would tend to favor men—or so the argument goes. This, of course, does not address the differences in strength among individual men or women—or among men as a group or among women as a group. World War II's impetus for women to work in factories showed that women, famously depicted as Rosie the Riveter, had the strength and endurance to master traditionally male roles in heavy manufacturing.

We should consider other explanations of the male as breadwinner that have to do with ideology and social power. One scholar describes "an unfortunate marriage between patriarchy and the industrial capitalist system" that allowed the husband to be the dominant figure within the nuclear household.[6] This role as provider also played into—and reinforced—a modern understanding of masculinity.

For many of us who grew up on reruns of *Leave It to Beaver,* the male breadwinner model of family organization seems to be the long-enduring norm that recent practice has overturned. Scholars debate, however, just how standard the male breadwinner family ever was. They point out that it was only the rise of the formal labor market in the past two centuries that allowed such a clear separation between paid and unpaid labor. In agricultural society, in contrast, women and men both undertook manual labor in the fields, and the economic return on the labor of any one person was not so simple to determine.

During industrialization, a debate raged on what wage a worker should receive. For those advocating a free-market solution, the proper wage is the one at which supply meets demand. This is a situation in which everyone willing to work has a job at a wage that employers are willing to pay, and employers need no further labor supply. How would anyone know whether this "equilibrium wage" was enough to provide for a family? Marx gave his famous account of the subsistence wage, which was enough to make workers willing to work for the capitalist because it allowed them to survive as they sought to provide for their loved ones. But if unwilling or unable laborers complained or underperformed, there was a "reserve army of the unemployed" standing at the factory gates ready to replace them.[7]

The debate about subsistence is intertwined with the focus on justice. What is a just wage? Catholic social teaching weighed in on this debate, starting with Pope Leo XIII in 1891. The pope emphasized that all workers, because of their dignity as persons, were due fair treatment by their employers. The pope was careful to emphasize an organic harmony among workers and employers. He thus explicitly rejected socialism, which he believed incited laborers into social conflict. He argued that the family was essential to protect, and men should be able to earn enough to provide for their families.[8]

In America, John A. Ryan spent his career arguing for a "family living wage." Ryan, who served as an important adviser to President Franklin D. Roosevelt, came to be known as "the Right Reverend

New Dealer." Ryan's approach, widely viewed as progressive for his day, was based on the male breadwinner model:

> Now, the support of the family falls properly upon the husband and father, not upon the wife and mother. The obligation of the father to provide a livelihood for the wife and young children is quite as definite as his obligation to maintain himself. If he has not the means to discharge this obligation he is not justified in getting married. Yet marriage is essential to normal life for the great majority of men. Therefore, the material requisites of normal life for the average adult male include provision for his family. . . . In the case of the wage-earner . . . the adult male laborer has a right to a family living wage.[9]

Ryan thus states as clearly as anyone the ties between bread-winning and the male provider role. But there are further questions to be addressed: What size of family is envisioned, and should the same workers be paid differently according to the needs of their families? Ryan offered a calculation for a basic family. He also went on to argue that all adult males deserved this same wage, notwith-standing the number of children—if any—each had.

Ryan argued that women, unlike men, did not have the natu-ral duty to provide for their families and thus were due only a wage sufficient to support themselves living "away from home." There was no shame in this gender-based wage differential—it was, in-stead, part of the moral argument.

In practice, women did receive lower wages than men in fac-tory work. These wage differentials notwithstanding, many work-ing-class women and children labored long hours alongside men.[10] The male breadwinner model remained a luxury for families that could survive on one income.

With the massive entrance of women into the formal labor force over the past forty years, the sole-breadwinner family has be-come less and less common in practice. Among married women whose spouse is present, 60 percent are working outside the home; this is roughly the same figure of all adult women who are in the labor force.[11] The lone breadwinner model remains a norm that is most readily attainable in upper income brackets. In the majority of two-adult households, both adults work.

The notion of breadwinning is still very much present among us, but it tends to convey different pressures along gender lines. For men, the social expectation to be a provider persists. But do the math—given the lack of a rise in the average wage (after adjusting for inflation) over recent decades, the only way for household income from labor to increase is to work more hours. And that has been accomplished, for the most part, by women entering the workforce. Many men may feel a need to be sole breadwinners, but if they ever could afford it, they can certainly not do so in today's economy.

Those men and women who have a strong sense of duty to be the breadwinner are hit especially hard by unemployment. Michigan, home of the American auto industry (devastated by long-term shrinkage and recent shocks), has experienced increased cases of depression and higher demand for mental health services.[12] Given the self- and socially imposed pressures to provide, is the opposite of a breadwinner a "loser"? This is the sentiment of many would-be breadwinners.

The men I know in my father's generation, born in the wake of the Great Depression, acutely feel such a strong duty to provide. They worked long hours and took pride in their work. They tended to wear this responsibility not as a burden but as a noble calling. There is much to admire in this commitment to family, to the duty to provide.

At the same time, this self-understanding was (and is) also unhealthy. There is a fine line between work as a calling and work as a matter of proving one's worth. Max Weber tried to analyze the Protestant work ethic in terms of the drive of Calvinists and Puritans. These Protestants were anxious, Weber asserts, to prove their status with God. Although Calvinism properly calls people not to anxiety but to gratitude, Weber may well have been onto something when he saw Protestants practicing work as if their life—and the lives of their loved ones—depended on it.[13]

Some of these men who grew up in the Depression era are, ironically, facing a recession just as they finally decide to retire. Many have had trouble letting go of the role of breadwinner, of provider. If work gives a sense of worth and contribution, then retirement seems like a step into a role of uncertainty or perhaps even worthlessness. It is sad to acknowledge that these men would probably have been better off in financial terms to have stopped working a few years ago, cashing out some of their 401(k) plans when the market was high.

As the ideal of the male breadwinner family fades, women tend to have a different relationship than men do to the idea of providing. Women's sphere was traditionally the domestic one. Children were dependent on their mothers to provide them food to eat from the moment they entered the world (and before). Women were supposed to provide not only nutrition but security, manners, and education as well.

In contemporary times, many women continue to bear a disproportionate burden of household chores and child-rearing duties and have now taken on the additional pressures of providing income from the formal labor market, too. This twin burden to provide has been called different names, including "working the second shift," as sociologist Arlie Hochschild has put it. While men, on average, work a few more hours at home than they used to, women continue with a disproportionate share of household labor combined with full-time work beyond the household.[14]

Both women's and men's economic roles are complicated. Not all women are wives or mothers, of course, but they experience common gender-based assumptions and practices in the workplace. Men face new pressures to share in housework and child rearing alongside the breadwinner expectations that the average male wage cannot meet. Many men and many women cannot provide—at least not in the ways that social expectations appear to demand.

What are we to do about this stark reality? We need to return to valuing people not for their economic contribution alone—even as we understand the important role of participation and contributions of various sorts in human well-being. We need to continue to work on establishing a minimum wage that is indeed adequate for persons, male or female, to support themselves and at least two dependents. And we need to emphasize the positive aspects of interdependence on one another to make ends meet.

Compared to breadwinning, *stewardship* is a term with a more obvious theological resonance, and a more technical (if narrow) meaning in church contexts. Every member of the clergy and of the church budget committee can tell you that stewardship is the season in which people fill out pledge cards that commit them to giving a share of their economic goods to the church. For many churches, Stewardship Sunday is the annual day when a visiting preacher is called in to do the "dirty work" of talking to Christians about money. It is hard, certainly, for the local pastor to speak about giving more when, as is often the case, the vast majority of the church budget goes to support the pastor's own salary. So once a year, the church tries to bring in someone to talk openly about money.

This vision of stewardship is too limited. Etymologically, the word comes from *sty-warden,* or keeper of the sty. When I discuss the word *sty,* I always recall the only context in which I regularly heard it used. My mother would say to me, when I was a kid, "This room is a pig sty. Clean it up." I suppose that, at least by parental standards, I was a poor keeper of my sty. The concept of stewardship (just as my mother did) reminds us that it is not just our sty, barn, or house. And it's not our money. We are God's stewards. Stewardship connects, then, to the very notion of economics. It is about tending to God's household, using the resources at our disposal to care for the earth and its inhabitants, including human beings. God provides the resources in creation, but we are called to steward them to good uses.

The concept of stewardship shapes the Old Testament, or Hebrew Bible. No concepts better reflect stewardship than the twin ideals of the Sabbatical year and the Jubilee year. According to numerous biblical texts, the Israelites were instructed by God to make the seventh year holy, or set apart. Just as God rested on the seventh day, the earth was supposed to lie fallow and rejuvenate every seventh year. And the seventh year created freedom for slaves and liberation from debts; all debts were to be forgiven (Exodus 23:10–11; Jeremiah 34:13–14; Deuteronomy 15:1–6).

The Jubilee year is the Sabbatical year on steroids: It is the forty-ninth year (seven years times seven) or the fiftieth year (to round out the calendar after seven cycles of seven years). And it requires the liberating practices of the Sabbatical year—plus the return of all property to its original ownership. The author of Leviticus explains the reason for the Jubilee: "The land shall not be sold in perpetuity, for the land is mine; with me you are but aliens and tenants. Throughout the land that you hold, you shall provide for the redemption of the land" (Leviticus 25:23–24). The earth is the Lord's; so is every plot and parcel of real estate.

Picture the late Pope John Paul II joking around with rock megastar Bono. This happened in 1999, and the photo is still posted on Flickr and across the Internet. Bono received an audience with the pope as a result of the pontiff's appreciation for the singer's commitment to fight international poverty. Bono and John Paul II were allies in the Jubilee 2000 campaign. This was a global effort to encourage private and public banks and the governments of the industrialized countries to forgive the debts of impoverished countries. These public figures used the biblical image of Jubilee, which coincided with a contemporary focus on the new millennium. They tried to motivate church leaders, celebrities, and global development advocates to push for a fresh start for the developing world. The Jubilee 2000 movement helped bring foreign debt and international poverty into the consciousness of citizens and onto the agenda of various summits of the G8 countries, the eight most powerful economies in the world.

You might ask, as I do: *But were these ideals ever put into practice in biblical times?* That is a good and interesting question, but it may not be the key point of the text. Scholars debate the issue, and the general consensus is that the ideals were probably never fully practiced. Still, they framed a vision of the world in which people are stewards called to care for the earth without claiming absolute ownership over it.

OWNING

But even if we don't own the creation, many of us believe that we own particular parcels of it. To own something is to have a claim to it, to have mastery over it. We want the legal papers to back us up.

The classic discussion of ownership appears in the major work of the political philosopher John Locke, his *Second Treatise on Government,* published in 1690. Locke begins by suggesting that we know from biblical texts that God created a world in which people held all goods in common. But Locke then argues that this situation was bound not to last for long. For God created human beings with reason, and their reason dictates that people should find the means to support their own life. They should provide their own bread. Locke asserts that a just government should be formed, by the consent of the people, that would allow people the freedom to make this happen. The state should provide people with political security, but citizens also need to be able to provide for themselves in economic terms. Locke suggests that they need to be allowed to hold property. He sees the pursuit of property as vital to meeting basic needs, including food, water, and shelter.

Thus Locke argues that God approves of private property, even if creation started out as a common resource. His argument proceeds in this way. People have a right to, and ownership of, their own body. When humans use their bodies to produce things, they have an ownership claim over those goods. For each individual, Locke famously wrote, "The *Labour* of his Body, and the *Work* of his Hands, we may say, are properly his. Whatsoever then he removes out of the State that Nature hath provided, and left it in, he hath mixed his *Labour* with, and joyned to it something that is his own, and thereby makes it his *Property.*"[15] When people mix their labors with the land, they own the product that results. Locke believes that it is right and good that people who labor should enjoy the fruits of those labors. He worries about what later social scientists describe as the diffusion of responsibility, or the lack of individual incentive, that results when goods are held in common. His very understanding of society is based on the vision that individuals are pursuing their own security and well-being, and they enter into society only when it is in their interests to do so. Their economic effort should contribute to their own condition, and ownership helps make that happen.

Locke's framework is much celebrated, and rightly so, as a way of understanding what ownership and private property mean. Yet this is often the only passage that we hear from Locke. Elsewhere, however, he makes key assumptions and adds important caveats to this framework.

First, Locke suggests that people have a right to property that they help produce, but only "where there is enough, and as good, left in common for others."[16] *Enough and as good.* He gives examples in which people pick acorns and "other fruits of the Earth" that otherwise would go to waste. People are entitled to pick as much fruit as they can as long as they eat it before it spoils. That is, people are entitled to hold as much property as they are able to use. As long as people do not take more than that, then there will be enough for everyone.

Locke's further examples of land and water show that he believed there is an abundance of each. He wrote of the uncultivated land and argued that God made the world good so that humans could benefit from it—to make good use of it. But a second time, Locke employs the phrase "enough, and as good" remaining for other people.[17]

Ownership and private property, then, even in the work of their great defender Locke, are not absolute rights. Unless it is qualified, ownership is an assertion of ultimate authority to have and to use a good as the owner sees fit. Locke claims that ownership and property rights have caveats concerning reasonable and limited use. He sees the importance—even the theological importance—of leaving enough for everyone else. Catholic social teaching extends this point, introducing the concept of a "social mortgage," by which the right of private property is always subject to the common obligation to meet the basic needs of all persons.

Ownership of economic goods always fits within the prior commitment to human dignity and the meeting of human needs. Locke begins with all goods being held in common and then, as a prudential matter, accepts that property can result when people mix their labor with creation. When understood this way, ownership is close to the concept of stewardship within God's creation.

Are Locke's assumptions still correct—that in a world of over 6.5 billion people, there is enough land and water for everyone to use and still leave "as much and as good" for all? In my community, most every summer we are told to ration our water usage. During declared water savings periods, no one is permitted to water a lawn on Mondays, Wednesdays, or Fridays. (For first offenses, we would only be fined.) Other communities experience rolling blackouts or limited electricity usage—such as a community in Nicaragua that I visited where the electricity was only turned on from six to eight o'clock in the evening.

We want to imagine a world, and help create a society, in which there is plenty to go around. Ownership is a means for making that happen, by giving people incentive to create products that they can use. We can go further by saying that ownership helps promote the creativity and productivity that brings important goods into existence.

But here the spirit of Jubilee comes into the picture. Ownership is never absolute, because creation is not ours. We are stewards, caretakers. Owning things is always also subject to the basic needs and well-being of all people. In the cases when there is not enough to enable all people to take as much as they want, then we should constrain ownership by addressing communal needs. How to do that at the global scale, where population growth pushes the limits of agricultural capacity, is a question I take up later as a dimension of sharing the creation. For now, I reiterate that there is enough to go around, but only if people take what they need, not all that they want.

MAKING SENSE OF PROVIDING

It is by now a familiar joke, and it is only funny because it raises the toughest questions of human suffering and dependence upon God to provide: A man was standing on his roof, shouting pleas to be rescued from his home because of a sudden and terrible flood. A fire truck came by, and a firefighter swung his cherry picker over to the roof. "Jump in!" the firefighter said. The man said, "I'm waiting for God to rescue me." Then, after the waters rose higher, a police officer in a rowboat approached. "Swim over to the boat!" The man declined, saying, "I'm waiting for God to rescue me." Then a Coast Guard pilot dropped a rescue basket down from his helicopter. "Get in the basket," the rescuer said. "I'm waiting for God to rescue me." Then the waters rose over the man's head, and he drowned. In heaven, he confronted God: "Why didn't you rescue me?" God spoke:

"You fool! Who do you think sent the fire department, the police, and the Coast Guard?"

So what does it mean to have faith in God to provide? We have already recognized that it does *not* mean sitting around waiting for God to make miracles. It calls human beings to strive, as God's agents, to provide for themselves—and for their neighbors.

The understanding of providence is, ultimately, a doctrine of comfort. Or better stated, it is a doctrine of hope. I believe in a God of providence who does not will that almost 3 billion people should live on the edge of economic destitution, as they currently do. I believe in a God who created an earth capable of hosting the 6.5 billion people currently alive, and likely far more than that. I believe that God does not wish for any of us to experience the anxiety associated with economic instability or exhaustion.

But believing in God to provide requires an attitude of hope that translates into practice. We see that hope in action when the biblical Jubilee vision brings strange bedfellows together to work for debt forgiveness at the local and global levels. When church leaders offer job training programs to local unemployed and under-employed people so they can provide for their families. And when women and men strive to provide both material and nonmaterial goods, like love and compassion, to their loved ones without allowing the turbulent economy to drown them.

Chapter 5

LABORING

*God saw everything that he had made,
and indeed, it was very good.*
—Genesis 1:31

A mid-level executive at a bank was called out of a meeting—
a meeting he was leading with the employees in his division.
His boss and the HR director took him down the hall to
tell him, "You are no longer with the firm. Times are tough and we
need to restructure. Thank you for your service." He had worked
for that bank for twenty-six years.

Employees at a national church headquarters were summoned
into the offices of their respective supervisors to be given the news that
their contracts had been terminated, effective immediately. The supervisors told these now-former employees that their e-mail addresses
were being disconnected as they met, and that they would have an
escort accompany them as they packed their desks and departed the
premises. It didn't seem to matter that this church denomination had
issued public statements about economic justice and about the dignity
of workers. Leaders in the world of nonprofit and faith-based agencies have adopted "the corporate way" of dismissing workers. They
need to be hard-edged, after all, if they are going to run their organizations "like a business."

These stories are troubling, especially because there is little that is unusual about them. Practices such as these had become the norm even before the recession. The group layoffs and plant closures of the downturn have just driven home the point: Employees are expendable.

Contrast those vignettes with this one. "I cannot imagine a more satisfying life than being able to say that I love my job and believe I have made a positive difference for my community." These were the remarks of the founding director of the Virginia Poverty Law Center upon the agency's thirty-year celebration. He went on to declare that his community of colleagues were invaluable to him and that he had been able to integrate this work with his family life. ⌈This was an account of work as central, work as vocation, work as valuable beyond money.⌋

And consider a home inspector I met when my family moved recently. As he was climbing around fallen insulation in the attic, he told me that he loved his job. In fact, he holds a master's degree that would allow him to pursue a more lucrative career, but he has chosen to inspect homes, and teach other inspectors the trade, because he enjoys setting his own schedule and he has found it to be fulfilling labor.

For most people laboring entails more time and is more central to life than any other economic activity. It is the source of much reflection and many jokes, from the cartoon "Dilbert" to the hit show *The Office*. Work involves a tension, if not a paradox. The process of making things, or repairing things, or teaching things—human activity of all sorts—is a fundamental part of life. It is an intrinsic good. But when labor is also an exchange relationship for money, it becomes an instrumental good, that is, something that serves as a means for something else. ⌈Can work be, at the same time, both intrinsically valuable and a means to other goods?⌋

When asking people *What do you do?* we are really asking *What kind of job do you hold?* And with that opening question, those who work beyond the bounds of the formal labor market scramble for legitimacy. "My job is to raise two healthy children," someone might say. "I escaped the rat race and am letting the government support me," a retiree jokes.

We should understand labor broadly as any and all human activity that intends some productive outcome. This allows us to say, almost without exception, that laboring is a practice of every human life. Indeed, the term also denotes the very process of giving birth. Laboring is essential to life itself.

From its first pages the biblical account moves quickly from creative activity to the drudgery of work (Genesis 1:1–3:24). In the beginning, God labors by creating all that is. "God saw everything that he had made, and indeed, it was very good." God makes humankind in God's image, and as an integral part of this act, God gives people the responsibility to be stewards of the animals of the field, of the air, and of the sea, and of the earth itself. God soon places the human being in the garden of Eden "to till it and keep it," and at this point of the story, this kind of human labor remains good in the same way that God's creative activity is good. Here we have a vision of laboring as creating or contributing to God's creation through purposeful activity. Work fulfills a number of human capabilities; it allows people to commune with nature, to make and keep the earth, and to contribute to the very order of creation.

Things change quickly with the story of the serpent's temptation and Adam and Eve's succumbing to it. Once they eat the fruit of the tree of the knowledge of good and evil, Adam and Eve suffer God's punishment regarding two vital human activities—childbirth and work. Indeed, the concept of human labor comes to invoke both the toil in the fields and the pain of childbirth. This ominous passage has disproportionately influenced our thinking about laboring.

And to the woman, God declared, "I will greatly increase your pangs in childbearing; in pain you shall bring forth children." And to the man God stated, "Because you have listened to the voice of your wife, and have eaten of the tree about which I commanded you, 'You shall not eat of it,' cursed is the ground because of you; in toil you shall eat of it all the days of your life; thorns and thistles it shall bring forth for you; and you shall eat the plants of the field. By the sweat of your face you shall eat bread until you return to the ground, for out of it you were taken; you are dust, and to dust you shall return" (Genesis 3:16–19).

This story of the fall of humankind, and the ensuing decline of labor from good work to toilsome chore, must not be read in isolation, as if God's punishment and divine-human alienation are the final words in the biblical narrative. On the contrary, human laboring can be part of the redemptive process by which humans discover their true calling in an overall purposeful life. The more fundamental word about laboring is its relation to God's creative activity. Our responsibility to manage God's household is a high calling—not mere toil.

Still, due in no small part to the Genesis account of the fall, laboring bears the resonance of being a necessary evil. Simplistic economic models tend to back up this view. In this chapter, however, while acknowledging the hard realities associated with human labor, I put the question in hopeful terms: How can we make a good living through thoughtful and faithful work? How do we frame our labor, paid and unpaid, so that it fits within a theocentric vision of life? In what ways can work of all kinds contribute to our capabilities and help us contribute to a good creation?

TOILING

"Vanity of vanities! All is vanity. What do people gain from all the toil at which they toil under the sun?" So begins the teacher Qoheleth in the biblical book Ecclesiastes (verses 1:2b–3). It is as if Qoheleth sees a community of people living out the curse of Genesis, chapter 3. Labor is toil. Surely everyone has moments or periods of work at which they feel empty, useless, and exhausted. For others, the vanity or meaninglessness of work is their norm.

The accounts of labor during the early Industrial Age are legendary: Men, women, and children worked from sunrise to sunset; some fell asleep eating their dinner as they lay in bed; the soot poured out of factory stacks and made it hard to breathe. Working-class neighborhoods were typically downwind of factories, because this was the cheapest real estate. After all, if you could afford anything else, would you choose to breathe the black air?[1]

Thanks to health and safety standards that have developed across the twentieth century, much about this account has become anachronistic for labor practices in the United States and other industrialized nations. A notable exception to the successful implementation of labor standards, however, remains the conditions that many undocumented migrant workers continue to endure. Migrant farmworkers' narratives are complicated—many are undocumented by the U.S. government, and this is precisely the reason they have fewer resources and protections to depend upon in the labor market. Their plight stands as a reminder that legal guarantees for workers are not a given—they have to be instituted and implemented. Farmworkers' labor conditions are also a call to extend those protections to all workers.

Toiling means long hours for people across the economic spectrum. Data confirm the common view that Americans tend to work an excessive number of hours, and that annual per-capita hours of labor increased significantly in the past four decades. Among the "advanced" or industrialized economies, the United States and Japan post the highest number of hours worked. Compared to Western Europe, from Iberia through France and from Germany to Scandinavia, Americans work longer hours. It is interesting to note, however, that the economies in transition from socialism into capitalism—such as Poland, Hungary, the Czech Republic—significantly exceed America's average labor hours. The social costs of catching up economically have been high for these countries.[2]

It is a hopeful sign that there is no definitive relationship between levels of economic development and hours worked. The factors are complex, and they appear to have more to do with culture and history than in any iron laws of economic well-being. No doubt, many people have little choice but to toil for their bread, especially in the current economy. Yet the place of labor within a well-lived life, shaped at both personal and public-policy levels, is not a straitjacket. Stated positively, people can make decisions that help shape the place of work in their lives.

PERFECTING EFFICIENCY

Across the global economy, the recent recession has led to job losses, work slowdowns, and unpaid leaves. But the employees who remain on the job have had to fill in for their missing colleagues, often covering multiple responsibilities into the foreseeable future. This is one of the underreported aspects of the recession: People retaining their jobs are working harder than ever before. Companies are stretching to be more efficient with their downsized staffs, so they ask for more effort. And employees want to show that they are essential to the enterprise, so they labor on. After all, they know they are expendable. (Except for, as people say only half jokingly, the IT or computer folks.)

Streamlining production through cutting or retraining workers is nothing new, of course. Frederick Winslow Taylor issued a classic work in 1911: *The Principles of Scientific Management*.[3] Taylor had been accepted to study law at Harvard, which placed him on the trajectory to follow his affluent Philadelphia family. But due to his problems of deteriorating eyesight, he had to forgo that possibility and began to work in an industrial career as a patternmaker and machinist. He progressed from apprentice to laborer, foreman, and chief engineer, educating himself through correspondence school with a degree in mechanical engineering.

Taylor took labor efficiency to new heights, issuing in excruciating detail the findings of his time-and-motion studies. He analyzed how to make widgets with the fewest possible steps. He did not invent the view that labor is an input contributing to the production of outputs as efficiently as possible. Indeed, this was a fundamental component of classical economic theory. But Taylorism, as it came to be called, instructed managers on how to put the concept into full practice.

Taylor's approach included the presumption that workers were not capable of understanding the processes at which they worked well enough to increase their productive rate. This could only be comprehended by managers, who were able to see the big picture, as long as they followed their own scientific principles. The managers would then have to compel workers, according to Taylor, to follow very precise step-by-step directions in order to increase efficiency.

Taylor's vision of work is thus starkly different than alternative perspectives that identify workers as the best source of information and innovation. Why would we not believe that people who spend years or decades of their lives doing certain jobs understand those processes thoroughly and even have ideas to do them more efficiently? But Taylor believed workers did not have the capacities or perspectives needed to innovate.

In fact, there is a certain irony between Taylor's biography and this conviction. He did not trust most workers to understand the processes that he had mastered, for his own part, through practical experience as a machinist.

Contrast Taylorism with the management technique of "walking around" in order to ask line workers how they understand their jobs and what they think are ways to improve efficiencies. Tom Peters and Bob Waterman suggest that excellent management happens when leaders take the time to leave their corner offices, or cubicles of whatever size, and venture out to ask the kinds of questions of people who know their part of the company better than anyone else. Great CEOs rack up hundreds of thousands of miles a year, they note. And they wear out pair after pair of shoes. Successful leaders of smaller companies know their employees by name and probably in more personal detail than that.[4]

Leaders who send the clear message that they want to hear from their employees inspire excellence. But they must be genuinely willing to listen. Otherwise, they simply incite what Joanne Ciulla calls "bogus empowerment." This occurs when leaders create the illusion that they care what their people think but in reality give employees little or no say in their companies.[5] (Many "Dilbert" cartoons come to mind—and so, too, episodes of *The Office*.) Employees are often rightly suspicious of actions of "enlightened executives" who want to communicate a new spirit of openness. Workers will care more about actions than about words. In this case, employees might ask, literally, do leaders walk the walk?

So how do we know when management by walking around occurs in practice? And what happens when it fails? When I was eighteen, I wanted to find a summer job to earn some money for college. I took the best-paying position I could find. This involved drawing on my father's role as financial vice president of a small paint factory, Perfection Paint and Color Company of Indianapolis. (It is now defunct, and I would like to think that the company's closure had nothing to do with my working there.)

Perfection Paint hired me as a stock boy and shipping assistant. I went into that job pretty full of myself, preparing to head off to college. That attitude quickly changed, however. I was soon humbled by carrying five-gallon paint buckets that I could barely lift and stacking boxes into stockpiles eight feet high.

The men in the shipping department of Perfection Paint were kind to me but not effusively so. After all, I was a privileged kid from management—the VP's son—who was spending the summer with them. As one of them told me, with neither warmth nor animosity, "You will work here for a few months and leave as soon as you can. We're stuck here for the duration."

I soon realized that these guys were my lifeline. First of all, they explained what the real dangers of the job were. We were not moving Tinker Toys, after all. Instead, paint and tinting dyes were heavy, toxic, and flammable. In addition to basic safety, the shipping employees shared techniques and strategies to get work done efficiently. This was not advice that could be stated in any official manual; it had to be taught on the job. Why restack paint boxes when you could "walk" the stack with the blade of the two-wheeled dolly or even with the outer side of your foot? I learned at least fifteen uses for a utility knife and a whole lot of ways to wield a tape gun. They even taught me (when our supervisor wasn't around) to drive a forklift.

There were some processes in the paint factory that didn't seem to be efficient. I don't now recall the details, but the order-filling process involved a number of redundancies. The stockroom was poorly organized. It seemed that I was moving the same stack of paint two or three times simply to get it out of the way. And we wasted packing material at the loading dock.

I summarized the culture of the paint company in this way: "Perfection Paint: Where perfection is our name, not our philosophy."

I told my dad that there were ways to improve stocking and shipping. Because I was his son, I had the opportunity to sit down with the company president at the end of the summer to discuss these things. If the guys in shipping had known this, it would have just confirmed their suspicion that I had been a spy for management. But we didn't talk about anyone in particular. Instead, I shared ideas with the president for improving shipping efficiency.

Most of the ideas were not mine, however, and I did not portray them as mine. Instead, the permanent employees knew that there were better ways to do the work that they had been assigned.

They realized that there were redundancies, and they knew that the rules were wasting their time.

Why didn't these shipping employees speak up to improve efficiency? They didn't believe that it was worth the effort. The operations vice president and the staff supervisor did walk around occasionally, but they didn't communicate a spirit of openness to new ideas. Perhaps employees would get disciplined or even fired for questioning their bosses. No one wanted to find out, so they carried on as usual.

This experience at the paint factory taught me that Taylorism is the wrong approach to understanding human labor. People can become more efficient at pasting a label on a paint can, but it doesn't happen through a manual prepared by outsiders or managers alone—especially when input from longtime employees is not invited. People are not machines, or not merely machines. We know when we are being treated as such, and we have a tendency to shut down when that happens.

Developments in human resource management and industrial-organizational psychology have helped companies realize that human morale and motivation are far more complicated than setting higher quotas for widget production. Insights for more humane workplaces often don't get translated into practice, however. Just ask Barbara Ehrenreich. In her book *Nickel and Dimed,* Ehrenreich recounts the ways in which she and her coworkers were demeaned in a series of minimum-wage jobs she held during her experiment to live on that pay. She had to urinate into a cup for a drug test in order to work at Walmart and take a test to establish that she would not question authority. She couldn't drink water as a housekeeper in the homes she was cleaning.[6]

As long as people view human labor principally as an input into a production process, we will also tend to understand work as a means alone. Isn't that what a labor market is all about? Workers supply labor to earn money, and companies demand labor to produce goods and services. The market wage is where supply meets demand. This is what we learn in introductory economics. The outcomes from human labor, and not the labor itself, produce utility, according to this account.

Thinking on the Job (or Not)

A friend of mine sat down with me for coffee. He told me that he has been working in the mortgage industry for three decades. He has moved around a few times as banks and brokerages have merged. Recently, his firm's new "parent" bank decided to consolidate its processing centers around the country, cutting back from over eighty such centers to two.

This news was a striking blow to my friend and his colleagues. First, this consolidation will move the processing of a loan further away from the relationship between the customer and the mortgage representative. The service quickly becomes less personalized for the customer and less under the control of the mortgage agent. Second, the consolidation of processing centers means that "specialists" will spend their entire day doing the same step on dozens or hundreds of loans. It is the assembly line approach applied to the mortgage industry. It is the specialization of labor that Adam Smith wrote about and F. W. Taylor and Henry Ford put into practice. But it is also likely to lead to the alienation of labor. Marx is famous for discussions of such alienation, but Adam Smith worried about it even earlier:

> The man whose whole life is spent in performing a few simple operations, of which the effects are perhaps always the same, or very nearly the same, has no occasion to exert his understanding or to exercise his invention in finding out expedients for removing difficulties which never occur. He naturally loses, therefore, the habit of such exertion, and generally becomes as stupid and ignorant as it is possible for a human creature to become. . . . His dexterity at his own particular trade seems, in this manner, to be acquired at the expence of his intellectual, social, and marital virtues. But in every improved and civilized society this is the state into which the labouring poor, that is, the great body of the people, must necessarily fall, unless government takes some pains to prevent it.[7]

This is largely why Smith favored subsidizing public education—as a way of keeping workers from this degraded condition.

Bear in mind that the jobs in the mortgage-firm scenario are of the good, white-collar kind, employing college graduates in air-conditioned offices and providing health care and retirement benefits. In the university setting, we professors emphasize that our students need to learn critical thinking instead of specific technical skills, so that they will be prepared to adapt to the changing workplace within a changing world. Unfortunately, many of the jobs that college graduates are finding do not ask them to think at all.

Much white-collar work has now been routinized into a set of decisions. Thinking on one's feet is not on the menu. Despite what we teach in college, there isn't time for employees to exercise critical, problem-based judgment. In his book *Shop Class as Soulcraft,* the philosopher-turned-mechanic Matthew B. Crawford recounts his brief stint as a "cubicle worker" writing summaries of journal articles for a database company. He was told not to think too much on his own but instead to follow a recipe for quickly drafting an article "abstract." Whether it was accurate or not seemed less important than whether it was produced efficiently. Crawford notes that his lunches with coworkers, their daily escape from the cubicle world, often devolved into a cynical and hilarious comparison of the ludicrous things they had slipped into an article summary that day.[8]

Have you ever gotten caught in what I term a "call-center vortex"? You call an airline, or an insurance carrier, or a utility company. First, you have to navigate the computer-generated options. *Press 1 for domestic travel, press 2 for international.* What if your question is not on the menu? I have learned to say "representative" or dial "0" even before I get stuck. That usually (but not always) triggers a connection to talk with a real, live human being.

But that can be when the real fun begins. The call-center representative often is only following the same menu on a screen that you were being fed via the automated voice system. The fact that the employee may be talking to you from anyplace between Bangor and Bangkok only exacerbates the lack of actual attention to your problem. Whatever their nationality, the representatives are trained not to think outside of the lines. I have learned to say "May I speak to a supervisor," because that can sometimes connect me to a person who has more familiarity with the big picture. Often it requires understanding the big picture—and having the green light to exercise independent judgment—to get work done.

What is it like to be a call-center representative doing this work? To answer that question, the documentary filmmaker Sonali Gulati ventures into the telemarketing centers in India. We learn from Gulati that these call centers are staffed largely by twenty-somethings who are straddling Indian and U.S. or European worlds. The call centers serving the United States largely operate at night in India, halfway around the globe. So the employees have their own worlds turned upside down, sleeping during the day, working at night, and donning American names and accents because these things help them to be successful at work. Hence Gulati names her short film *Nalini by Day, Nancy by Night,* after she meets a real person with that identity—or identities. Gulati paints a fascinating picture of young, ambitious, fun-loving Indians who form a strong bond of community.[9] This portrait resonates with that of the Academy Award–winning movie *Slumdog Millionaire,* in which a call center's employees rally around their coworker who becomes a famous game-show contestant. And it resembles the hip and hard-working culture of Silicon Valley—albeit in a lower wage bracket.

The Indian call-center workers, like Matthew Crawford and his colleagues in the article-summary business, are well aware of the constraints placed on them at work. They have to follow a script, and as long as they stay in this work, they basically do as they have been told. But they cope by making fun of the work and of themselves. Sometimes, they manifest their resistance by sabotaging the process. A database writer makes up stuff about his articles; call-center workers make bogus calls or, alternatively, help customers beat the system to find the best deals available. These workers don't stop thinking critically; they simply channel that thinking in ways different from what they would have chosen had they enjoyed more fulfilling jobs. It would be possible to read these narratives in a cynical way—to argue that cubicle workers are oppressed or even dehumanized in the work that they do every day. Crawford tends to read much of white-collar work with this lens. For my part, I read Crawford's story, and especially Gulati's, as showcasing the human spirit of resiliency.

Thus, at one level, it might be easy to say that it doesn't matter too much what jobs people secure—they will find ways to make the most of them. Taken to the extreme, this approach would lead to quietism, or acceptance of just any kind of work. We must strongly reject such a view. We can appreciate the human capacity to make the most of situations without accepting those situations as given. The question then becomes, How do people find good jobs, given the various kinds of pressures we face in searching? What practices of reflection and searching should we do to find work that fits our theocentric understanding?

A how-not-to example illuminates the point. It's the story about the way a consulting firm regularly hired the best students graduating from the university where I teach. Its recruiters would arrive on campus in the early fall, just as the seniors were beginning to think about life after college. The company's interviewers would meet dozens of candidates and extend an offer to the very top group. They enticed our best students with a bonus of $500 and a laptop computer.

Had these students sold their inheritance for a bowl of soup, as Esau did in biblical times? (Genesis 25:29–34). At a minimum, many who took the deal were selling themselves short. How do I know? I talked with them afterwards, and they told me they knew they had "settled." Of course, some of the seniors had been preparing for a career in business consulting, and for them, this was their dream job. But why had the others accepted employment in a field they did not want to pursue? Because they did not know how to turn it down.

In practical terms, my students were unprepared to pass up a "real job" that came with a shiny new laptop and five hundred bucks. A well-paying job promises a way out of a financial hole. And, during their entire senior year, they would be able to answer that inevitable question from parents, professors, and classmates: "What are you going to do next year?" They could make the succinct reply, "I have a job. I will be an associate with Big Consulting Firm X."

It may sound dramatic to compare these college-student job seekers to Esau. Esau said he was famished, and when his brother

Jacob offered him stew in exchange for his birthright, Esau replied, "I am about to die; of what use is a birthright to me?" (Genesis 25:32). Are students that desperate? Unlike Esau's view of his case, the employment prospect for most graduates is not an issue of survival—although we must never forget that for many people in America and around the world, employment is, in fact, a matter of life and death. The anxiety that entrants into the labor force experience can be debilitating. Many adults face school loans and credit card debts that hang over their heads. Debt is a powerful and scary thing. And so it comes to pass that many people sell themselves short because of the very real anxieties of living in tough financial times.

It is always a joy to know people who are devoted to work that fulfills their sense of purpose and that contributes to the common good. A former student with a passion for politics found her way onto the Virginia governor's staff. Another graduate is CEO of a statewide organization that works to build inclusive communities across lines of race, culture, religion, and sexual orientation.

What do these people share in common? They have drawn on their moral and faith-based convictions to pursue lives of meaningful service. They enjoy decent but not affluent lives. They model a life of relative simplicity without parading their choices. And they have a conviction that they are doing exactly what they want and need to be doing.

Discerning Our Callings

The Christian tradition has a great word to reflect all of this: *vocation*. The word comes from the Greek word *klesis*, through the Latin words *vocatio* (calling) and *vocare* (to call). In the New Testament, calling most frequently refers to the general way in which God invites humans into a life of faith. In medieval times, the notion of vocation was used within the church to refer to positions within religious orders. Vocations led people into monasteries, not into the manor or market. The Protestant reformers Martin Luther and John Calvin changed all that. They developed the notion of the vocation of all Christians to work "within the world" in response to the monastic understanding. Vocation is thus closely related to the priesthood of all believers: All Christians are called by God to do God's work in the world.

This is hence a wide definition of *vocation*. But its modern usage has been narrowed again, in a number of ways. First, the term usually refers only to a paid occupation or career, and hence *avocation* becomes a term for one's hobby or interest. (Can paid work not also be interesting?) Second, *vocation* usually refers only to certain types of specialized, generally respected careers and occupations, including ministry. Curiously, though, *vocational school* typically refers to job-specific or trade-specific training that stands in contrast to college education or college preparatory work. Whether it refers to labor in specialized professions or to trade school, *vocation* is usually employed as a narrow, technical term, not as something that everyone has.[10]

When we see it through a wider lens, however, vocation includes the various contributions that each of us make within our communities. These contributions entail more than our occupations. They involve all aspects of life. And everyone's contributions count.

In this way, the two senses of laboring discussed earlier—childbirth and working—come together. God calls us, collectively, to raise (if not actually give birth to) children—children whom we help prepare to live full and good lives. When a child is baptized, all members of the church pledge to share responsibility for raising the child within the faith. To be sure, the parents will do much or most of the work—and it is certainly work. Child rearing remains an economically and socially underappreciated form of labor, but it is a calling nonetheless. We should see caring for children as a clear part of our vocation, or, as Bonnie Miller-McLemore frames it, one of multiple vocations to which people are called. Other activities beyond paid work and family life, including but not limited to child rearing, are also part of vocation. Thus, the reflective practice of vocation invites us to focus on all of the ways that we contribute—or could contribute—to our communities.

Vocation has experienced another form of narrowing. As the etymology makes clear, if a person is called to some form of work and life, then surely someone must be doing the calling. The Christian tradition affirms that the caller is God. It is this aspect of vocation that imbues it with its sense of purpose. God calls each of us. To pursue one's calling is to serve God in the world.

The Presbyterian minister Frederick Buechner writes, "Vocation is where your deep gladness and the world's deep hunger meet."[11] It has to do with sharing our own energy and passion with near and far neighbors in a way, ultimately, that glorifies God. John Calvin stated that we do this through a variety of activities. "We know that people were created for the express purpose of being employed in labor of various kinds, and that no sacrifice is more pleasing to God, than when everyone applies diligently to one's own calling, and endeavors to live in such a manner as to contribute to the general advantage."[12] Although people do it in different ways, everyone can contribute to this general advantage, or the common good.

It is important for each of us to ask whether our current positions and roles allow us to fulfill our callings. Some Christian interpretations of work and vocation have suggested that people should seek to glorify God in their roles even if they are being oppressed in them. Luther famously denied the rights of the poor to revolt against their lords. The sociologist Ernst Troeltsch wrote that early Lutheran understandings of vocation "only demanded the securing of the necessaries of existence and the protection of the food-supply by the civil authority; apart from this, it requires the patient endurance of the injustices of the world."[13]

But the Reformed tradition in particular has encouraged people to understand that their life and work of faithful response to God should be lived out *per vocationem* and not merely *in vocatione* [through positions and not merely in positions].[14] In other words, people should reflect on whether the particular positions in which they find themselves allow them to make meaningful and faithful contributions to their community. They should not be stuck in positions—either by political or economic forces.

An immediate objection arises. What are people supposed to do when they are stuck in demeaning jobs—continue in a bad work situation or instead choose unemployment? Do we say that people who work for a company that makes a carcinogenic product are fulfilling their vocation? Or do we suggest, alternatively, that it is better that they quit rather than make products that are harmful to others? These are not good choices.

Are people who are unemployed living out their vocation? The economist Amartya Sen has pointed out the negative effects on well-being that unemployment creates. Stated the other way around, labor is itself an important source of human satisfaction because people desire to be able to contribute to their societies. And human labor offers, at its best, an opportunity to express human creativity through making or remaking things. Sen rightly notes that even staunch supporters of market capitalism fail to acknowledge these vital, intrinsic aspects of working that are too easily lost in discussions of unemployment's additional negative effect of lost income. Something more than money is lost when people desiring to work are unemployed.

We must affirm that all people are equals before God and that the vocation of each should also be considered equal. It is possible that some people have not discovered their vocation or that financially tough times make it difficult for people to live out their vocation. In any period, people with different educational backgrounds and social networks have different opportunities available to them. Indeed, this leads me to emphasize the need for good public policy and a just society in which all people have a fair shot at finding good work. We even say that it is part of the vocation of each of us—especially those of us who have had educational or economic advantages—to shape society such that everyone has the opportunity to fulfill their vocation. Vocation and justice must be closely intertwined.

Still, it is admittedly a luxury to be able to leave your job if you do not believe it is contributing to social justice. The point is not to criticize people for staying in jobs that are not contributing to society—though it is reasonable to hope that people working for companies producing harmful products, or using deceptive or illegal means to produce goods, would seek alternative sources of employment.

Similarly, vocation invites people to choose non-employment-related activities that also contribute to the common good or, at a minimum, do not violate the basic standards of justice. Going out for drinks with one's friends on the weekend seems perfectly good and fine, unless the partying leads to behaviors that disrespect others. Playing golf is a sport that many people enjoy, but being a member of a segregated country club does not meet the minimum standards of justice.

At the most fundamental level, vocation invites conscious reflection upon one's own life within a theocentric worldview. *Do my activities and positions fit well with God as the center of value? In what ways am I contributing to the common good? Am I using my capabilities as best as I can to promote a good and just society?*

These are precisely the kinds of questions that my students who took the first lucrative job they were offered did not undertake. They faced a number of compounding pressures to land a "good job," but many of them acknowledge that they settled for consulting when other forms of work would have been better for them. Many of us miss opportunities to reflect carefully on our work and activities—and on those occasions, we, too, settle.

We can do better. The process of discerning our vocation is intended to help us meet our potential. The steps of preparing for ministry, for example, are designed to help people find their calling. In discussing ministry as vocation, church leaders emphasize that there is both an internal, personal, or even secret sense of call and an external affirmation of call. That is, individuals discern that God is inviting them into ministry but that is only a first step. A divinity school professor once quipped that some of his students appeared to have mistakenly overheard God's call to the person sitting next to them. The personal, internal call must also be affirmed by other people or by the community as a whole. This external call process is put into formal practice in some church denominations through committees on the preparation for ministry that work with those exploring ministry.

Thinking in terms of internal and external calls is useful for many kinds of work and activity. How wonderful it is occasionally to get an unsolicited note from a student or a colleague offering words of encouragement for my teaching. From the other side, as a parent, I have e-mailed and communicated in person words of gratitude to my preschooler's teachers. They have a call to be doing exactly what they are doing, a fact that is clear to parents and other observers of their good work.

External affirmation of one's vocation is indeed vital, and it serves to save us from what could become excessive navel gazing. I often wonder if the secular emphasis on self-reflection and introspection can actually impede people from finding their calling. It can be stultifying to have the same conversation over and over again in one's head about work, career, and commitment. Vocation calls people into self-reflection, to be sure, but it should always, as Buechner writes, be focused on the match between one's own gifts and passions and the world's needs. Other voices—friends, neighbors, family members, and perhaps coworkers—have a part to play in emphasizing not only the world's needs but also how well a person's talents can best address those needs.

The practices of vocation, then, are not just about personal reflection and contemplation. They also include ongoing conversations with trusted others. As in the example of ministerial preparation, there may be some cases in which a formalized process of communication and discernment is fitting. But in most cases, what is needed is the weaving of conversations-in-progress into our daily activities. In some cases, a "discussion" may stretch over years or decades as people pursue their callings over their whole life cycle. The challenge of this informality, of course, is that the urgency of pressing daily routines can crowd out our capacity to focus on why we are doing what we are doing. This is partly why the practices of recreating are so important and fit so vitally with these reflections upon laboring. For laboring and recreating, at the most fundamental level, together fit into being good stewards of God's creation.

Chapter 6

RECREATING

❧

After the fire a sound of sheer silence.
—1 Kings 19:12b

Amid the noise, busyness, and labor, we must find time for recreation and reflection. Time is money, we are told. But time is also a precious, priceless resource given to us by God. In the language of capabilities, being well rested, having sufficient time for play, and participating in religious or spiritual practice are all significant parts of living a faithful and healthy life. Not every minute should be an economic commodity. In positive terms, establishing a rhythm of good work, worship, and rest allows us to live out our vocation within God's creation.[1]

LOSING TIME

Have you noticed all of the economic imagery we use to describe time? The historian E. P. Thompson argues that only in the modern Western world do persons *spend* time, instead of passing it, or merely living within it.[2] Many of us are not only spenders of time but in a busy world we suffer from time-deficits and accumulate time-debts to people we love and projects we value. As finite persons we realize that our stock of time is limited—we live on borrowed time.

The most frequent of these economic expressions is the claim that "time is money." Something about this phrase, "time is money," has captured our imaginations because it describes the frenzy of contemporary life. More than that, it encapsulates the perspective that labor—the work-for-pay variety—is the default activity of human beings, and that other activities, such as recreating, bear costs. This is all even clearer in its original context—advice offered by Benjamin Franklin. "Remember, that time is money. He that can earn ten shillings a day by his labor, and goes abroad, or sits idle, one half of that day, though he spends but six pence during his diversion or idleness, ought not to reckon that the only expense; he has really spent, or rather thrown away, five shillings besides."[3] In Franklin's counsel, recreating involves wasting money.

Best-selling books have told us what we already knew: Ours is a rapidly moving and changing consumer world, a world that one scholar has called "McWorld" after McDonald's, Macintosh computers, and the like.[4] The world is flat, another public thinker writes, and everyone can join in the global competition for economic prosperity.[5] We tell time not merely in hours and minutes, but in seconds and nanoseconds. We are "overworked Americans" who have not gained but rather lost leisure time despite the massive technological gains of the past fifty years.[6] (I have already noted that people of other countries racing to catch up are working even longer hours than Americans are.) We are a society whose children suffer from a parental "time-deficit" that leaves parents feeling guilty and children in great peril.[7] Women find themselves doubly pulled by increasing participation in the labor force and by household work that still falls disproportionately on them. While the contributing factors are diverse and debatable, one thing is clear: Time is scarce, and Americans are more and more aware of the so-called opportunity costs associated with each choice about how to spend it.

We should see life as more than the combination of working and the costs of not working. To develop a perspective in which recreating fits alongside laboring and the other economic practices, we must confront the difficult and various relationships between time and money in our everyday activities. How do we balance our commitments at work with commitments at home? How can we move beyond both home and work to become involved in community life?

The economic framework has been influential in how many of us think about time. Evaluating the costs associated with time within well-defined inquiries in economic science is a valuable exercise. This economic approach helps illuminate how modern Westerners make decisions. At the same time, there are social costs associated with viewing time as a tradable commodity with a price tag. My aim is to understand this important approach and only then to argue that it has drawbacks when it is employed beyond its intended purpose. I want to help shift our thinking from asking, "What is the cost of time?" to "What are the costs—to us, ethically—of seeing time as money?"

THINKING ECONOMICALLY

The economic view of time begins with the assumption that time is a scarce resource held by all people. Each individual must choose to allocate some amount of time to each of various activities, including working in market or nonmarket sectors and engaging in leisure. In the economic model, people make choices about time allocation by seeking to maximize their happiness, or their utility. Time is treated like other resources granted to individual human beings. We possess it and can spend it. We can trade our money for another's time. Of course, it is not possible for us to buy another person's time in any direct way as if to subtract from that one person's life span and add to ours; so time is not a good like an automobile that can be purchased directly. But as anyone who has ever hired a teenager to cut the grass or to shovel the driveway knows, we can purchase the labor of another in order to allocate our own time to more "utility-producing" activities.

One principal decision that people face, as noted in Chapter Five, is how much time to spend in the formal labor market and how much to work in nonmarket labor, especially within the household. Though not counted in official economic statistics, household labor is important to consider for two reasons: In any scenario, someone has to do it, and in reality, women are still bearing the brunt of it.

Holding household labor aside for a moment, we can next look at the "labor-leisure" trade-off described by economists. Persons can "spend" time at leisure, or they can "sell it off" by working at paid labor. The worker provides labor in the production process in exchange for earnings. A person who makes the decision to supply labor is trading away that time in order to purchase other goods. It is a commodity exchange: one's time for wages, and these wages are assumed, in turn, to be used to buy consumer goods or services. Income can, of course, be used for saving or charitable giving as well.

One implication of this economic approach is that time spent on leisure—or in the care of children for that matter—could have otherwise been spent in supplying labor in the market. Such non-market activity thus has a "cost" vis-à-vis the market—this is indeed the opportunity cost. So Ben Franklin was right: If a person spends an afternoon playing golf or working at a homeless shelter, the opportunity cost is the amount of wages or salary that person could have earned by working in the market, which is additional to the incidental expenses incurred in that activity. An important implication, as one economist frames it, is that each individual's "wage rate is not only the price of labor, it is also the price of leisure."[8]

Thus in this framework, recreation has a price tag. The price rises as one's wage-rate increases. For example, an executive's leisure might "cost" $500 per hour while a manufacturing worker's leisure might be valued at $20 per hour.[9] If people have similar labor-supply behavior, those who receive higher wages tend to work more hours than people drawing a lower wage. This helps explain why persons with a high salary potential find it difficult to take time off from work in "good conscience."[10]

As noted in Chapter Five, in contrast to leisure, labor is not treated in this framework as an end in itself. It is merely treated as a means to two ends—for companies, labor is an input in the production process whose ends are goods and services; for individual workers, labor is a means to obtain money, which is used to purchase goods that provide utility. In the economic approach, then, there is no emphasis on the intrinsic value of work. Of course, no economist would deny that work can have positive, intrinsic value for some or many persons, but such a fact is not a part of the basic approach.

Thus the standard economic approach provides an odd view of time: Leisure is assumed to be an end in itself, but its cost is determined by wage-rates. Persons supply labor not because they might enjoy their work but only because they want to do other things with the income.

Such an approach to time may help social scientists accomplish their limited goal: to explain and predict human actions. The place of economic theory, Nobel laureate Milton Friedman argues in a classic essay, is precisely to explain and predict outcomes by assuming people behave "as if" they viewed the world in this way.[11] It is not necessary, he asserts, to know what actually motivates people or to give an accurate "anthropological" account of who the human being is.

But what if people have taken economic thinking seriously in how they really do make their life decisions and allocate their time? In a word, the predominant economic approach has arguably had some formative influence on us. The perpetuation by economists (and others) of such a theory may very well promote thinking of work principally as a means to acquire consumption goods and to think of leisure as a "costly" activity.[12] To be sure, the impact of this economic approach on the public's view of time is not direct. As one of my friends in public policy once told me, many people don't know the difference between Milton Friedman and Milton Berle. But even if they don't say, "I won't take a vacation because my economics professor told me it is too expensive," they can still apply the concept of opportunity cost in ways that shift behavior in this direction.

The point is not to blame economists but rather to contest the economic approach's capacity as a worldview to account for the intrinsic value of time-bound activities—including work and leisure, among other activities. We should not ask economics to do what it is not framed to do. This means that we must look to other approaches to view work and leisure in fuller perspective.

ESCAPING FROM EFFICIENCY

Well-meaning critics of America's overworking often remain captive to economic-based imagery for time. Some are calling for the "investment" in children and even for seeing children as "capital" to which resources, including time, must be devoted.[13] Others, also well-intentioned, struggle to show the benefits for labor efficiency and for personal health gained from more rest and relaxation. Although each of these perspectives has value, they do not tell the whole story. For they tend to import economic logic into the very spheres of life that can provide a haven from the quest for efficiency and constant calculation.

The popular notion of "quality time" with children and other loved ones is a recognition that we must carve away, or protect, some valuable time with family, however short it might be. Yet using this term can unwittingly create pressure to spend time with family or friends as *efficiently* as possible! Meanwhile, despite all the talk about quality time, one study suggests that total contact time between parents and their children has dropped 40 percent since the sixties.[14]

As Schor argues, the quest for better and better time management is an approach that tends to blame the victim. If we are feeling the time bind, it must be because we aren't organized enough. At the very least, the time-management approach tempts people to try to more efficiently squeeze more activity into an already chaotic schedule. There is nothing inherently wrong with time management, of course, but it may keep us from just saying no to additional activities, and perhaps to living beyond our means.

Being still, reflecting, and even just loafing may be inefficient. But they are part of any well-lived life. They also stand as a witness against the idol of efficiency. H. Richard Niebuhr once wrote about what he called "the grace of doing nothing"; in that context, he was resisting a political impulse to do something when doing nothing was the better way to go. We could learn to apply that concept amid the economic pressures always to be doing things. Idleness is a gift, and it can fulfill basic human needs such as communing with creation even if we can't readily measure such things in costs and benefits.

DIALING IT DOWN

There is commercial noise all around us. Wherever you are reading this book, if you pause, you can probably hear traffic, or an air conditioner, or other sounds of human activity. The noise takes many forms. The electronic gadgets are just one kind. Commercials blare on TV much louder than the programs they interrupt. There is also the "visual noise" created by commercial culture. Billboards crowd many landscapes. Many urban and highway horizons resemble the outfield wall of a minor league stadium—a continuous line of local companies' and major corporations' logos.

E-mail has come to signify the constant cacophony of our working life and our home life. But many people now act as if e-mail is too slow—not instantly gratifying enough. BlackBerrys and smart phones deliver text messages directly into our consciousness. There is now a field called "interruption science," which studies how these and other new technologies intervene in our daily routines. The average manager at work, research suggests, undertakes over a hundred different tasks a day and spends less than five minutes each on them.[15]

Where can we go to find peace and quiet? The prophet Elijah did as prophets do, and he went up on the holy mountain to find some refuge (1 Kings 19). He had been despondent and afraid, because Jezebel was chasing him to kill him. He had wandered in the desert for forty days and forty nights. On the mountain, Elijah managed to secure a quiet spot in a cave. But when he woke up, stretching his arms and emerging slowly from the rocks for some nice peaceful mountain air, he got an earful. First a great wind—a hurricane force wind. Then an earthquake—a life-jarring earthquake. After that, a fire—the kind that burns but does not consume. And what comes next? The biblical story offers a rich phrase: "after the fire a sound of sheer silence." Other biblical translations call it a sound of gentle blowing or a gentle whisper. Elijah knows immediately it is God's still, small voice. Elijah could hear it because of the silence.

Where do we go for the silence? Gordon Hempton is a botanist. He lives on the West Coast, on the edge of Olympic National Park. He studies sounds around the world and specifically, the sounds of quiet. In his travels to national parks and remote areas across the United States and beyond, he has discovered something that is so striking that it is almost hard to believe. By his count, there are less than a dozen places in the entire country that are free from human noise. He defines a quiet place as any one where you or I could sit and not hear a human-made sound in fifteen minutes. There are almost none of these quiet places in the United States, and there are none at all in Europe.[16]

In many areas otherwise (still) untainted by humans, jet airplanes flying at some 35,000 feet overhead interrupt the silence. It seems that many of us have trained ourselves to tune out much of the soundscape. From the time that they were two years old, my children have interrupted almost every form of outdoor play to point upward and exclaim, "plane!" Because we adults are bombarded with sounds, we have to filter out many of them (such as airplane noise) just so we can cope with the noises that have a more direct bearing on our well-being. We don't take in, in other words, many of the sounds that surround us.

We often create distractions for ourselves. Many people leave the television on in their houses. A friend who does this tells me that it helps her keep in touch with the world, and others report that it makes them feel less lonely. Although this way seems particularly noisy to me, we all have our methods of avoiding the silence—not to mention avoiding good communication with other people.

Much as the botanist and acoustic expert Gordon Hempton treks into the woods with his sound equipment, we too need to venture out to find the quiet places. There may be only a few such places in our lives. They might include reading, prayer, running, or walking. We must each seek out some holy silence—literally, time set apart—in which we might hear ourselves and listen for God. We have built our lives so that we don't often hear it, yet God's still, small voice may be speaking. Finding silence can also help with the discernment needed to continue shaping our respective vocations.

The spirit of Sabbath, of celebrating the day set apart for rest, can be one quiet place. The Jewish and Christian faiths each emphasize the Sabbath dimension of life as a way of naming and addressing the human needs for worship and for leisure within a well-lived life. Worship is part work and part leisure, time set off from other daily activity and non-activity to give thanks explicitly for life. Even God took the seventh day off from creative activity, not to rest as much as to marvel in the natural wonder .

I confess that for my family, after a long week of rushing around from meeting to meeting, from day care to elementary school, and from gas station to grocery store, the relative silence of Ellwood's coffee shop is often more appealing to us on Sunday morning than going to a morning of activities and a worship service at church.

Our congregation is typical in depending upon many words in the worship service. We assume that the Word comes to us only through our human words. While God's Word is indeed communicated in the biblical texts, in the preacher's words, and in the spoken prayers of worship, it can also be expressed in the sound of sheer silence. My pastor has tried to include a period of brief silence during worship. It is amazing how sixty seconds of silence seems like ten minutes. People reach for their bulletins. They shift in their chairs. They look around. The service as it is currently framed makes silence seem out of place.

This is the cultural context that many American churches and individuals face. Luther and Calvin reframed a doctrine of vocation that understood daily routines of family, church, and marketplace as part of a faithful life. It is relatively easy to find silence in monastic life. For my own part, I have spent some of the most spiritual moments of my life in quiet retreats—at the Taizé Community in France and at Gethsemani Abbey in Kentucky. Other people love to retreat from their routines and visit the beach or the mountains (presumably without the fires or earthquakes).

Yet if we are to live out a faithful vocation in everyday practice, then such occasional retreats can only be part of our approach. Similarly, vacations—as wonderful as they can be—are about vacating our everyday experiences to get away from it all. We must, in addition, find space for recreating within and amid the daily routine. Indeed, a vision of vocation requires more than merely a balance of labor and recreation. It is a question of an integrated life in which work and play fit together. We should make time for work, family, civic engagement, and church commitment. Time dedicated to the various nonmarket activities shouldn't always be evaluated in terms of forgone income.

BUILDING FENCES

Our current notion of vacations is not a universal concept; it depends upon a modern understanding of individual workers who choose to take time off. "The vacation is an artifact of a particular time and place," Michael Walzer writes. "It isn't the only form of leisure . . .

the major alternative form survives even in the United States to-day. This is the public holiday. When ancient Romans or medieval Christians or Chinese peasants took time off from work, it was not to go away by themselves or with their families but to participate in communal celebrations."[17] *Free time* in other epochs meant freedom from religious holy days or civic holidays, not freedom from work. The starting assumption in some cultures is communal life; our starting place, in contrast, is individual work. Even if it were possible, however, we should not try to return, nostalgically, to an earlier time in which the market (along with every other aspect of life) fit within a highly ordered civic-religious calendar.

We should also not underestimate the social (and even quasi-religious) meaning of many American holidays that we do celebrate. Memorial Day and Labor Day, for instance, serve as bookends for the summer plans of many American workers, with July 4 the one major public event in between. The unifying benefits that a more fully shared calendar might offer would come at significant cost for a diverse society. Whose holy days should count, and how would their observance avoid the First Amendment's prohibition against religious establishment? (We could easily get distracted here on the myriad issues related to Christmas as a religious and national holiday.) Which holidays should get national recognition? Establishing the Martin Luther King Jr. federal holiday was worth every bit of the fifteen-year political struggle, but it was no simple process. Beyond occasional, extraordinary additions such as this one, citizens are not going to reach consensus upon any major changes to the public calendar.

We must find ways to create areas of nonmarket time within our public and our personal routines. There are many levels on which to do this. At the public level, it involves what the theologian and economist Daniel K. Finn calls shaping a "moral ecology" around the market. In overall terms, we need norms and institutions that keep the market in its proper place in our lives. This means making sure that there are appropriate fences, or constraints, within which the economy operates. For Finn, these fences include governmental regulation to ensure fair practices within market exchanges; the provision of basic goods and services for all people, regardless of their productive capacity; the morality of individuals and groups;

and a strong civil society. In building and maintaining such constraints around the market economy, we can enable people to live their lives as citizens, religious adherents, family members, hobbyists, and so on.[18]

The Sabbath is one example. It would, in my judgment, be nostalgic and unfitting to revert to a society in which the economy, commerce, and retail would completely shut down on Sundays. It is also a practical impossibility. Yet it seems vital that businesses allow people who celebrate their Sabbath to opt out of economic activity on their particular day of rest. At the same time, creating such a moral ecology that allows for Sabbath observance by individuals is not one that individuals can accomplish alone. Just ask the Christians who brought suit against Walmart and the Jews who challenged Sears about how difficult it is to honor the Sabbath when your employer tells you that you cannot. In each case employees told their supervisors that they could not work on their respective holy day, and the supervisors refused to budge. Ultimately these two cases went to court, and in both instances the companies agreed to settlements favorable to the employees.[19] Thus it required public—legal—action to change an ecology in which economic activity typically trumps everything else. Even after the legal framework has been set, however, it still takes a certain amount of initiative—courage, even—for workers to request that their employers grant them an accommodation allowing them to take time for Sabbath. Or for special family time. Or other personal needs.

Ukrop's is a family-owned chain of grocery stores in Richmond. Founded in 1937 by Joe Ukrop, a Baptist, the grocery was "based on the golden rule—treat others as you yourself would like to be treated." Because of the Ukrop family's religious convictions, the store does not sell alcohol and it is closed on Sundays. (This is a particularly interesting case, because although Ukrop's stores are closed on Sundays, a few employees work on Sundays, doing restocking, cleaning, and so forth.) The small chain is a Richmond institution, with its fans and detractors, which has carved out a strong customer base due to its high-service model and high-quality food. For twenty years, the chain enjoyed the largest market share in the Richmond area, but in 2009 it was surpassed. One of the reasons that experts cite for this relative loss of market share is that other, national grocery chains marketed themselves as the Sunday alternative to Ukrop's. Robert S. Ukrop, the current president and CEO, states that "market share is not our thing," emphasizing that the chain's value commitments are more fundamental than the financial results.[20]

There is no denying that individual workers and individual firms might find themselves at a financial disadvantage if they set self-imposed constraints such as not to work or do business on the Sabbath. It is also possible in some instances that values-based or faith-based companies can find a "niche market" for their way of doing business. It is not necessarily the case, for example, that a firm that closes on the Sabbath would have a net negative effect from that commitment. They might instead draw people to their company who share that value-framework.[21]

So-called blue laws requiring the mandatory closing of companies or stores on Sundays (or Saturdays or Mondays) would be a way of limiting work hours while keeping the economic playing field level.[22] Some scholars have argued that the resident aliens in Israel were required, like the Israelites, to take a Sabbath day of rest not only to honor God but also so that they wouldn't have the advantages of working more hours than their hosts.[23] (The resident aliens already had a tough time in Israel even before they were told that they were required to honor their host's Sabbath laws.) I have already stated the moral problem associated with trying to enforce a single day of rest for all members in the economy, since that would compel members of minority faith groups, and people of no professed faith, to follow the Sabbath of the majority group.

A better approach is to devise ways to limit total working hours. In some law firms and medical offices, junior professionals race for the most "billable hours"—to the point of affecting their own health and well-being. It would take a system-wide agreement to change the disadvantage that employees face when they individually refuse to join in this race to work long hours. A number of these professions have debated limits on working hours, for a different reason: public welfare. Medical doctors and airline pilots who work too many hours are a danger to their patients and their passengers. But it takes institutional bodies beyond particular hospitals and airlines to make the changes. In the case of medicine, the Accreditation

Council for Graduate Medical Education has implemented a modest policy, limiting medical residents' work schedules to eighty hours per week. In terms of regional airline pilots, the February 2009 crash of a Continental Express flight, in which pilot fatigue was determined to have been a contributing factor, has led Congress to push the Federal Aviation Administration and the airlines to put a legal limit on pilot workdays.[24]

This situation fits the description of what economists call a "prisoner's dilemma"; all could be better off with more free time, but in the absence of cooperation, an undesirable outcome—overwork—is reached. Mandatory days off or required vacation time would help solve this dilemma. Such an initiative would of course incite controversy since it apparently impinges on people's freedom to work as much as they want to. But it would also increase freedom in other important ways—in the same way that taking a Sabbath increases the freedom to wonder at creation and literally to re-create.

Family-friendly policies of companies are also a positive development toward strengthening the moral ecology of markets. Such policies include on-site child care facilities, flextime work schedules, and job-sharing arrangements. Some of these items merely shift but do not reduce the number of hours worked, and in overall terms these policies have been implemented by firms as a competitive edge, an attempt to become an employer of choice. In some instances, it requires government action to establish fair and consistent policies across workplaces. For example, the Family and Medical Leave Act of 1993 allows employees to take up to twelve weeks of leave (albeit unpaid) from their jobs for personal health reasons or to care for a loved one, including the birth of a baby or adoption of a child.

A friend of mine recently increased her part-time work to a full-time commitment to her employer. She did so for one reason: She needed to be eligible for health care benefits, which are presently only open to full-time employees. She had loved her earlier situation, in which she had struck a balance between being with her young children and laboring part time in a paid position. But when her spouse's employment changed, she needed to pick up the health care coverage for the family. The full-time versus part-time distinction does not have to be as strict as it currently is. Employers could make benefits roughly proportionate to hours worked, thus giving companies no incentive or disincentive to hire part-timers in relation to full-timers. Individuals and religious congregations might join together in pressing for better benefits packages for part-time workers; this would allow many people to allocate their time better between work, family, and community.

The moral ecology around the market could also be strengthened by public attention to the economic conditions that compel both parents in two-parent households to work and that often require many people to hold second jobs merely to make ends meet. Progress here would involve raising the minimum wage to a "living wage" level. Addressing the disparate causes of the continued lag of women's wages behind men's wages remains another critical issue. Unless people can earn a decent living in a reasonable number of hours at work, no ethical emphasis on vocation will effect a more balanced and prioritized life. Establishing a living wage is something that neither individuals nor individual companies competing in the marketplace can accomplish. Instead, it requires coordinated, collective action. Churches have been key actors in living-wage movements across the country. Note that this is not only a matter of just labor conditions; a living wage would also allow workers to spend more time in recreation and other activities beyond the workplace.

MAKING SPACE FOR RECREATION

The practices I have considered thus far require collective or public action. Ironically, creating the social conditions in which it is easier for everyone to recreate will require significant political and civic engagement. This is part of what I mean when I write that the vocation of each person includes helping make it possible for others to pursue theirs. I started with this public level because those practices are too readily overlooked, especially given the survival orientation many people have adopted solely to meet the pressing demands of work and family. But individuals can do a number of things on their own to integrate recreating into their daily routines.

First, the workplace itself offers occasions for sociality. Amid the intensity and stress of the economic downturn, when the threat of pink slips is an ever-present reality, it is almost anathema to recall that work can be fun. The relationships created around the water cooler are significant for many if not all workers. Our coworkers are people with whom we spend a great deal of time. Despite the ratcheting up of employee time pressure, we can and we must continue to find ways to build "pockets of inefficiency," to borrow a phrase from the sociologist Arlie Hochschild, into each working day for leisurely interaction with coworkers. These pockets of inefficiency have long been called coffee breaks.

Yet, however much we value workplace friendships, they are principally instrumental. At least they start out that way, and these relationships can be dramatically shifted by a third party—the employer—at almost any time. The company can move people to other units or simply move them out. And, of course, workers themselves make changes in their employment situations. Thus, although socializing as a part of one's paid laboring can play a part, it cannot be the whole solution to recreating.[25]

Other practices associated with recreating have to do with arranging a work-family-community routine that fits together well. For some people, living near their work or even working from home is a good way to integrate work and personal time. For others, this is a nightmare. When I was in graduate school, I placed my desk right next to my bed—partly because I lived in a studio apartment and had few options. But after a while I realized that I never escaped my work. Even when I was sleeping, I could reach out and touch it. Friends and colleagues tell me that they prefer a strict separation between work and personal time—and some fight valiantly against pressures to be accessible at all hours via an iPhone. Thus, for some people, integration means overlap. For others, it means healthy separation.

Many practices of leisure have become highly commercialized. Sports can be equipment-heavy and expensive. Golf clubs are now a capital investment, and innovations and the corresponding marketing create pressure to buy a new set every year or two. Many people desire to golf, so they buy new clubs. But because they are too busy at work to make time for a four-hour round, they use the equipment very infrequently. As soon as they proceed to keep up with the Joneses with new clubs, they sell their old, slightly used ones. With the help of Craigslist or yard sales, people can buy almost-current, like-new clubs for a quarter the price of new ones. That's good news for bargain hunters, but for the busy workers who buy and then sell the new stuff, this expense suggests misguided choices about balancing work and leisure.

The vacation industry is built upon the commercial message that it's possible to build exotic travels into even short breaks from work and school. Hence the five-day and even three-day cruises to the Caribbean or along the Mexican Pacific coast. Given that we dedicate our everyday routines at home and work to squeezing in activities, it should be no surprise that we would also try to be efficient in packing in as much stimulating activity as possible into our vacations.

But in contrast to these commercialized forms of leisure or vacation, recreating does not require spending a lot of money. The best things in life may not be free—most activities require at least minimal expense. But they are probably inexpensive. My own kids have as much fun riding the public bus and riding bikes in our neighborhood as they do when we try to take them places, whether around the city or out of town. The challenge that I face is escaping the multitasking modes that I have adopted at work. The spirit of Sabbath and the message of silence overlap here: Recreating requires the capacity to be present in the here-and-now. And, even though we might try, being present is not something you can accomplish by trying harder at it. It calls for a process of trying less.

A lesson I learned from Brother Émile of the Taizé community is a helpful practice: When we are trying to rid ourselves of distractions, either in silent reflection or in other ways of recreating, we do not need to get anxious when thoughts keep running through our minds. Instead, we can write down those scattered ideas as they arise. The very act of naming them in this way can help clear the distractions and allow us to become more present to our surroundings.

Finally, it bears emphasizing that the practices of recreating tie closely into the practices of discerning desires. The more content we can be with fewer material goods, the less we will feel pressure to work excessive hours at paid work, which fuels the work-and-spend cycle. The more we are able to live with a messy house or a less-than-perfect yard, the more time we have to relax and enjoy people around us. Such practices allow us to not keep up with the Joneses. Instead, we let the Joneses go to the mall without us.

These practices create spaces for recreating in work life and family life that are not shaped by opportunity costs and other market calculations. We must also keep the wider community in view. Our personal and collective time pressures have made it increasingly difficult to contribute our time in volunteer work and public life; President Obama, like his predecessors, has called for a renewal of this voluntarism. Such civic engagement—from service projects to activism promoting the living wage—is itself a form or revitalization that reminds us that our respective vocations ultimately serve God and the common good.

As a way of conclusion, let us return to where we started: Is time money? Ultimately we must say time is much more than money. Time is a gift, an opportunity, for pursuing all the dimensions of a well-lived life. Prudential calculations of costs, while helpful for thinking through time-based decisions, should always be contextualized within the call to personal well-being and the common good. Many nonmarket activities—above all recreating—transcend market logic, and they deserve our valuing.

Chapter 7

EXPANDING THE COMMUNITY

❧

And who is my neighbor?
—Luke 10:29b

O ur communities extend beyond our family, church, neighborhood, and local area. Even national borders have new meanings in an ever-more-interconnected world. There are good theological reasons for viewing ourselves as members of a global community of human beings, each created in the image of God. The movement toward a worldwide economy offers the opportunity, at least, to help unify all of God's creation. Expanding the community to the worldwide level, however, requires us to understand ourselves to be not only global consumers but global citizens.

CROSSING BORDERS

How does the relatively abstract understanding of "one world"—a community in which everyone should be treated with dignity—become real to us? The best way I know is through person-to-person encounter.

My friend Jay once found himself trying to buy a nice hand-woven rug in a local market in Mexico. We had been volunteering in the Yucatan region as part of a young-adult service and mission trip from our church. I no longer remember the precise numbers, but Jay's conversation with the Mexican merchant (call him Diego) went something like this:

Jay: How much for this rug?

Diego: One hundred pesos.

Jay: I'll give you twenty.

Diego: How about fifty?

Jay: Twenty.

Diego: Thirty?

Jay: Twenty.

Diego (handing Jay the rug, with some exasperation):
Okay, twenty pesos.

It appeared that they had a deal, then, at Jay's price. So all of us were surprised—especially Diego—to hear what my friend said next.

Jay: Will you take fifteen?

Anger quickly appeared on Diego's face. He had negotiated in good faith with Jay, who had offered three times to buy the rug at twenty pesos. Diego had come all the way down to that price. Jay had broken a norm of bargaining by not being willing to make good on his offer.

Truth be told, Jay did not really want a rug. Without intending to offend anyone, Jay had thought this whole "negotiating thing" was a sport. For him, it was a matter of the fun of bargaining, the excitement of seeing new wares in the local Mexican market. For Diego, in contrast, this potential sale was a matter of his livelihood. He likely did not have the luxury of joking around about money. After all, he lived in a country in which the average annual income per person was then about $1,700, or less than $5 a day. Many countries are worse off than Mexico is. Yet, even today, some 20 percent of the Mexican people try to survive on less than $2 a day.

So this moment of bargaining—and misunderstanding and embarrassment—was more than a young American negotiating for a rug with a local Mexican merchant. It was an encounter of worlds, a collision of economic realities. My friend Jay is now a schoolteacher in Indiana; he and his family live a decent but modest life in the American middle class. I do not know how the Mexican merchant is doing. But the average income in the United States stands about six times that of Mexico. It is very likely that his standard of living is far below Jay's, or yours, or mine.

My friend Jay and I confronted global inequality face to face during our service trip south of the border, and we have returned time and again to that conversation. It is challenging for Americans to make ends meet in our own fast-paced, expensive economy. Trying to live faithfully is even more complicated when we situate ourselves in a world in which many people—billions of people—have nothing like the economic choices and opportunities that we might have.

In this case, the issue was not about billions of people; it was about Jay and Diego. Should Jay have paid Diego his original asking price of 100 pesos? He negotiated the price down to a "market" price, at which seller and buyer agreed to make the transaction, but was Diego so desperate that he had settled for a price far below what was fair? Was Jay, in effect, trying to steal the rug? Or, alternatively, should Jay have realized—before he ever opened his mouth to bargain—that he didn't really need a rug and so should have just walked right by? But wouldn't his money help to support the rug makers and sellers in Mexico? Thus, even if he didn't need a rug, should he still have bought at least one just to "help the economy," to help people like Diego? Or would such an attitude itself be patronizing—as if Jay could be some kind of savior for Mexico?

This encounter was not only about crossing the political border between the United States and Mexico. It also required crossing the economic border between the industrialized and developing worlds. To be sure, the promise of market exchange is that two parties meet as equals and freely trade their goods (in this case, swapping pesos for a rug). Yet, just as there isn't free movement across international borders, the exchange between Jay and Diego was mediated by a host of cultural, social, and financial barriers that made the two parties less than fully free. And, I am suggesting, the large economic inequalities between the two gave Diego less-than-equal bargaining power in the exchange.

Freedom and equality, the two greatest political and philosophical values, have a theological resonance. Because all humans are created in the image of God, their source of value—God—is the same for each. This is the theological grounding of equality. And bearing the image of God, each person should enjoy the freedom to act as an agent in economic affairs.

"Who is my neighbor?" This question prompted Jesus to tell the story of the Good Samaritan, and it is a question that can help us put into practice a commitment to equality and freedom in an unequal world (Luke 10:29–37).

"Teacher," a lawyer asks Jesus, "what must I do to earn eternal life?" He is really asking, "Is there a statute to follow, or some claim form to fill out?" Jesus responds with a question of his own. "What does the Hebrew law say?" The lawyer knows his law, so he recites in his self-satisfied way, "You shall love the Lord your God with all your heart, and with all your soul, and with all your strength, and with all your mind, and you shall love your neighbor as yourself."

And then the lawyer asks the key question: "And who is my neighbor?" But he asks it for all the wrong reasons. He wants to make himself appear smart, and even righteous and worthy, by debating with Jesus the finer points of Hebrew law. Indeed, the lawyer also asks the question to find out the limits of his neighborly duty. He hopes for, and expects, a strict definition. Perhaps *neighbor* means just those fellow religious people, for example, all the people in the lawyer's synagogue. Or perhaps *neighbor* means only the people who live in his neighborhood. When the lawyer asks the question, he expects to find out how far his love of neighbor has to go. Instead, Jesus tells a story about crossing the very borders that the lawyer had intended to circumscribe his obligations.

The story would make for good reality TV: A man is beaten and robbed, left bleeding on the side of the road. Who, if anyone, will slow down to help? The pious person and then the important person pass right by. They look down and away, embarrassed for not stopping and hoping that no one sees them walking by. One is late for a business meeting, the other for a prayer meeting. They are also afraid that if they try to help, they might get sued for mistakenly doing something that hurts the man more. Stopping to help might also cost them money if the dying man's HMO were to refuse him reimbursement for the lack of a referral form from his primary-care physician.

But in Jesus' story, the unexpected happens. An unknown hero rescues the dying man, taking him to the local health clinic and agreeing to cover his medical and food bills.

The hero is someone the listeners would never think of as a neighbor. He is one of the Samaritans, a group that broke away from the Jewish community of faith long before the time of Jesus. The Samaritans and Jews had an "us and them" relationship. Jews regarded themselves as "us," and Samaritans as "them." The Samaritans had their neighborhoods, and Jews had theirs. There were borders in Palestine, and members of each group knew their own place. Jews and Samaritans weren't supposed to mix, let alone help each other. This was the social backdrop for Jesus' story.

One summer when I was in divinity school, I lived in the town of Faison, North Carolina, just off I-40 on the way to the beach. When you counted me and all the other visitors, the population of Faison reached six hundred. The town had one main road and one stoplight. There are two principal products from this area: pickles and tobacco.

Three communities live in eastern North Carolina—whites, African Americans, and Latinos. The local political and economic power is held by the white establishment. A lot of the white families are farmers, but others work in the pickle production plants.

Another group in eastern North Carolina is the African American community. When I was there in the 1990s, blacks were not fully welcomed by whites, and there was hostility on both sides. Some white families are descendants of plantation owners, and some African Americans are the descendants of slaves, who later became sharecroppers. Just about the only place that whites and blacks seemed to me to commingle comfortably was at the local grocery store, the Piggly Wiggly.

There is a third group around Faison. Working for the farmworker ministry, I got to know the hundreds of Latinos and Latinas who had come as migrants to work in the tobacco and cucumber fields. They often lived in migrant camps or in old farmhouses off small country roads, often without signs or mailboxes.

The farmworker camps were easy to miss, but they are unmistakably a part of North Carolina. Many Latino and Latina migrants feel isolated and alone. Many, of course, are in the United States because they lack any good opportunity in their home country. They are earning money to support needy family members in their home country. For the most part, they do not integrate into the local cultures, and they change locales with the seasons.

As a visitor who had come to work with migrants under the invitation of the church, I was allowed to interact with all three communities. I got to work with whites, blacks, and Latinos. At no other time in my life, though, was I more aware that there are social borders that are not often crossed. Whites and blacks and Latinos lived in the same area but as separate communities. There were social customs about where to be and with whom, and about what situations were not acceptable. Blacks generally did not show up in white churches, and vice versa. Few whites or blacks frequented the authentically Mexican restaurant at the edge of Faison. The borders were not well marked, but they were known by everyone in town.

In biblical times, the Jews avoided Samaritan lands. They would go out of their way to stay out of Samaritan territory. Perhaps they avoided the other group's land in order to keep the division strong between two groups. Perhaps they did it out of fear. For whatever reason, Jews were willing to go the extra mile to avoid Samaritans.

One evening I met with a group of white Christians in Faison to plan a farmworker outreach event. A college student arrived late; she apologized, telling us that her father had forbidden her to travel the most direct route. Coming that way, she would have had to drive by the largest migrant camp. The father told his daughter to take the longer way, and to avoid contact with Latinos. The irony was that we had opened that church meeting by reading the parable of the Good Samaritan.

Who is our neighbor? I know the stereotypes—none of which are worthy of repetition—of African Americans, Latinos and Latinas, and white Southerners. Across the United States, we remain isolated from our neighbors; blacks and whites largely continue to live in separate neighborhoods. Latinos, and other immigrants, live in marginalized communities within many U.S. towns and cities, even though they make many contributions to civic life and the economy.

IMAGINING OUR NEIGHBORS

The most significant borders that Jesus addresses in his parable are not the lines demarcating Jewish and Samaritan territory or, for that matter, the river known on respective sides as the Rio Grande or the Rio Bravo. Instead, Jesus is talking about those borders that you and I construct in our minds. We classify people in ways that keep us from them, and them from us. Mexican and American. Black and white and Latino. Rich and poor. Neighbors and strangers.

In 1977, Egypt and Israel stood as archenemies, having fought four wars in thirty years. No Arab leader had made a public visit to Israel, and an enduring peace between the two nations seemed unrealistic. But President Anwar al-Sadat of Egypt indicated that if Israel were to invite him to visit, he would make the trip. Israel did extend an invitation, and consequently, against the criticism of many on all sides of the Middle Eastern fault lines, he made a historic trip. In Jerusalem, he addressed the Israeli Knesset, the national legislature, to confront the political and military matters that had long kept the two nations in conflict. In that speech, he made this statement:

> Yet, there remains another wall. This wall constitutes a psychological barrier between us, a barrier of suspicion, a barrier of rejection; a barrier of fear, of deception, a barrier of hallucination without any action, deed, or decision. A barrier of distorted and eroded interpretation of every event and statement.[1]

Such "other walls" are "the human walls of suspicion, fear, insecurity, mistrust, hatred, and uncertainties about identity."[2] These keep people from expanding their worldview beyond their own kind, and hence they are the borders that keep us from expanding our community.

The Samaritan crossed a number of borders to help the Jew in need. Notice that the priest and the Levite both had seen the injured man on the very side of the road on which they were traveling. There were no geographic barriers between them. They would have had to walk right over the man if they had kept walking straight. They actually cross the road in order to avoid the dying man.

With the Samaritan, the contrast is clear. He literally crosses the road to walk toward the injured man. But the imagined borders he overcomes are even more significant. If he as a Samaritan had attempted to help but not gotten the Jew to safety, he could have been blamed for the robbery and death. For all we know, the injured Jew might rather have died than receive the help of a Samaritan.

If we are going to love our neighbors as ourselves, we have borders to cross. Some of those borders are located on maps. Most of them are in our heads. The true neighbors are the people who dare to cross over religious and social borders to live together in peace. Many of the barriers are also economic. What are the obstacles—external to us and inside us—that keep us from reaching out?

We must expand our "moral imagination" if we are to live globally. Adam Smith emphasized the need for people to develop their moral sentiments, their capacity to envision and understand the reality that other people experience. Smith offered a vivid story to express his meaning:

> Let us suppose that the great empire of China, with all its myriads of inhabitants, was suddenly swallowed up by an earthquake, and let us consider how a man of humanity in Europe, who had no sort of connection with that part of the world, would be affected upon receiving intelligence of this dreadful calamity.[3]

Smith says the European would be sorry about the situation, but because he was not directly connected to these persons, his own life would not be significantly changed. Smith emphasizes his point by suggesting that if the cultured European knew that he would "lose his little finger to-morrow, he would not sleep to-night; but, provided he never saw [the earthquake victims], he will snore with the most profound security over the ruin of a hundred millions of his brethren."[4]

As Smith observed, without a sense of sympathetic (or empathetic) connection to other persons, we simply cannot have a proper moral understanding. Through our moral imagination, however, we can develop that understanding and be moved to act according to our moral commitments.

Expanding the community requires a change in our consciousness—in our imagination—as much as it requires a change in our political and economic institutions. Yet it is by no means clear that we are prepared to think of ourselves as global citizens, as citizens of the world, or as cosmopolitans. In fact, for most people, these phrases sound foreign and out of touch with everyday experience. National identity remains a chief stumbling block to expanding the community worldwide. Although it feels normal to call myself an American, it remains an abstraction, and a presumption, to declare that I am a global citizen. Yet it is unclear why, in principle, it's so much more difficult to envision my status as one human being among six and a half billion humans than to count myself as one American among three hundred million. Both collective units are tremendously abstracted from the dozens (perhaps hundreds) of people with whom I regularly interact.

But from our earliest days we are embedded in a set of nationalistic or patriotic narratives that form us as loyal citizens: The pledge of allegiance, the flags, the currency. I do not mean to say that national identity cannot be beneficial and healthy. On the contrary, I mean to lift up its importance. I also, certainly, acknowledge the significance of religious identity and affiliation as viable, vital parts of well-being. But it is possible, surely, to think of ourselves as Americans, as Christians, and as global citizens at the same time. At present, the global kind of identity does not have its own rituals and forms of education and initiation, making it seem more remote than the national and religious identities.[5]

I want to return to the story of my friend Jay and his marketplace encounter with Diego over the handwoven rug. That occurrence endures in my mind because I now realize that it was the "other walls" that kept Jay and me from understanding the reality that Diego was living. Quite simply, we were living in different worlds, and as suburban American high school kids, we did not have the capacity to imagine the reality that Diego was living in.

That marketplace non-exchange went awry, I now believe, because we did not recognize the full humanity of Diego and his Mexican compatriots.

Some people go on international service-mission trips and believe that they can instantly connect with the people they meet and proceed to help fight poverty by showing kindness toward their hosts for a week or a month. They can make a difference by building one church or clinic or school through their volunteer labor. As much as I want to embrace this narrative, I am haunted by one insight that I learned in my economics classes: Labor is the one resource that is in abundant supply in the developing world. I have done the math regarding a number of service-mission trips in which I have participated: In every case, the cost of the airline ticket from the United States to Latin America exceeded the value of the labor that each participant contributed to the mission. (And this is assuming that the labor the volunteer provided was at least as skilled as the labor a qualified local person could perform.) In other words, in financial terms, it would have been more effective for each volunteer to stay home and send a donation in the amount of the airline ticket.

But, you might reply, the main point is not the labor completed but the human relationships that are established on such trips. At this point, let's return to the question of cultural and imagined barriers among the parties. Are we actually able to transcend the differences and connect on a human-to-human level?

Critics of service-mission trips maintain that no such relationships are possible. The barriers are just too high. Further, they assert, the attitude of service to the world's impoverished is nothing short of patronizing. When the income ratio of "the helper" to "the helped" is in the range of 100 to 1, it can be impossible to establish a relationship based on equal moral worth.

I have already mentioned that I have continued to participate in service-mission trips, often as an organizer or translator. Thus, I have opted in practice for the view that believes these trips can make a positive difference. But my perspective is chastened by the critics who caution against condescension. American and other first-world participants in service trips should know that there is no way that their labors can justify the trip. One notable exception to this claim is the case of highly specialized medical doctors (or other professionals), whose expert work can save lives that otherwise would be lost, and who can dedicate a portion of their time to training local doctors to do likewise. I also emphasize that participants must be aware of their relative super-affluence, so that no one can simply assume that a cross-cultural encounter happens on an equal playing field. Indeed, this awareness of both global poverty (the condition of deprivation) and global inequality (the relationship between the poor and the affluent) is a key educational task that should be integrated into any service-mission trip. Mutual respect must be earned in spite of, and with eyes wide-open toward, the social and economic inequalities.[6]

CHALLENGING GLOBAL INEQUALITY

Building international bridges cannot happen until we confront the severe levels of global economic disparity. Inequality of income, for instance, is as severe in global society as it is in any particular country in the world. That is, consider the degree of economic disparity in some of the most economically unequal countries in the world, like South Africa, Guatemala, and Brazil. These are nations marked by economic instability and social fractures. As just one example, in South Africa, carjackings are a regular occurrence, and in response, some car owners have installed flamethrowers to ward off would-be attackers. When we view the whole world as one society—which is precisely what globalization encourages us to do—we learn that global economic inequality is at least as severe as inequality within any nation.

Today's increasingly interconnected citizens are more likely to take note of this global inequality and its implications.[7] As part of thinking globally, we now make international observations alongside the social comparisons that we already undertake at local and national levels. The economy creates interactions across global income classes, and new media technologies have broadened people's "frame of reference" beyond national borders. In earlier eras, except for frequent international travelers, people did not regularly see the reality of severe global inequality—at least not in the vivid colors in which we can now encounter global poverty on television. More significantly, U.S. television programs are increasingly pervasive around the world, replete with product placements and lifestyles of conspicuous comfort. Residents of the developing world see not the so-called typical American family; they see the Hollywood version, wealthier and more consumeristic than the actual people. In this respect, the globalization of people's consciousness can have negative effects, particularly on people living in abject poverty who see affluence whenever they interact in the global economy.

Someone might reply that such increased feelings of relative deprivation on the part of the poor are little more than envy. But the experience of relative deprivation is not merely a matter of envy. As I noted earlier, appearing in public without shame is an important human capability, and the actual goods needed for a person to appear in public will vary from society to society—as the scope of our economic and social comparisons globalizes, the goods that people perceive that they need to appear in public also shift. It is appropriate to want to understand yourself, and to be understood, as a full participant in your society. This is fundamental for human well-being.[8]

As for the global affluent, a group that includes most U.S. citizens and readers of this book, there may be negative and positive effects of globalization in our social comparisons. First, we realize that we are, in global terms, better off financially than many or most people in the world. By conventional analysis, this makes us feel fortunate or well-off. Of course, if the economist James Duesenberry and others who pioneered the discussions of relative well-being are correct, we spend very little time looking below us. We aspire, instead, to follow the Joneses in the next-up income class. At the same time, we may well experience empathy, however faint or fleeting, with the persons we know are living on less than a dollar or two per day. To have knowledge about that suffering diminishes our sense of well-being.

Thus high levels of global inequality have negative effects on the agency of the poor and the affluent alike: The further apart the experiences and life conditions are among various persons, the less likely they are to be able to engage one another.[9] As we increasingly ingrain into our consciousness a vastly unequal world, we globally privileged persons share at least one important attribute with the global poor: We perceive ourselves to be incapable of making change. How many of us truly believe that we can make a difference in combating global poverty? It is not just a play on words to say that to believe we can alleviate global poverty requires radical faith.

It may turn out that seeing ourselves as part of one world has a net positive effect on human well-being, especially for the well-off. But the complex positive and negative factors, especially severe inequality, deserve our focus and reflection. We should seek to understand them all, but also recall that Christian faith calls us to pay particular attention to those dimensions that undermine the well-being of our most vulnerable global neighbors.

MARKET EXCHANGE AS BRIDGE BUILDING

Some proponents of the free market suggest that the best way to address the needs of the poor is to trade with them. Most economists and development experts agree that access to markets is a means by which millions, or perhaps billions, of people have escaped abject poverty. Even harsh critics of the market have embraced its antipoverty potential: The Brazilian theologian Leonardo Boff had preached that oppression results from the imposition of the global economy on the developing world. In the early 1990s he began declaring that oppression means exclusion from the global market and that, in light of the collapse of socialism, a more participatory form of economics is needed.[10]

But participation in the global free market is no guarantee of poverty reduction. I have noted that the market mechanism tends to exacerbate inequalities, yielding returns on each input into the marketplace—land, labor, capital—in proportion to what people bring with them. It is also possible that market engagement could lower the number of people in absolute poverty while increasing global inequality (if, say, the affluent disproportionately increase their wealth while the poor see modest gains). Those providing "unskilled" labor receive relatively small returns. Development economists have argued convincingly that the most effective antipoverty strategy is not either-or—either pro-market or pro-government. Rather, countries that have encouraged free-trade policies alongside strong social safety nets have had the most success in terms of human development.[11]

In other words, people need to have certain capabilities—including being well nourished, well educated, and in good health, and having access to basic goods and services—before they can take advantage of the market's opportunities. My economics professor Charles Ratliff used to recast the adage "A rising tide lifts all boats" by asking, "What if you don't have a boat?"

Opening up the labor market is, ideally, a way of expanding the community, both domestically and internationally. In principle, growing the world economy is a win for all parties. Bill Clinton articulated as well as any leader that promoting global aid and global trade together was good public policy, arguing that the world's poor could become consumers of American products. Economists, viewing the problem from the other side, provide convincing models for how exclusion of certain people from the labor market is economically inefficient. And yet, in the United States women and African Americans were long excluded from certain fields, and many fields remain disproportionately filled along lines of race and gender. In Virginia's segregated public education system, prior to the eventual successes of the Civil Rights struggle, the highest-paid African American teacher in a school system earned less than the lowest-paid white teacher.[12] The goal here was not efficiency; it was racial inequality. It was a grossly inefficient practice, discouraging talented African Americans from entering the teaching field. When an open and free labor market operates, in contrast, it creates opportunities—and workplace interaction—for people of all backgrounds.

But again here, the key is whether people are in a position to take advantage of opportunities in the market. The greatest American political philosopher of the twentieth century, John Rawls, struggled for language to describe an ideal society in which all people could take advantage of economic opportunities: "Equality of opportunity" is not enough, Rawls contended. It must be "fair equality of opportunity." With the qualifier *fair* Rawls meant to say that people require not only legal access to jobs and careers—they also need to have the background, experiences, and wherewithal to exploit in practice the opportunities that exist in principle.[13]

The ideal of free trade is confounded by the reality of national borders and the lack of free movement of labor. Free trade typically only means the free movement of capital and goods across borders. In practice, at least, it does not permit the free movement of people to follow job opportunities. Indeed, when workers from Mexico,

Central America, and elsewhere seek higher wages in the United States, they must either enter the legal immigration or guest-worker queue, with a low probability of success for unskilled workers—or enter as "undocumented" workers with few legal protections. We take it as a given that citizenship and national borders trump the free movement of labor, but it is certainly possible to imagine a society in which laborers could travel to another region to pursue economic opportunity. After all, this is the situation we have among states within the United States. And, more remarkably, such is the economic reality that is coming to pass across national borders within the European Union. The free movement of labor would help allow the market to embody the equal opportunity that it purports to present.

The market offers promise to expand our community globally in another way—the exchange of cultures with people quite different from us. When we trade grain and textiles with people across the world, we probably also import their ideas and customs. John Stuart Mill, the nineteenth-century political philosopher, may have said it best:

> But the economical advantages of commerce are surpassed
> in importance by those of its effects which are intellectual
> and moral. It is hardly possible to overrate the value, in the
> present low state of human improvement, of placing human
> beings in contact with persons dissimilar to themselves, and
> with modes of thought and action unlike those with which
> they are familiar. Commerce is now what war once was,
> the principal source of this contact. . . . Before, the patriot,
> unless sufficiently advanced in culture to feel the world his
> country, wished all countries weak, poor, and ill-governed,
> but his own: he now sees in their wealth and progress a
> direct source of wealth and progress to his own country. It
> is commerce which is rapidly rendering war obsolete, by
> strengthening and multiplying the personal interests which
> are in natural opposition to it.[14]

To the extent that the exchange of cultural ideas and practices is mutual, this is a crucial point. Yet we must also pay heed to the reality that cultural encounters are not often the encounter of equals. When Americans hold cross-cultural meetings with poorer nations, the exchange is not necessarily reciprocal. You do not have to believe that America is an imperial superpower to understand that the influence of American cultural practices and products have a disproportionate impact when they come into contact with other cultures. The open exchange of goods and ideas is desirable as long as we also promote those capabilities that enable people to exploit the market's opportunities.

Making Global Neighbors

Like it or not, globalization has changed and is changing our life. Yet we have significant choices to make in order to influence *which* global processes will take precedence. Our individual and collective practices can indeed impact the ways in which the global order takes shape. The fight over Internet norms, regulations, and property rights, for example, will determine just how democratic the World Wide Web is, and consequently, how "flat" (or fair) the world might become. To take another example, social activism and academic criticism have helped revise the respective approaches of international financial institutions like the World Bank, the International Monetary Fund, and the World Trade Organization. The leadership efforts of the United Nations Development Programme, with the help of selected national political leaders and a web of celebrity and nonprofit organizations around the world, have had at least measured success in injecting severe poverty into international political discussion.

Take, for instance, the international movement against extreme poverty, known in Britain, Ireland, and Europe as Make Poverty History and in America as the ONE Campaign. This movement is largely made up of young adults and even teenagers who are Internet-savvy and who care about ending poverty in this generation. Bono, of the band U2, has become the most visible face of this movement. But it is the millions of people in the United States and around the world who fill its ranks and constitute its real force. Critics contend that even Bono, one of the most recognizable and influential creative artists on the planet, cannot make a positive difference against extreme poverty. If Bono is powerless, so the thinking goes, certainly we ordinary citizens are, too! I have heard many of my students—and myself sometimes—saying that widespread economic problems are just too big for any of us to tackle.

Yet the ONE Campaign and related efforts, including the official United Nations Millennium Development Campaign, have indeed helped to place global poverty on the agenda of governments and nongovernmental agencies around the world. No single person has exercised sufficient agency to make this happen. But together, celebrities like Bono, philanthropists like Bill and Melinda Gates, and citizens like you and me have made progress against poverty.

Bono's work against extreme poverty models some of the key ideas of this chapter: crossing borders, stretching our moral imagination, calling people to put their faith into action. A Christian seeker who has never pulled his punches against the institutional church, Bono has appealed to the Christian story to motivate people against poverty. Indeed, he has drawn upon the story of the Good Samaritan on various occasions. He once stated, "When it comes to Africa, we're not just crossing the road to avoid the man who needs help. We're catching a bus in the other direction."[15] In a more constructive way, Bono appeals to the ideal of human equality. Indeed, he almost always grounds his appeal to equality in the moral claim that all persons are equal before God, created in God's image. For example, he has explained his commitment to social justice as "the journey of equality. Equality is an idea that was first really expressed by the Jews when God told them that everyone was equal in His eyes. . . . I'm not sure we accept that Africans are equal."[16]

Bono's moral argument moves from moral equality to widening the scope of our community. In his own words: "So the next step in the journey of equality is to get to a place where we accept that you cannot choose your neighbor. In the Global Village, distance no longer decides who is your neighbor, and 'Love thy neighbor' is not advice, it's a command."[17]

To put this global ideal into practice, Bono realizes that he must address the intense loyalties of nationalism. Rather than strictly oppose patriotism, Bono attempts to reappropriate national values to make them truly global. As one notable example, during U2's 2005–06

Vertigo world tour, Bono built upon the imagery from his song "Pride/ In the Name of Love," about the American dream of Dr. Martin Luther King Jr. to extend King's dream to those in extreme poverty around the world. After singing this song, Bono would say:

> Sing for Dr. King, for Dr. King's dream
>
> For a dream big enough to fit the whole world
>
> A dream where everyone is created equal under the eyes
> of God
>
> Everyone. Everyone.
>
> Not just an American dream or an Asian dream or a
> European dream.
>
> Also an African dream.
>
> Also an African dream. Africa.
>
> From the Bridge at Selma in Mississippi [sic]
>
> To the mouth of the river Nile
>
> From the swamplands of Louisiana
>
> To the high peaks of Kilimanjaro
>
> From Dr. King's America
>
> To Nelson Mandela's Africa
>
> A journey of equality moves on, on, on, on.[18]

Bono embraces a strategy of promoting obligations to "the least of these" around the world while expanding, rather than opposing, the ideals of America. Such a strategy is not unlike Dr. King's own appropriation of both Christian and American ideals in a struggle for justice. He is stretching our moral imaginations in order to expand our community.

The ONE Campaign had, as of mid-2009, built a network of over two million supporters. In 2006, the movement helped make happen the Live 8 concerts, with concerts on all seven continents just prior to the meeting of the G8, the eight most powerful economies. At that meeting, the G8 leaders committed $50 billion dollars annually to debt relief for impoverished countries, and some leaders credited Bono's efforts in this outcome. The movement is not perfect, and both Bono and the organization are open to critique. Bono is, after all, an affluent celebrity who enjoys expensive wine and sports cars. To be a member of the ONE Campaign requires little more than sending an e-mail or text message. Yet serious people, including world leaders such as Bill Clinton and economists such as Larry Summers and Jeffrey Sachs, have praised both Bono's understanding of the issues and the effectiveness of his campaign.

This example of progress through concerted, coordinated action is a promising sign. Of course, there is significantly more work to be done by many people if the UN's Millennium target goals for 2015—including cutting extreme poverty in half—are to be met or even approximated, but citizens working in concert have made real advances. If we can make headway on the global economic level, then we can more easily see that at the local and national levels, our actions can also increase our individual and communal capabilities.

Expanding our community is not just a matter of reaching out across the world (though it is certainly that). As I have already highlighted, in the discussion of migrant farmworkers in the United States, the local is global. Our disparate faith traditions have never existed in such variety and diversity in one society at one time. The "other" is our next-door neighbor. Of course, many of us feel the tensions of multiple religious and moral traditions within ourselves. Our interactions and market exchanges with fellow citizens (whether in the local or global sense) do not require us to agree with others on all matters.

In my midsized American city, communities of citizens from across the world enrich our public life. But we are not close to being unified as one community. Commerce is a promising way in which people can connect across their demographic differences. Indeed, the celebrations—the Greek festival, Armenian festival, Second Street festival, the Hispanic celebration, festival of India, and so on—play a prime role in educating other Richmonders about minority communities in the area. Economic and civic events alone are not going to create equal conditions, however. In addition, webs of local organizations must work together to expand the community, particularly by promoting more humane economic conditions for marginalized groups. Some of these provide direct service to people in need, while others advocate for changes in public policies in order to make permanent and systematic changes in the opportunities available for a broad cross-section of people. For example, Richmonders

Involved in Strengthening our Communities (RISC) brings together religious congregations from across races and theological perspectives to advocate for more just and responsive public services, including affordable health care for the poor and uninsured, affordable and accessible housing, public transportation, and economic development. And Colaborando Juntos ("Working Together") is a network of social-service providers that have coordinated their work so that Latinos and Latinas gain knowledge about and access to means of support in the local area.[19] Participating in such networks and organizations can help individuals team up in their local areas to expand the reality of one community.

We can also practice expanding the community through our purchasing decisions. Richmonders can buy crafts, jewelry, and pottery at a shop called AlterNatives, confident that all the profits from their purchases go to the Highland Support Project in Guatemala. This project helps the people of Tejutla San Marcos, Guatemala, through a variety of initiatives from women's support groups to stove building to reforestation of the surrounding area.[20] It would be impossible, certainly, to track every dollar and every purchase that we make in the hopes of connecting with the producers or providers of our goods and services. But every time that we are able to do this, through the local farmers market, the local bike shop, or the international cooperative, it is an opportunity to humanize the market.

I believe firmly in the power of cross-cultural interaction locally and internationally. For the latter to take place, of course, requires travel. For my own part, international experiences have indelibly shaped my life and understanding of the global economy's vices and virtues. But make no mistake about it: It is a privilege to be able to travel frequently—a standard intercontinental ticket exceeds the annual income of some two-fifths of the world's population. Not only is airline travel expensive, it is also environmentally unfriendly. Thus in order for international experiences to take place, we are likely to exacerbate global inequality and environmental damage. This stands as a challenge to all of us with the means to travel to ask ourselves if our trips fit within the approach to economic life that we are developing. Is the travel likely to promote our own capabilities or those of others? Are there ways to ameliorate the negative effects, such as through carbon offsetting? How can we arrange our travel so that it promotes the crossing of cultural and economic borders rather than reinforcing stereotypes, whether it is of the primitive natives or of the ugly Americans?

The Christian story is a global one, even as it concerns our everyday local affairs. Indeed, we recognize that the global and the local overlap in almost everything we do. Christian faith should expand our vision globally—not to view every person as a potential consumer in a global market but instead as a neighbor endowed with human dignity. In opposition to narratives that portray national identity or even religious identity as primary, the Christian story portrays all human beings fundamentally, then, as moral equals created in God's image.

The global economy has the promise to enhance, in some ways, the conditions of human dignity and solidarity. But this is not a given, and economic systems should always be subject to the kind of moral analysis suggested in this chapter. Make no mistake: Whether we acknowledge it or not, we are already living globally. The question is how we will do that. Our everyday practices, from how we treat the people we encounter face-to-face in the marketplace to how we work for humane conditions for migrant workers and fair-trade policies, make all the difference in the world.

Chapter 8

DOING JUSTICE

❧

I will make justice the line, and righteousness the plummet.
—Isaiah 28:17

Doing justice is a fundamental practice for living faithfully in the global economy. Even when we realize, though, that there is economic injustice in the world, it is difficult to pinpoint its exact contours. The Old and New Testaments give us important perspectives on economic life but provide few precise guidelines. The Bible does not specify, for instance, what should be a fair price for a handmade Mexican rug. Yet to implement effective and faithful practices against injustice, we must do better than saying, "We know it when we see it." We must delve more deeply into how to do justice.

Biblical texts offer some fundamental ideas—principles for building a sound and solid groundwork. The author of Isaiah, for example, dreams of a better day for God's people. Lamenting that his faithless leaders have sought military assistance from foreigners rather than trusting in God, he envisions a new Jerusalem that is built on "a sure foundation." How can people construct this kind of secure and healthy society? God declares, "I will make justice the line, righteousness the

137

plummet" (Isaiah 28:16–17).[1] Justice provides the architecturally sound structure upon which people can flourish.

It is remarkable, though probably no coincidence, that Adam Smith used a similar metaphor in talking about justice as he created the intellectual framework for modern economic thought. He believed that justice was foundational for society and the economy to operate. Smith remarked, in fact, that justice was more essential than charity. He contrasted justice with beneficence, that sense of mutual love and affection. Smith writes:

> [Beneficence] is the ornament which embellishes, not the
> foundation which supports the building, and which, it was,
> therefore, sufficient to recommend, but by no means neces-
> sary to impose. Justice, on the contrary, is the main pillar
> that upholds the whole edifice. If it is removed, the great,
> the immense fabric of human society . . . must in a moment
> crumble into atoms.[2]

In the biblical accounts and in that of the founder of modern economics, doing justice is about setting up and maintaining an orderly system of economic life. Acts of charity, outreach, and kindness have a vital part in helping us create communities in which we would like to live, but not even these can take the place of a just structure.

Determining what such an architecture of justice looks like poses plenty of challenges. At the local, state, and national levels, government bodies can establish and enforce a system of laws and standards. We already know that the economy is transnational, and even global. At the global level, however, there is a "structural discontinuity" between political bodies and the economy. Briefly stated, the economy is global, but government is not. Short of a global state, which is neither practical nor desirable, international justice will have to be cobbled together through international financial institutions, mutually agreeable bilateral and multilateral treaties, precedents of practice, and appeals to morality.

Church bodies and Christian theologians have provided many accounts of justice in the modern economy. Some of the approaches are generally favorable toward free-market capitalism and others are more sympathetic to the critique offered by socialism. Almost all share a critical distance from the economic order, evaluating the strengths and weaknesses of particular economic systems. I will draw on these rich traditions to offer principles and practices that help us promote justice in economic life.

The Roman Catholic Church offers the most cohesive tradition of writings, broadly known as Catholic social teaching. A key date is 1891, when Pope Leo XIII issued the most famous papal encyclical on the economy. Leo XIII, who served as pope from 1878 until his death in 1903, was no modernist, rejecting the excesses of individualism and the freedom of thought. In significant contrast to his predecessor, Pius IX, Leo XIII believed that the church needed to create a critical but appreciative interaction with the social, economic, and political changes in the modern world. It is telling that the pope named his major encyclical letter *Rerum Novarum,* or "Of New Things."[3] His main concern was the effect of the modern industrial economy on workers; the subtitle of his letter was "On the Condition of Labor." Leo XIII began a tradition of social and economic encyclicals written by popes and bishops' councils. Pope Benedict XVI issued his *Caritas in Veritate*—Truth in Justice—in July 2009.[4]

Parallel to this Catholic social tradition has been a series of writings by Protestant thinkers and institutions. The period 1890–1914 was the height of the Social Gospel in the United States and Britain. In this movement, theologians and church leaders across the spectrum recognized the social problems being caused by industrialization. At the same time, they expressed optimism in the capacity of industrial and technological progress to raise the standard of living for all people. Protestant writings on economic justice across the twentieth century increasingly incorporated the perspectives of marginalized groups.

What the various Catholic and Protestant approaches have in common is a critical reflection on an economy of unprecedented scale and degree of specialization. They face the shared reality that industrialization has changed the rules of the game. They write with an awareness that capitalism is an all-encompassing phenomenon—and that socialism is an alternative that many workers are familiar with. In fact, Leo XIII's *Rerum Novarum* states explicitly that the church needs to engage with these economic issues and look out for the well-being of workers—or else they might be seduced by socialism. And the early post–World War II period, especially the 1960s, was for each tradition a momentous time. The Second Vatican Council opened the Catholic Church to all aspects of global society. Pope Paul VI declared, in 1967, "Today the principal fact that we must all recognize is that the social question has become worldwide."[5] The ecumenical and international spirit opened up the Catholic Church to regional bishops' councils and "liberation theologies" that attended carefully to economic, social, and political contexts. The World Council of Churches, the ecumenical body including many Protestant denominations and Orthodox churches, addressed numerous issues of faith and social life, including the economy, in this period.

The Roman Catholic tradition has stated articulately that economic life must establish three kinds of justice: *commutative, distributive,* and *social.*[6] That is, there should be fairness in exchanges, there should be a fair distribution (or redistribution) of goods, and the economic system as a whole should be fairly organized to allow each person to contribute to the common good. These rather abstract principles help us think about human capability and well-being beyond our own individual or family concerns. Let us examine examples that model each kind of justice.

PRACTICING COMMUTATIVE JUSTICE

The vision of justice as a structurally sound system translates into fair and open economic exchanges. The communal laws recorded in Leviticus and Deuteronomy apply justice to everyday practices in the marketplace. "You shall not cheat in measuring length, weight, or quantity. You shall have honest balances, honest weights, an honest ephah, and an honest hin: I am the Lord your God, who brought you out of the land of Egypt" (Leviticus 19:35–36). (In case you don't regularly measure in ephahs and hins: The former is about a bushel of dry goods, and the latter is about a gallon and a half of liquid.) The Levitical codes were serious about fairness in market transactions; in fact, a colloquial way of reading this passage is, "You shall not put your thumb on the scale, by God."

In any market-based transaction, a number of ethical conditions must be met in order for it to be a just exchange. Some conditions must have occurred before the goods and services ever get to market. First, the items for sale must have been produced justly. What does this look like? The makers must receive fair compensation for their work. I cannot sell you a widget that has been produced with slave labor or with other unlawful labor practices. This includes just treatment of the people who transport and sell the widgets, because they, too, are acting on behalf of the seller. In addition, the producer must follow legal and moral guidelines to protect the environment and animals as well as to uphold health and safety standards in the workplace. Mainstream movies now include this line in the film credits: *No animals were harmed in the making of this film.* In this vein, widget makers should be able to make these statements: *No animals or workers were harmed in the making of this product. If any environmental damage was done in the production process, restoration has been made, as verified by an independent third-party organization, and the cost of restoration has been incorporated into the price of this widget.* Of course, this is too much text to appear on a product label, but these practices are a necessary condition for justice.

Once the goods get to market, the buyer and the seller must have fair claim to the items they are offering to exchange. As a buyer, I cannot use money I have just stolen from the bank. Likewise, the seller cannot offer for sale goods that have been stolen. And both parties must enter freely and willingly into the transaction with good information about the products changing hands. That is, in a fair market exchange, the sellers and the buyers alike must use neither coercion nor deception.

The trouble with these ethical standards is that in a global marketplace, it is hard for either sellers or buyers to know whether the conditions have been met. Many sellers claim that they do not know, and are not culpable, if they hire a subcontractor who uses unjust labor in the making, transporting, or selling of widgets. The buyers, by definition, are more removed from the production process: If they do not even know in what country their shirts are made, how can they divine what the workers were paid or whether the factory polluted the water table?

Still, given the technological and informational capacities of the global economy, the problem is not one of knowledge; it is, instead, an issue of responsibility. At each stage in the production process, the assembler or manufacturer should be able to account for the practices of all parties involved to that point in the process. In other words, if companies embraced the commitment to make sure their products had been produced justly, they could collect the information to justify their practices. We are not going to return, of course, to the days of knowing the baker and the butcher and all the other suppliers of goods as our local neighbors. Instead, we will need to utilize tools of global technology, communication, and networking to help verify information provided by sellers about justice in the production process. We can depend increasingly on watchdog groups, Web sites, and human rights organizations that monitor the practices of the larger corporations.

Students at some of the leading major universities with high-profile athletics programs began to ask, in the late 1990s, about their schools' ties to Nike. These college students noticed that the athletes for whom they cheered were wearing Nike swooshes on their jerseys, and they learned that their universities had exclusive marketing deals with the shoe-manufacturing giant. They also understood that Nike's subcontracting factories in Indonesia and elsewhere in the developing world had provoked criticism for their labor practices, including low wages, unsafe or unhealthy conditions, and child labor.

The students formed United Students Against Sweatshops (USAS) to coordinate this work. The group used the student voice at their universities—such as the University of Michigan, the University of Wisconsin at Madison, and the University of North Carolina at Chapel Hill. Students realized that they have significant economic power, particularly when they coordinate their actions. They purchase university T-shirts and sweatpants, and they spend even more on tuition, room, and board. The leaders of USAS on these high-profile campuses sought to convince their respective university administrations to pressure Nike to change the labor practices at its manufacturing plants. The student activists thus helped trigger a coordinated chain effort to address labor standards. The chapters of USAS secured agreements from some universities to disclose the nature of their licensing contracts with Nike and other apparel providers. The efforts were not fully successful, and they are ongoing. But the short history of the USAS suggests that consumers can use the mechanisms of the market itself to make changes in market practices. The students used the power of the purse to put economic pressure on their own schools to alter Nike's instructions to its subcontracting factories.[7]

This type of information gathering and monitoring can be done through the most high-tech means at our disposal. Guaranteeing that these conditions are met is an essential part of commutative justice in a largely impersonal economy.

Yet, as helpful as new technology is for setting the rules of exchange, commutative justice is more than a transaction that is monitored by third parties. In its ideal form, commutative justice requires, in the words of the ethicist Jon P. Gunnemann, "an exchange between two individuals who inhabit a world of shared meanings (that is, shared understandings and expectations about the goods they exchange) and who are mutually knowledgeable about these meanings and goods. Such exchangers are peers."[8]

In Chapter Seven, I noted the example of AlterNatives, the cooperative store that sells crafts made by Mayan residents in Tejutla San Marcos, Guatemala. In that case, the store sets up a mutual relationship of peers through the person of Guadalupe Ramirez, a native of Tejutla, and her husband, Ben Blevins, a native of Richmond. These two figures serve as the liaisons between the producers of the goods and their purchasers. They can confirm, personally, that the transactions are made according to the standards of commutative justice. Indeed, as noted, this enterprise accomplishes far more in terms of community building than "merely" upholding the practices of just exchange.

Unique circumstances would be required to replicate this program, which was formed because of particular personal relationships. Thus we should also lift up efforts that are scalable upward, in an effort to ensure that just exchanges take place in and among many locales.

Two of the most established "connector" organizations are Ten Thousand Villages and SERRV International. Each was formed in the late 1940s and was founded by a Christian denomination. Each preaches the message of economic and human development for people around the world who otherwise would be economically disenfranchised. Each promotes the making and selling of crafts by creating long-term exchange relationships with local producers based on paying them a fair price for their goods.[9]

SERRV was started by the Church of the Brethren with the mission of helping economically vulnerable Europeans in the reconstruction efforts after World War II. The organization's mission shifted in ensuing decades toward promoting the production of crafts in the developing world. It establishes relationships with partner organizations, currently in thirty-six countries, who employ thousands of artisans who make the products. Through its sales on the Internet and via stores and religious and other nonprofit organizations, SERRV establishes a steady market for these unique crafts. At the same time, it can work with its partner community-based organizations to make sure that the artisans receive a sustainable, fair wage. SERRV claims historical ties to the Church of the Brethren and partnerships with Lutheran World Relief and Catholic Relief Services, but is an independent organization. In 2008, SERRV had almost $10 million in sales of its products to buyers in the United States.

Ten Thousand Villages has a higher profile than SERRV in many communities across North America because it has its own retail stores—more than eighty in the United States and another seventy-five in Canada. This retailer claims roots to 1946, when Edna Ruth Byler began selling needlepoint and crafts made in Puerto Rico to her circle of family and friends around the Mennonite Central Committee headquarters in Akron, Ohio. This ministry took on the name SELFHELP: Crafts of the World. In 1996 it was renamed Ten Thousand Villages, which evokes Mahatma Gandhi's quote: "India is not to be found in its few cities but in the 700,000 villages . . . we have hardly ever paused to inquire if these folks get sufficient to eat and clothe themselves with." Ten Thousand Villages buys from artisan groups in thirty-five countries (and, it is worth noting, sells some SERRV products in its stores). Retail sales have topped $20 million annually.

Each of these organizations, with related but distinct missions, puts principles of fair trade into practice. They define *fair trade* as paying wages that are sufficient to enable people to achieve basic levels of human development. Although the literature of these organizations does not invoke the capabilities approach, they are promoting a type of sustainable development that leads to the expansion of human capabilities. It all begins with a dependable, decent wage. SERRV and Ten Thousand Villages are part of a network that organizes itself under the banner of fair trade.

Are not all market transactions that are freely entered into by both parties fair? Is that not the very definition of commutative justice? This is indeed what many proponents of the free market claim: that if I enter into the marketplace and make a trade—of my labor, my money, or some product—with another trader, it is a mutual, voluntary exchange. After all, basic laws protect against coercion and deception. If an exchange is free, it is also fair. Free trade, in this view, *is* fair trade.

This is the point at which we must ask what options the exchangers have. How voluntary is their choice? Members of the fair trade movement will point to situations in which people living in extreme poverty—and recall that there are about 1.4 billion such people—have very few real options. They may enter into a work arrangement for $1 per day to make a craft good, but this is because they have no viable alternative. This reminds me of the story of the man about to be executed. "Would you like to die by electrocution, hanging, or the firing range?" asks the executioner. These options produce no good choice.

Amartya Sen lived through the period of the 1940s in the Indian subcontinent, when cultural and religious separatism led to violence and the Partition of India. The violence became real to him, he recounts, at one moment during his youth in Dhaka (now in Bangladesh):

> One afternoon in Dhaka, a man came through the gate
> screaming pitifully and bleeding profusely. The wounded
> person, who had been knifed on the back, was a Muslim
> daily labourer, called Kader Mia. He had come for some
> work in a neighbouring house—for a tiny reward—and had
> been knifed on the street by some communal thugs in our
> largely Hindu area. As he was being taken to the hospital
> by my father, he went on saying that his wife had told him

not to go into a hostile area during the communal riots. But he had to go out in search of work and earning because his family had nothing to eat. The penalty of that economic unfreedom turned out to be death, which occurred later on in the hospital.[10]

Given his financial desperation, Kader Mia's agreement to work in a neighborhood so dangerous to him was hardly voluntary.

Amid the reality of economic vulnerability, the *market-clearing* or equilibrium price may well be lower than what would allow people to escape their condition. In these situations, is it fair to pay people that market-clearing wage? Free trade proponents would say yes; the fair trade movement would say no. Free traders tend to believe that the market wage will necessarily allow people to subsist, and they also think that such employment, better than none at all, can set a person on the "ladder of development," as economist Jeffrey Sachs calls it, that will eventually allow them to climb out of poverty.

I applaud the fair trade activists. They are creatively using the market mechanism to connect producers with buyers willing to pay an amount above the equilibrium price.[11] They are also witnessing to the conviction that no matter what the market conditions or where people live, people deserve to be able to earn a decent living. They are building sustained exchange relationships that promote trust and mutual understanding, things that expand the economic and moral community. The consciousness raising that they are doing with purchasers in the United States and elsewhere is helping expand the market (even with higher prices than would be possible if artisans received lower wages) for such goods.

Some readers might agree that it is a moral imperative to ensure adequate economic means for every person but still insist that these are responsibilities of the government, not of the market. To the extent that economic desperation drives a person into an exchange and affects its terms, this is a matter of commutative justice. It is true, however, that people would be less vulnerable on low wages with a strong social safety net than with a weak or nonexistent one. This is a question of distributive justice, which I consider next.

Distributive justice concerns how a society or community shares its goods, its roles, and its responsibilities. Determining what a just distribution is takes us beyond what the market does best, which is focused on fair and free exchanges among individuals. Economic science analyzes how goods and services can most efficiently be exchanged, whatever their initial distribution. But if we are to care morally about more than what the distribution of goods should look like—not only in some "initial" distribution but in ongoing ones— then we have to make evaluations based upon some ethical or theological framework. As economists rightly say, this is a normative, not a descriptive, exercise.

This leads us back to the practice of valuing, asking what criteria or principles we will use to determine what the distribution of economic goods should be. It brings us to theological or theocentric commitments. One way of approaching distributive justice is to ask, *How would God have us act so that we bring the current unequal realities more in line with the conviction that all people, created in God's image, are worthy of dignity?* The answer is not absolute equality of income, wealth, or any other economic good. Rather, we should strive to constrain social and economic inequalities enough that everyone can interact with each other as moral equals. This, indeed, is the vision we articulated with the practices of expanding the community.

In a world of vast economic inequalities, then, how do we help bring about the conditions of moral equality? Theologians, particularly from Latin America and other developing countries, call for particular attention to the needs of the least well-off. They have named this concept *the preferential option for the poor.* They have called Christians and other people around the world to practice this option, or choice, for and with impoverished people in their personal and collective actions.[12]

The preferential option for the poor is first a theological doctrine—it reflects who God is. Who opts for the poor? God. How do we know who God is? The theologians, such as Gustavo Gutiérrez, Leonardo Boff, and Ivone Gebara, call people to look to experience—not just their own but also those experiences reflected (indeed, canonized) in the Bible.[13] The biblical writers emphasized God's care for the economically vulnerable precisely because economic injustice was prevalent. In the book of Deuteronomy, God is described in this way: "God of gods and Lord of lords, the great God, mighty and awesome, who is not partial and takes no bribe, who executes justice for the orphan and the widow, and who loves the strangers, providing them food and clothing" (Deuteronomy 10:17–18).

God loves the orphan and the widow, those who have traditionally been excluded in Israelite society (and in ours). In this passage, paradoxically, is the declaration that "God is not partial" alongside God's practice of showing favorable care for the orphan, widow, and stranger. God's equal love for all people translates into preferential care for those with the most needs.

So the option for the poor is a theological doctrine grounded in God. Jesus is identified in Luke's Gospel as the one who comes to realize God's option for the poor, which is given in the vision of Isaiah: "The Spirit of the Lord is upon me, because he has anointed me to bring good news to the poor. He has sent me to proclaim release to the captives and recovery of sight to the blind, to let the oppressed go free, to proclaim the year of the Lord's favor" (Luke 4:18–19).

This liberating vision is played out in Jesus' ministry of healings of and actions done for the outcasts in his society.

The option for the poor calls us to act. Those who feed the hungry, clothe the naked, free the oppressed, and so on, according to Matthew 25, are those whom God favors. Individuals, churches, and societies are called to opt for the poor because God has first opted for the poor. The work that God instructs in the Hebrew Bible and that Jesus lives out in the Gospels continues through the choices and commitments that we make to work alongside the poor and the marginalized in our own time.

Thus, who opts for the poor? First God; God enacts this option in the life, death, and resurrection of Jesus; the option is transmitted by the Spirit into the life of the churches, and thus Christian groups and individuals are called to exercise their wills by committing to care for the those in need. As Gutiérrez says, the option for the poor is not optional within the Christian message—it is rather central to who God is and what churches and individuals are called to be.

How do we understand this notion of preferential care? Afflu-ent Christians have had a tough time with this notion, which seems to imply that God loves the poor more than them. No doubt about it: This doctrine is supposed to make wealthy people uncomfortable. Not uncomfortable in some emotional, woe-is-me way but instead uncom-fortable in the sense of calling people to put the commitment to the poor into practice. We should understand the preferential option to be rooted in the universality of God's love for all people—in a world in which some people have greater social and economic needs than others.

Thus, God calls us to apply a theocentric understanding of uni-versal equal love through personal and collective practices that ex-press preferential attention or care. How does this look in practice? This is especially challenging when we move from church to public policy. In 1963 Pope John XXIII wrote this: "Every civil authority must take pains to promote the common good of all, without prefer-ence for any single citizen or civic group. . . . Considerations of jus-tice and equity, however, can at times demand that those involved in civil government give more attention to the less fortunate members of the community, since they are less able to defend their rights and to assert their legitimate claims."[14]

For redistribution to be morally legitimate, the redistributor must be a recognized authority. Robin Hood may have had a moral cause, but his means—stealing from the rich—was morally suspect. We are called to regular acts of individual giving and charity, as we have seen in the discussion of vocation and discuss further in Chap-ter Nine, on sharing. Governments, acting on legitimate authority, should be the agents of any redistribution.

Rebecca Blank is one of the leading economists in the coun-try. Author of *It Takes a Nation: A New Agenda for Fighting Poverty*, she served on President Clinton's Council of Economic Advisors. Later, she was dean of the Gerald R. Ford School of Public Policy at the University of Michigan, and now serves as under secretary for economic affairs in the U.S. Department of Commerce. She is also a faithful Christian. Blank has lived a professional life advocating for public policies that benefit poor people, and her "avocation" has been explaining to Christians why they should embrace such a com-mitment as part of their practices of faith. Blank asserts that it is not just up to the generosity of the faith community—she has estimated that if religious congregations were to take over from government the current social safety net in the United States, each congregation—Christian, Jewish, Muslim, and all the rest—would need to contribute $300,000 annually, which is more than most congregations' budgets![15] It is a question of the scale of the economic and of financial need of the poor—it is too massive without truly public support. She writes:

> We should value the redistributive ability of government. Governmental institutions give us the ability to address inequities or injustices. They provide a way to serve the "widows and orphans" in our community. This is particularly important in a larger and more complex society, in which individual outreach may not be satisfactory and where we need to create public organizations or programs to deal with the needs of those who are not able to be economically self-sufficient through the market.[16]

Blank thus supports pressing public leaders to craft public policies that attend to the needs of the most vulnerable. She asserts that Christians and other citizens can disagree about which specific policies will be effective, but this should not obscure agreement on a basic commitment to redistributive public policies. A policy such as the Earned Income Tax Credit, which in effect is a negative tax on, or a positive supplement to, low wages, is consistent not only with distributive justice but also with social justice, which I discuss next, because it promotes social contribution through work at an adequate wage. But as Blank points out, distributive justice means caring for widows and orphans—many of whom are either elderly or very young and should not be expected to work. Distributive justice, and the preferential option for the poor, includes a commitment to support public policies that guarantee conditions worthy of each person's dignity, regardless of ability to work.

PRACTICING SOCIAL JUSTICE

Social justice entails working for conditions that allow every person to contribute in some way to the societies and communities in which they live. When we take the big-picture view of a complex economy and well over a billion people in poverty, it is easy to believe that we can make little difference. In one sense, a powerful politician in the United States and an impoverished person in America or Angola share in common the experience of living in a world that seems fully beyond control.

Thus, social justice requires faith and practices of hope. We have already emphasized that working for justice is a part of each person's vocation, but we need to see that our efforts are not in vain. Let us examine one kind of social-justice initiative based upon the combined agency of people with economic means and people without such means: microcredit.

An entrepreneur or team of entrepreneurs wants to start a small bakery and needs the capital to buy equipment. Another group in another village wants to raise farm animals as a small business but lacks start-up funding for animal feed and other supplies. For people such as these, typically without collateral or access to capital, receiving a small loan—perhaps $50 or $500—expands their opportunities to contribute to, and benefit from, economic and social life.

The best-known microlending institution, the Grameen Bank of Bangladesh, has granted millions of women small loans to begin local enterprises, thus reversing the vicious cycle of economic deprivation. The bank (and Muhammad Yunus, its founder) received the Nobel Peace Prize in 2006 for this work. Yunus goes so far as to declare that credit (or access to credit) is a basic human right.[17] Having access to credit is not only a right; it is also a human capability. Having access to credit enables people to gain access to other important goods, services, and social opportunities. It allows formerly marginalized people to become participants in the economic and social life of their communities. That expansion of human capabilities is what social justice is all about.

Another program, the Microcredit Foundation of India, has helped make small business loans available to more than 250,000 people in Tamil Nadu in south India. Almost all of these loan recipients are located in rural villages, and most are women. The secret of this program is its communal aspect—the women come together to share the risk of the loans they receive. More than that, they share their stories together. The Microcredit Foundation refers to these circles of women as *self-help groups* and to the loan recipients as *members*.

The entire program is structured around group participation and accountability. The Foundation encourages the formation of "self-help groups" of twenty women who will work together and who will be mutually accountable for the loans they take out from the bank. Because of this model of mutual accountability, microcredit programs typically have a near 100 percent rate of loan repayment.

The self-help groups sponsored by the Microcredit Foundation of India meet twice a month, under a rotating leadership model that gives all participants a chance to run the gatherings, and they learn the basics about banking, interest rates, borrowing, and investing. The women borrow money together, and with some assistance from the bank, they establish local cooperative businesses that produce goods or services for the village or nearby towns. The women themselves must draw upon their own skills and knowledge to produce a simple good or a service—examples include purchasing cows for their milk, or tailoring garments, or growing and selling local produce. Once the women's groups have successfully borrowed and repaid the loans, they then have a positive credit history, a money-making business, and an understanding of economic processes.

The Microcredit Foundation of India has an interesting history. It focuses on the agency of rural women who otherwise would not be able to participate in the global economy. But it was founded largely through the efforts of an influential banker and business leader, the late K. M. Thiagarajan of Chennai (Madras), India. Thiagarajan had been the longtime chairman and CEO of the Bank of Madura, at which bank he began a microcredit initiative. A devout Hindu, Thiagarajan spoke of his work as a calling to make financial means accessible to the rural villages surrounding his large cosmopolitan city. He declared that the purpose of the self-help groups is not simply to make good borrowers but to help form good and able citizens who can enjoy a better life in their villages.[18] Thiagarajan recognized that increased agency was often one of the by-products of women's involvement in the self-help groups.

Microcredit initiatives, which are rapidly expanding across the world, help bring about the conditions for social justice. They directly address a key aspect of the needs of impoverished people—credit that opens doors to basic economic goods and services. Second, they usually focus on women, and always on people with few economic resources, who in India and elsewhere suffer disproportionately in terms of income, education, and health. Third, they typically involve the participation of an outside agency (such as a commercial bank or a nongovernmental organization) that engages with the participants, not wholly out of a sense of "philanthropy," but rather out of a desire to earn a reasonable return while providing credit to persons who otherwise would have to borrow from high-interest moneylenders or remain economic outsiders. All of these aspects combine to allow people formerly without agency to play a contributing part of social and economic life.

One of the most significant critical questions for the micro-lending movement around the world is the issue of sustainability. How do groups of five, ten, or twenty people remain intact over the years? Can women who receive small loans successfully prepare themselves to receive standard loans for individuals? Thiagara-jan emphasized that many self-help groups that he helped form in Tamil Nadu were still functioning five years later and had moved on to address various community-development projects beyond the loans.[19]

The potential for the expansion of such a model of self-help groups and small loans is nearly endless. The Microcredit Foundation of India boasts fourteen thousand small groups in dozens of villages in Tamil Nadu, improving the lives of over a quarter of a million people. But Tamil Nadu has sixty-six million residents. Surely there is room for expanding the efforts to provide technical, financial, and labor support to tens of thousands of local initiatives to fight local poverty.

Microcredit made its name in places such as Bangladesh and south India, but it has quickly expanded globally. Indeed, increasing the agency of the disenfranchised through access to finance also can give agency to those of us privileged enough to be reading (or writing) a book about the challenges of economic life. My friends Rick and Jennifer recently visited Peru as part of Rick's work. They spent a number of months there, and they got to know a taxi driver, Marco, who struggled to make ends meet as a driver for a company. He wanted to buy his own used taxi and work for himself. Rick and Jennifer are people of faith, and they decided that as part of their relationship with Marco, they would loan him $1,500 so that he could pay off his debt for the taxi. They offered an additional "reverse interest" option to Marco, giving him the incentive of a 10 percent rebate, or $150, to pay the loan off on time. Rick and Jennifer reached out—via e-mail, Facebook, and a blog—to their circle of friends and neighbors, inviting us to participate in this loan. They would keep us updated on Marco's business and personal situation. They expressly stated that they understood this loan to be part of their Christian call to live faithfully during their stay in Peru. It was about helping the taxi driver build the capacity to have gainful employment. Marco wants to contribute his labors, but he needs the capital to be able to do it. Rick and Jennifer found their own participation in microcredit to be valuable, and they have multiplied their efforts under the organizational name CuscoGracias.[20]

Most of us do not have the opportunity, or occasion, to spend time living in the developing world. We cannot engage directly in such loans, so we need liaisons like Rick and Jennifer—even on an institutional scale. This is where organizations such as Kiva and Oikocredit come in. Kiva is the best-known of these organizations, having become the darling of the likes of Bill Clinton and Oprah Winfrey. The concept is tremendously simple: Kiva—the word comes from Swahili, meaning unity, agreement, or even covenant—helps connect entrepreneurs in the developing world with "social investors" in the industrialized world. Kiva has, literally, a world-class Web site that allows an investor, with two clicks, to review a list of potential entrepreneurs to support. Kiva works with microfinance institutions in countries across the world to verify the entrepreneurs' projects, prospects, and progress. Social investors gain regular updates on the entrepreneurial effort and the investment. The sense of agency and, to a lesser extent, of relationship that investors and entrepreneurs can gain is a testament to the wonders of Internet technology.[21]

Jessica Jackley and Matt Flannery co-founded Kiva. They each describe Christian faith as fundamental in their motivation to create their company. Jessica had interned at World Vision, an international Christian organization, and Matt's family had ties to World Vision as well. They had been inspired by the work of Muhammad Yunus and the Grameen Bank. They applied their abilities and connections to build up their Web-based structure.[22]

The lesser-known Oikocredit is less trendy than Kiva, but it has reached 16.8 million people through its loans. When it was founded in 1975, it reflected the cutting edge of the Christian ecumenical movement. Oikocredit—which incorporates into its name the Greek word *oikos* for world or household—arose from conversations in the World Council of Churches at a time when economic development had come to be seen as a vital part of mission in global church and society. Progressive-minded Christians in Europe sparked the planning for the organization.[23] Today, would-be investors across Europe, the United Kingdom, Ireland, and North America can click and invest in Oikocredit. Or they can support microfinance associations directly in particular countries. "For as little as $20, anyone with a computer and a conscience can invest in alleviating global poverty." Church denominations and other institutional investors also place their capital in this enterprise. Oikocredit talks about "maximizing social investment," and financial investment is just one part of this. Microfinance is efficient, but the goals toward which it aims are more in line with human capabilities than with finances alone.

Social justice will be realized when we have set up a local, national, and global infrastructure that allows all people to contribute their talents and creativity to the common good. Microfinance is one innovative mechanism allowing people to develop their agency. This example also shows that progress toward social justice can also help achieve more just exchanges (for example, between lender and borrower) and hence support commutative justice. While the social and financial returns of the enterprise should benefit various parties, microlending may well also have the effect of reducing severe inequalities, thus promoting distributive justice as well.

KEEPING OUR HOUSE IN ORDER

Doing justice is a vital practice of faith. It establishes the basic infrastructure that holds together our various levels of household, from our domicile to the whole of creation. The examples we have examined for commutative, distributive, and social justice are illustrative and, I hope, illuminative: They can shed light on all of our exchanges, on our thinking, acting, and voting on public policies, and on our own agency and that of others as we seek to contribute to our communities—local and global.

Justice can seem impersonal, and in some ways it is. We must see it, even when we talk of person-to-person exchanges, as a system that orders our lives in ways that allow us to flourish. In addition to the architectural images of justice as the pillar, foundation, or infrastructure of society, we also are familiar with justice as blind to personal attributes. These images of justice occupy our public debates over our own legal justice system—whether judges should be seen as umpires, interpreters, appliers of the law, or in some other role, and what criteria they should use to decide cases. Although partiality for or against demographic groups is widely seen as unacceptable, the debate rages on concerning whether the law can be blind to differences of race, gender, or other factors in societies in which those attributes have mattered historically and continue to shape people's identities.

And yet, justice is deeply personal, in the sense that it can shape every human relationship. There are tensions between structural questions of fairness and personal interactions with loved ones. After all, none of us can have an interpersonal circle as large as the expanding moral community, so we all have partialities and preferences. Notwithstanding these tensions, justice and charity are and should be closely connected. In the most recent papal encyclical on the economy, Pope Benedict XVI frames justice within the wider framework of love. "If we love others with charity, then first of all we are just toward them. Not only is justice not extraneous to charity, not only is it not an alternative or parallel path to charity: justice is inseparable from charity, and intrinsic to it."[24]

If we are to show love toward neighbors, we must work for justice for all neighbors. Justice creates the conditions under which everyone has the opportunity to pursue their own goals and interests, including relationships with their loved ones. This is a theocentric view: God loves all humans equally, but we live in an unequal world in which people have various and disparate needs. God shows preferential attention toward those with the greatest needs, and so should we.

Chapter 9

SHARING

❧

It is a question of a fair balance between
your present abundance and their need.
—2 Corinthians 8:13b–14a

Let them gather all the food of these good years
that are coming, and lay up grain.
—Genesis 41:35a

We share material goods within households, and we share much more than that. At home, we must figure out how to share things such as bank accounts, chores, meals, the living room, the bathroom, and the back yard. In the global household, this translates (more or less) into sharing financial markets, labor markets, food production, civic life, environmental management, and recreation. Ultimately, we share community. In theological terms, this connects, of course, to *communion,* in which people come together to share in the body of Christ, eating from a common loaf and drinking from a common cup. These are material elements that give physical, not just spiritual, nourishment. In the story of Jesus' feeding of the five thousand, we have seen that human sharing is an integral part of God's providing for all. From the domestic household to the global one, God calls all people to be companions—from *com,* "with" and *panis,* "bread"—those with whom we share bread.

This is not easy, and it appears to run against our self-interest, which surely must be part of our economic thinking. Faith-based calls to share our individual resources can seem idealized—none more so than the Book of Acts. But just how naive is this biblical account? Acts recounts the stories of the Christian community just after the life, death, and resurrection of Jesus. These followers grapple to understand what they had experienced with Jesus and what had happened to him. Amid puzzlement, frustration, and amazement, they try to find their way. Indeed, this community is known as the People of the Way. Their sense of shared struggle draws them into a tight-knit community, and this requires economic sharing. "Now the whole group of those who believed were of one heart and soul, and no one claimed private ownership of any possessions, but everything they owned was held in common. With great power the apostles gave their testimony to the resurrection of the Lord Jesus, and great grace was upon them all. There was not a needy person among them, for as many as owned lands or houses sold them and brought the proceeds of what was sold" (Acts 4:32–34).

This post-resurrection story makes me wonder the following: Is it more difficult to believe in the resurrection of Jesus or to believe that this community held their goods in common? It is one thing for the Son of God, the human-divine Jesus Christ, to be raised to new life. That is part of our longtime faith tradition. It is quite another for people to share credit cards, car keys, and food.

Did they really share everything? There were doubters then and there are doubters now. The text says that a good man, Barnabas, sold his field and gave the proceeds to the apostles for the community's use. But then—in a passage less frequently read—Ananias and his wife Sapphira sell their property but turn over only a portion of the money to the community. They were keeping some of the money for themselves—call it their own rainy day fund. Peter challenges Ananias directly for his dishonesty, saying that not only has Ananias lied to the community, he has also lied to God. When Ananias hears this declaration, he simply falls down and dies. Sapphira also has a chance to tell the truth; she does not, and so she also promptly drops over and dies (Acts 5:1–11). (How different have been the reactions of current-day embezzlers and Ponzi schemers, who "lawyered up" to protest their sentences even when they admitted wrongdoing.)

Economic living is, ultimately, a communal practice. Community, in fact, is one of the most important goods that we share. It is not a *zero-sum* good in the way that many consumer goods are. If I eat the whole pie, none is left for my friends. But if I engage more fully in the life of my community (whether it is a neighborhood, church, or civic club), chances are that others will reciprocate and also enjoy more of that same shared good. Community is thus a *positive-sum* or expanding good.

Participating in the life of a community is a central capability. We have a genuine need to belong in social groups, whether they are families, school organizations, friendship networks, civic and neighborhood associations, or congregations. Participation and membership are intrinsic goods, fundamental parts of a flourishing life. And they are also instrumental goods. Recall that in the example of the Microcredit Foundation of India (and various programs across the world), self-help groups provide the community of support and accountability that make the lending program work. The members not only share their finances, they share their time and commitment. And let us not believe that the benefits of community are only for the economically vulnerable. We all need others to shape us in directions that are healthy. Communities can get caught up, of course, in the same ways that individuals can in consumerism. A good friend recently told me about his family's search for a new church home. He found that he "didn't seem to have nice enough shoes" to fit in at his affluent local church. So it is not just any community that will serve a person's overall well-being.

Alongside the other economic practices—discerning desires, laboring, providing, doing justice, and so on—sharing stands as an integral and integrating part of living faithfully in the global economy. In sharing the creation, sharing goods, sharing at home, and sharing with future generations, we shed additional light on the other practices.

SHARING THE CREATION

On July 7, 2007, the ethical challenges of sharing the planet were visible for all to see. They were transmitted in vivid, HDTV color from concert venues on all seven continents into my living room, and yours. The Live Earth concert organizers, led by Al Gore, were creatively harnessing the technologies and resources of the world economy to attack one of the world's most pressing problems: global climate change. Gore and his team had recruited the latest, hippest celebrities and musicians to shout out the "inconvenient truth" of global warming and the human factors contributing to it. Thanks to the organizers' savvy promotional campaign, the concerts reached an audience estimated at between 1.2 and 2 billion people, especially the younger generations. The organizers called it the largest entertainment event ever held.

There they were: the Dave Matthews Band, Keith Urban, and Bon Jovi in New Jersey, Genesis and Madonna in London, Shakira and Snoop Dogg in Hamburg. And hundreds of other performers at a dozen venues. The performers did not travel to the nearest concert venue; they crisscrossed the planet to provide, presumably, an international mix of performers at the key venues. To transport these artists and their support personnel around the world, the environmental costs of air travel in particular were staggering. One organization estimated the total "carbon footprint" of Live Earth at 75,000 tons— thousands of times an average Westerner's annual environmental impact.[1] On the positive side, the concerts were carbon-neutral, according to the organizers. In a practice known as carbon offsetting, the participants funded the planting of about 100,000 trees to make up for the damage caused by the travel and venue activities. The trees, especially if planted in the tropics, will absorb and break down carbon dioxide, removing it from the environment.

Was the promotion of the world's largest rock concert a good way to decry the ecological damage of the global economy? Do our means match our message? As one critic posed the ethical question, would we throw a pig roast to promote vegetarianism?[2]

To add to the moral ambiguity, during the U.S. broadcast of the event, the television emcees delivered a segment about the environmental impact of disposable plastic water bottles. Within a few seconds of their plea to stop the excessive use of plastic water bottles, the next-up musical act performed with a row of water bottles lined up behind them. The sense of irony must have been present even for the most avid supporter of the event. The performers' practices did not line up with their stated values.

Lest we criticize these celebrities too quickly, however, we must confront our own ecological practices. Live Earth's moral quandaries are simply ours, writ large. Like the organizers of Live Earth, most of us are contributing far more than our fair share to global pollution. Even if you, as an individual, contribute only one-fourth of the U.S. average to global greenhouse gas emissions, you are exceeding the current international average. And that current per-person usage needs to go down if the world is to reach sustainable levels. So let us acknowledge just how challenging it is to think about, let alone put into practice, sharing the creation.

In the effort not to offend constituents, some Live Earth performers suggested that solving global warming was just a matter of small habits, like turning off the stereo when not using it. Such practices matter a great deal. But we intuitively know that the moral and theological challenges of globalization are greater than changing the kind of light bulbs we use—even though this is a good thing to do. How can we most effectively and faithfully live within a global economy that is properly constrained by the moral and physical ecology? We require a wider-angle lens to examine the economic, political, and social contexts in which we and our institutions are located.

The psalmist gives us the theocentric fundamentals for sharing creation. "The earth is the Lord's and all that is in it, the world, and those who live in it; for he has founded it on the seas, and established it on the rivers" (Psalm 24:1–2). We are stewards, not owners in any ultimate sense, of the land, air, and waters. Yet do we and our institutions put this conviction into practice?

When nations negotiate international climate treaties, the parties do not begin from any such perspective. Instead, the negotiations typically start with the status quo of national boundaries and economic production patterns. Industrialized nations, which generally have greater per-capita consumption and energy-use figures than developing nations, proceed as if they are entitled to maintain their current practices. The developing nations similarly pursue their own economic interests first and believe they are entitled, just as the industrialized nations were, to increase their emissions and other environmental damage as an unfortunate by-product of economic growth.

The Kyoto Protocol is the most significant climate agreement, having been ratified by over 180 countries. The protocol sets legally binding guidelines on the industrialized nations, which are the largest polluters, by which they must reduce by agreed-upon targets the level of greenhouse and other harmful gases from their 1990 levels. In contrast, the developing nations agreed to follow only general, nonbinding commitments. The United States signed the protocol in 1998 but never ratified it; hence, the agreement has no legal force on American practices and U.S. administrations and private corporations have received much international criticism for this failure to join the international effort. Many critics of the protocol, including U.S. leaders, have claimed that the differentiated approach for industrialized and developing countries means that the former are getting the short end of the stick.

A theocentric understanding of sharing the environment gives a different view. No individuals or countries have a right to pollute. Management of the creation is a responsibility, not an entitlement. Citizens and leaders in each locale and nation have a responsibility to look after human well-being and the welfare of other animals and the natural environment. It is a question of integrating and often balancing these goals. Individuals, corporations, and governments can rightfully pursue their economic well-being, but not by exploiting the natural world. The fact that many people already benefit economically from their own polluting is no justification to continue those practices.

From a theological standpoint of the preferential option for the poor, the need to produce agricultural and other basic goods for economically vulnerable persons outweighs the desire of more affluent people for other consumer goods. Because there are higher proportions and degrees of economic vulnerability in the developing countries, these nations have some justification to be bound by relatively more favorable environmental regulations. There is no excuse for gratuitous pollution, however, and even processes that address basic needs should be as ecologically efficient as possible.

The U.S. government should take a leadership position in environmental matters. Whether or not the senate should ratify the Kyoto Protocol—and no one expects America to come late to the party—is less important than whether the government commits to future talks on various international agreements. China has now outpaced the United States in gross quantity of greenhouse gases, but Americans far exceed the Chinese on a per capita basis. Churches and individuals should continue to lobby their leaders to have the country participate more fully in global agreements.

In economic terms, all producers should incorporate the "full cost" of environmental damage into their accounting. Economists describe negative external effects (or negative externalities) as those costs borne by outside parties who share in the adverse environmental effects of a production process, such as the farmer whose water is contaminated by waste pumped into a river by a factory upstream of the farm. Full-cost accounting for such ecological damage would require the factory, in this simple case, either to change the process so as not to pollute or to compensate the farmer (and other affected parties) for such damage. Most or all of the costs borne by producers would eventually be passed along to consumers, and the governmental costs of regulation and protection would be paid by citizens. This full-cost accounting would be a part of environmentally just sharing.

The responsibilities of sharing the creation extend to the institutions of civil society. Higher education can and must play a leading role. A number of universities and colleges across the country declared that they would enact on their campuses a "year of sustainability." It isn't clear whether any of the organizers of this initiative recognize the irony of focusing in the short term (2008–2009) on a concept about long-term endurance. Critics called this to the attention of the schools' administrators, however. One journalist wrote a story about the initiative under the headline, "Sustainable for a Year."[3]

Davidson College, an elite liberal arts college that adheres to its Presbyterian identity, was one of the campuses that joined this sustainability commitment. Deflecting the criticism, Davidson's leaders asserted that the yearlong initiative was intended to build momentum for a movement that would, in fact, became an ongoing part of the campus culture. The college implemented an array of policies. On the very question of water bottles, they enacted into policy the recommendation to reduce plastic: All official events would use tap water instead of the bottles. This change saved the University $10,000 last year. The water-bottle policy was combined with less visible but more significant energy savings—particularly through improvements to the physical plant. And Davidson implemented a number of educational initiatives, within and beyond the formal curriculum, about ecological issues. The faculty established an environmental studies concentration, and student affairs founded a small residence, Eco House, for a group of students to practice sustainability and to educate the campus.[4]

Davidson's efforts are notable for their comprehensive approach. They are also representative of the actions of campuses across the United States to take a public leadership position on environmental change. Davidson joined six hundred schools in signing the American College & University Presidents Climate Commitment. Many campuses used the recession as a moment at which to cut inefficient practices and move toward green policies of energy conservation. And campus leaders have taken increased initiative to raise the public profile of environmental education. Universities have the means to share knowledge—in the classroom, in the residence hall, and through Internet technology. Just as important, campuses are a kind of model community, and they depend on a significant degree of social engineering. They are an ideal context in which to implement and teach about sustainable economic and environmental practices.

At the same time, higher education faces unique challenges as this kind of model community. Its institutions share, in fact, in the conundrum that the organizers of Live Earth faced. The educations that they offer students bear significant environmental cost. How do colleges and universities employ their resources in ecologically responsible ways? Students travel from far away to be on campus; the more elite the institution, the greater the distances their students travel. In turn, schools send students abroad, at least once and sometimes more. Colleges don't put it this way in recruiting and admission brochures, but in the process of providing a world-class, international education, harm to the environment is done in order that educational goods will result. (To be sure, the educational enterprise can also provide positive effects for the local economy.) So colleges and universities may well exacerbate ecological challenges even as they equip students to address them.

Churches face similar dilemmas. The most visible challenge results from what I call *church-preference individualism*. We tend to think of attending church as another consumer good that will help us fulfill our tastes and preferences. And thus we do not choose to attend the nearest church, or even the nearest church in our denomination. Thus, church shopping leads to local Sunday traffic patterns that resemble the global crisscrossing of the Live Earth artists. That latter event was a one-time spectacle; church traffic is an enduring blight. Energy usage by churches is often ecologically inefficient, as many local congregations cannot afford the one-time costs to upgrade their outdated physical plants to become more efficient. Yet if churches are to be sites that promote environmental sustainability, they should put into practice what they preach.

At the personal level, our desiring contributes to shopping and consuming, and these, in turn, result in polluting. President George H. W. Bush famously said that the U.S. lifestyle was not up for negotiation.[5] Yet Americans cannot assert that *everyone else* needs to consume less because there isn't enough clean air to allow everyone to live the lifestyle that we have already staked out. We need better education about our own consumption patterns and ways to share the creation more equitably.

The challenges of personal consumption pertain to the everyday decisions that individuals make, but they also have to do with the choices available to consumers in the first place. It is difficult to be environmentally responsible as a computer user when your machine is designed under "planned obsolescence." Within three to five years, every desktop, laptop, and notebook computer will have become an old jalopy on the information superhighway. We should press for transformations in the legal regulation of computer waste and in the capacity of computer hardware to be upgradable with technology advances. In the meantime, we can dispose of the machines responsibly through community computer recycling programs.

Through our own purchasing power, we should opt for goods with the least environmental impact. Again, though, we can only purchase from the choice set that is available to us. Conversely, that choice set is partially shaped as companies respond to consumer demand. When Costco introduced a new milk container in 2008, it did so with a "green" marketing blitz. The plastic jugs are almost square, and thus they are environmentally friendly because they can be stacked and transported more efficiently than rounder jugs. Costco's ads attempted to preempt the inevitable criticism from consumers who were just fine with their comfortable old milk jugs.[6] Consumers and their advocates can signal their willingness to go green through their purchases and other communication with producers. Producers must be willing to opt for and then promote ecological alternatives. This example points to the kind of intentional coordination among producers, retailers, and consumers that will improve the ecological cost of consumption.

Commuting and home energy are two other key aspects of personal ecological practices. They contribute to the two largest sources of carbon dioxide pollution in the United States—buildings and transportation. The former accounts for 38 percent and the latter 34 percent of emissions. People cannot change their home energy practices all at once, but through such practices as doing an "energy audit," we can at least learn what aspects of our home are leading to inefficiencies or excessive waste.[7] Most of us cannot sell our SUV and buy a Prius tomorrow—though the federal government's cash for clunkers program produced an all-at-once push. Experts dispute, in any case, whether such sudden transitions produce a net positive effect. But over time, as American and other drivers' buying habits change—in concert with tougher "CAFE" federal gas mileage standards—we can make private transportation more efficient.

At the same time, the movement toward public transportation must become a greater priority. The high-speed rail system in Spain, for example, has spectacularly transformed that country, fueling its economic development in the past two decades. The travel time from Madrid to Barcelona on the new AVE train (which means *bird,* from "to fly" in Spanish) is three hours. Before high-speed rail, the train service took nine hours. Businessmen and many others had to fly by plane. Now they fly on the tracks, which is much more economical and ecological.[8] The easy critique is that American distances are too great for train travel. When new trains average over 100 miles per hour, as they do across Europe and Japan, a train system over much of the United States is no longer a pipe dream.

The economist Robert Frank suggests eco-friendly consumption decisions are also ones that promote genuine well-being. If individual consumers keep pursuing the latest gadgets, we speed up the race for more and more individual goods. We run faster and faster to keep up with the stuff of the Joneses, but in terms of happiness, we are just running in place. To escape the race, we must pool our resources to pursue those *public goods* that can benefit the whole community. Public parks, schools, and road and sidewalk projects are examples of goods that do increase the happiness of people.[9] This is because such commonly held goods do not depend on keeping up with the Joneses. Instead, they involve cooperating with the Joneses to build a park where people of all backgrounds and ages can exercise, relax, and play. Investing in these public goods changes the equation—combining our impulse for material goods and our impulse for communal participation.

Sharing the creation requires a broad set of practices in our institutions and our individual lives. These discussions of government, civil society, and personal behavior merely suggest the array of practices needed to tackle our ecological problems. They are all part of stewarding the creation from our current situation, in which each of us is currently taking more than our fair share.

SHARING OUR GOODS

Christian economic practices are rooted in the joyful, grateful response to the God of grace. God gives life, and life abundant. We misunderstand that abundance when we interpret it as material prosperity. It is better understood as life lived in human community that enables us all to realize our God-given capabilities. Money and other material goods help make that possible, but possessing wealth or goods is not the real goal. Rather, we aim to develop our own capabilities and to contribute to meeting the needs of others.

Our giving occurs in a variety of ways, at a variety of levels: from individual gifts in the church offering plate and to charitable groups over the Internet, to engagement in public debates about health care and education, to support of domestic and international antipoverty efforts. All of these are active responses reflecting gratitude to God, who provides for our life and the lives of all others.

How much giving is enough? In a world of 6.5 billion people, 1.4 billion of whom are experiencing absolute poverty, how much should we give, and to whom should we give?

Peter Singer, a world-renowned ethicist at Princeton University, develops an answer that challenges each one of us. His response is based on the philosophical framework of utilitarianism.[10] He makes a number of reasonable assumptions, including these: We should seek to maximize overall utility, or satisfaction, in the world; the utility or satisfaction of each person should count equally, regardless of their nationality or where they live; and utility derived from each dollar of income tends to decrease for any person as income increases. In our world of vast economic inequalities and significant suffering, Singer argues that each of us should donate money to the point that our utility loss from a gift is as great as the utility to be gained by the recipient. In other words, I should give away my money otherwise to be used for luxuries and other consumer goods until my own well-being approaches the well-being of the world's poorest persons. If all people in wealthy countries followed this commitment, the well-being improvement for the poor would be greater than if only a few people act, and the giving burden, shared by more wealthy people, would be lighter on each. Notwithstanding how other people act, however, morality demands that each of us follow the principle of giving to the point of equal marginal utilities.

Singer has softened his moral criterion in the quest to get more people to follow it. (His strategy is thus consistent with his philosophy of maximizing utility.) While never renouncing his strongest moral position, Singer argued that people should at least be willing to give away all things that are not morally significant in order to help others who are suffering. (Is your iPod or second television morally significant?) Singer then weakened the position further to say that those wanting to live a morally decent life must give at least some share of their income to fight global poverty—whatever other charitable causes they support—and the wealthier you are, the more you should give. He has posted his progressive scale on the Internet, which begins with 1 percent of income for the middle class to 33 percent for those with annual incomes above $10 million. Singer has stated that, for his own part, he gives away 30 percent of his income to global anti-poverty organizations.

Singer summarizes his position as follows: "When we can save the life of an innocent human being at a modest cost to ourselves, we should do so." He draws this conclusion about current giving practices:

> If I am correct, the vast majority of us who live in developed countries are not living an even minimally decent ethical life. Almost all of us spend money on luxuries—after all, even bottled water is a luxury when the water that comes out of the tap is free. Should we be spending money on that, and on other unnecessary items with larger price tags, when the money we are spending on things we don't need could save a life?[11]

Singer's utilitarian arguments about the moral scourge of poverty call Christians to take even more seriously the theological claims about giving. Should not the affirmation of the equal dignity of all persons created in the image of God make at least as strong a call to confront global deprivation as Singer's secular approach does? The religious ethicist Eric Gregory—who, like Singer, is a professor at Princeton—asserts that although Christians do not embrace all of Singer's utilitarian framework, there are good reasons to accept his moral arguments about global poverty.[12]

The Christian call to giving goes even further than Singer does, however. We have already affirmed that all of our lives and our possessions belong to God. We are giving away what is not ours in the first place. Today's politicians gain popularity with constituents when they tell them, "It's your money." Theologically speaking, it's not our money. We are stewards. We are charged not only to care for our own lives and for our loved ones but to think in terms of the whole of God's household.

Thus, if we try to calculate what we need to do in order to live a morally perfect life, we will arrive at the conundrum faced by the rich young ruler who confronts Jesus. This ruler wants to know what he needs to do to inherit eternal life. Notice that this is precisely the question of the lawyer to whom Jesus tells the story of the Good Samaritan. In both cases, Jesus starts with the same answer—he should keep the commandments. (In one case, Jesus cites many of the Ten Commandments; in the other, he cites the "summary" version—to love God and love neighbor.) The ruler, like the lawyer, says he has kept the commandments—so what else should he do? Jesus sizes up the rich young ruler. Perhaps Jesus notices the nice clothes the man is wearing. Jesus says, "There is still one thing lacking. Sell all that you own and distribute the money to the poor, and you will have treasure in heaven; then come, follow me." What we read next is no wonder: "But when [the rich young ruler] heard this, he became sad, for he was very rich" (Luke 18:18–25).

I have this same reaction every time that I read Peter Singer's moral argument. His strong principle of giving—that we should give in radically equalizing ways, and at the global level—is convincing to me. To be sure, there are ways to qualify it. We do have local responsibilities that we must attend to and are well situated to influence positively. It is proper that we give some disproportionate attention to our own interests and to those closest to us. And, societies need to make ethical demands that selfish and sinful human beings can reasonably be asked to uphold. Yet even after we have accounted for all these items, we face a moral obligation to give far more than most of us do to alleviate and witness against human suffering.

This situation should not lead us into despair, however. Humility, yes, but not despair. The proper response to the challenge of global poverty, and to giving in general, is gratitude for God's grace. We cannot earn our eternal life through our actions and we will not attain moral perfection. But we can embody gratitude in our lives. That approach then shapes more generous actions.

In his writings to the Corinthian church, Paul exhorts his sisters and brothers to extend generous donations to the distressed churches in Macedonia. He writes that the Macedonians suffer extreme poverty but that they have shown him and others an "overflowing wealth of generosity." They are poor but tremendously hospitable. Paul turns, then, to his wealthier counterparts in the church at Corinth to ask their help. He requests them to be generous. Here is his principle for giving in a situation of economic inequality:

I do not mean that there should be relief for others and pressure on you, but it is a question of a fair balance between your present abundance and their need, so that their abundance may be for your need, in order that there may be a fair balance. As it is written "The one who had much did not have too much, and the one who had little did not have too little" [2 Corinthians 8:13–15].[13]

There is a resonance between this claim and Singer's strong moral principle. Note that Paul describes giving within a framework of long-distance (should we say, in this case, virtual?) community. This is not isolated giving—it is distributing resources within a community so as to achieve a fair balance, some approximate equality. Paul's theological point is that gratitude leads to generous sharing. He writes, "Each of you must give as you have made up your mind, not reluctantly or under compulsion, for God loves a cheerful giver" (2 Corinthians 9:7). Cheerfulness here is not a fleeting sentimentalism; it means the joyful approach that derives from gratitude.

The Christian tradition makes gratitude, as a disposition for sharing, more fundamental than any technical or formal requirement to give. The historical standard for the Christian practice of sharing, however, has been 10 percent of one's income. Tithing, from an old English word for *tenth,* has roots in the Hebrew Bible. After Jacob dreams about encountering God's angels on a ladder, he joyfully declares, "Surely the Lord is in this place—and I did not know it!"—and, in response, he decides to give back one-tenth of all that God gives to him (Genesis 28:10–22).

Stories such as this one were codified into the laws of Deuteronomy. The Israelites were mandated to present a tithe of all products at the sanctuary. These gifts were to be the "first fruits"—not the smaller or bruised fruits taken from the bottom of the barrel. The purpose of the tithes was the support of "the Levites, the aliens, the orphans, and the widows, so that they may eat their fill within your towns" (Deuteronomy 26:1–15). The tithe was intended, then, to underwrite the religious life of the community (through the Levite priests), and also to support the most economically vulnerable groups of the community.

We do not believe, and we must not believe, that our giving will bring justice to the world economy. Instead, such sharing combines with the work of doing justice—such as promoting equitable domestic and international policies—as a witness that God's intention is the well-being of all people and of the creation.

Giving can become just another form of self-serving satisfaction: We make ourselves feel better because we return to the church or to some other charity a portion of our earnings. Donating to other people can even sometimes become a way of keeping them dependent or subservient. A healthier account reminds us that giving regularly, as in the practice of "tithing," becomes a discipline that establishes order in our economic lives. It reminds us that giving should not be dependent upon the whims of how we feel (sympathy, empathy, or antipathy) toward another person or what economic desires we are having at a particular moment. Rather, we dedicate a regular portion of our income to the church and other institutions working for God's justice. In so doing we remind ourselves that all of what we have comes as part of God's own creation.

SHARING AT HOME

Economists have tended to focus on exchanges and activities outside the household and have thus left issues of intrahousehold distribution to non-economists. After all, standard economic analysis assumes that people act as self-interested agents within an environment of competition—such as in the labor market, product market, and so on. Within the household, most people agree, the assumptions of competition and self-interested behavior cannot account for the sharing that takes place. At their best, at least, households more closely model the sense of genuine community than larger societies do.

But it is a mistake to make a full contrast between the competition of the marketplace and the altruism of the household. The marketplace is not adequately modeled as a sphere of competitive self-interest. Contrariwise, the household is not a site of pure altruism. (How do I know? I live in one.) It is the same human beings who inhabit the marketplace and the domestic sphere, and even if they enjoy different kinds of relationships in public and private, they have the same moral psychology.

Within the household, people have their own individual interests as well as interests in others. Indeed, the very notion of self-interest is more complicated than simple models portray it to be, and my self-interest may well incorporate the hope for your interests to be met. Households are a sphere in which these overlapping interests are likely to occur.

Amartya Sen has proposed that we examine close personal relationships in terms of "cooperative conflict." Within a household, people typically do seek cooperation—by necessity, they share a host of economic goods—but there are also inevitable conflicts in the interests between and among household members. Individuals typically do care about the well-being of the whole, but they retain some degree (which varies by person) of self-interested concern. Actual practices reflect the interaction between altruistic and self-interested commitments.[14]

Sen's analysis is particularly germane for thinking about gender and cooperative conflict, especially in relation to the economic decisions about work outside the home and various household activities. Who will do what? We have already seen that the market wage often becomes the de facto way of valuing time. It is the opportunity cost of leisure. In the current-day U.S. labor market, the typical or median year-round, full-time female worker earns about 78 percent of the average year-round, full-time male worker.[15] It is thus more common, within dual-earning male and female households, for the man to out-earn the woman in the labor market. There are many exceptions, of course. Sen has shown that income disparity, within the framework of cooperative conflict, gives the higher-income earner more "negotiating power" in the relationship. Since labor within the household is unpaid when done by a household member (but not if you hire a housekeeper, nanny, or gardener), that labor carries less value in negotiations among household members. In the cases in which women earn less than men, typical gender stereotypes can be activated, and men have more economic and social power within the household.

Two friends of mine—married to each other with one child—find themselves in this familiar situation. She is a well-regarded and well-paid professor, but her salary pales in comparison to what he earns as a corporate vice president. When their child gets sick—or their day care provider gets sick—the married couple has to arrive at a decision. Who is going to miss work to care for their child? The standard answer in economics is that there is no dilemma here: both parties would decide together, and in harmony, on the outcome. And the most likely answer is that the wife should take off work. After all, that is the income-maximizing decision; his opportunity cost is greater than hers is. But in my friends' experience, that is another way of saying that his time is more valuable than her time is. (Notice that in this case, since both are salaried and not hourly employees, there is no direct advantage in market terms if she covers the kids instead of him; both receive their full salary in either case.) She rightly finds this frustrating, and she believes that, when this happens every time, she is getting the short end of the stick. The sense of sharing the parenting responsibilities—which contributes to relational well-being—is not easily incorporated into a calculation of opportunity costs.

Yet it is precisely this market-based valuing that predominates so much of our thinking of time allocation within the household. Many people are feeling the time crunch, but working mothers tend to feel it most of all. As this group has picked up, over recent decades, more hours in the labor market, working fathers have moderately increased their hours in work at home (domestic chores and parenting). Sharing at home is seldom borne evenly.

Children pick up on the distribution of household roles and chores. My wife and I have learned that children (at least ours) are not born with a natural propensity to share. In fact, *traffic cop* and *umpire* describe our parenting practices well. Kids need to see parents—and other adults—interacting in ways that model reciprocity and mutual respect.

The commitment to equal dignity and the expansion of everyone's capabilities should apply within the household as much as outside it. Economics as managing the household is not only a metaphor for the global economy—it also means each household and each family unit. The equal valuing of each member of the household cannot be accomplished by calculating labor-market wage rates alone. Sharing requires a form of valuing that transcends market analysis.

Whether in the public sphere or at home—or both—sharing becomes more complicated when we consider what we owe to future generations. In Qoheleth's reflections in Ecclesiastes about laboring, he writes, "Vanity of vanities! All is vanity. What do people gain from all the toil at which they toil under the sun?" He continued, "A generation goes, and a generation comes, but the earth remains forever" (Ecclesiastes 1:2b–4). That is a candid way of stating our own finitude. Qoheleth's grim tone captures important aspects of the toil that most people confront at some points, and many confront perpetually, in their working lives. Yet hope, not despair, should be the ultimate word.

Our labors are not in vain because we are contributing to a good beyond ourselves. We are managers of God's household, temporary caretakers, who are called to till it and keep it—and improve it. Managing a sustainable household requires us to plan carefully for the future. Biblical stories provide examples of good planning—and its opposite. Recall the rich fool, so happy with his possessions that he merely has to build bigger barns to store them. He hasn't planned for his own death, and so his heart is in the wrong place when he dies. But what happens to the earthly stuff he had treasured? Presumably, he hadn't thought to leave a will—of if he did, Jesus forgets to mention it in his parable. Is the stuff of any use to his heirs or neighbors? This example is one of poor stewardship. It is a man's failure to use his resources to help his own or others' genuine well-being.

Consider a very different biblical narrative about storage barns. In Genesis, Joseph interprets the pharaoh's dreams, warning him about a long famine that is to come. The years of drought would follow a period of plenty. Storage of nutritious food is precisely what is needed. Joseph advises: "Let them gather all the food of these good years that are coming, and lay up grain under the authority of Pharaoh for food in the cities, and let them keep it. That food shall be a reserve for the land against the seven years of famine that are to befall the land of Egypt, so that the land may not perish through the famine" (Genesis 41:35–36).

One of my friends, an economist, jocularly told me that this story reveals God's support for Keynesian macroeconomic policy: Joseph directs the pharaoh to become the automatic stabilizer! He is quite right that this act of preparation plays a stabilizing function. John Maynard Keynes dictated that government should increase its public spending in order to soften the effect of a recession. Governments should step in, he maintained, to smooth the economic cycle, spending in recessions and saving up in boom times.[16] Indeed, Keynes's ideas from the inter–World War period have become widely accepted. Richard Nixon reportedly stated, "We are all Keynesians now." (But I do not believe he meant God, too.) More recently, although political disagreement persists, most economists accept that governments have a responsibility to increase spending when private spending decreases. This is an important function of leadership and public policy. Some priorities, such as "green spending" on environmental technology and fuel efficiency, should have more money dedicated to them.

There is indeed a vital role for government to play in guiding economic life in order to plan for the future. Economists debate the pros and cons of deficit spending and the accumulation of national debt. But few economists believe the level of debt that the U.S. government is currently carrying—about $11.5 trillion in mid-2009—is healthy or sustainable as a long-term practice. Even before the economic stimulus packages of 2008 and 2009, interest payments accounted for roughly 10 percent of the annual federal budget, and combined with the interest accrued by the government from Social Security shortfalls, the United States was paying about a half-trillion dollars a year in interest. This borrowing can have the long-term effect of crowding out private investments, as the interest rate for credit goes up with government demand for it. Keynesian economics calls, in the short term, for public stimulus of the economy, which is highly justified. But beyond the economic recession, good stewardship will entail public efforts focused on reducing the government deficits that lead to further national debt.

There is also a more general message, of course, from the biblical message of preparing for the future. We must all be prudent with our material goods, expanding our time horizon beyond the immediate term.

But the current moment always seems so pressing. In America, the personal savings rate is lower than that of most other industrialized nations. At one point in 2005, the rate was actually negative, meaning that Americans were spending every penny of their disposable income and then were extending their credit card balances beyond their means.

Bank of America has a "keep the change" program to encourage savings. It promotes this as a simple way to save. The bank describes it with this promotional language:

> Each time you buy something with your Bank of America
> Check Card, we'll round up your purchase to the nearest
> dollar amount and transfer the difference from your check-
> ing account to your savings account. You get to keep the
> change—so every cup of coffee, gift, meal and tank of gas
> add up to more savings for you. What could be easier?[17]

"You get to keep the change" . . . but the money was already in your checking account. This is a gimmicky way to get people to move money from checking to savings—and who knows? Maybe it works. But it perpetuates the model of saving money by spending money. It plans ahead by focusing on purchases in the here and now.

Sharing with future generations requires storing goods—less of the consumer goods that the rich fool piled up, and more of those goods that Joseph described, goods that will sustain us and future generations.

Concern for the future also entails care for the creation. Our consuming and polluting habits have costs that will be borne for many years to come. When companies and countries do not properly incorporate environmental care and restoration into their production costs, they create an *earth deficit*. This is the term that the late cultural historian and Catholic theologian Thomas Berry used to describe the unaccounted-for damage or degradation to the environment from economic production.[18] The full balance sheet, to extend the economic image, must account for these items. And, of course, many of these costs will not be paid by the current generations. They will come to fruition, rather, decades or centuries later. The debate about nuclear power and radioactive waste, for instance, is complicated by the fact that most forms of minimal-risk storage require containment facilities that endure across generations. How do people guarantee that the proper processes will be followed, and is it fair to commit people in the future to undertake them in perpetuity? The literal storage of "goods" (which are "bads" in this case) can have a negative impact on the well-being of future generations. These are not the storage barns that the pharaoh dreamed about or that Joseph commended to the people.

With which people in future generations will we share? If we care about an equitable distribution of economic resources—and I have asserted that we do, on a global scale—then inheritance rights and recipients take on central moral significance. Bill Gates Sr., father of the Bill Gates of Microsoft, is one of the millionaires who has fought for the inheritance tax. Unlike most other wealthy Americans, and against his own (narrow) self-interest, the senior Gates has taken a high-profile stance to defend federal and state inheritance taxes from calls for their repeal. He believes that future generations—and he generally speaks about the U.S. context—should have roughly equal chances at success. Hence he promotes using inheritances for improving public education. Critics of inheritance taxes assume that the money that adults hold should be inherited by whomever they designate—and hence, when that right is taken away, it is a "death tax." Bill Gates Sr. has a different nomenclature for the inheritance tax: "To me the better nickname would be 'the grateful heirs tax.'"[19] *Gratitude* is the word.

Thus, what, precisely, do we owe future generations, and to whom do we owe it? There is no set formula, but our claims on economic resources are no firmer in death than they are in life. The passing from one generation to the next is an appropriate time to promote the equal conditions of all people to develop their capabilities and achieve a decent level of well-being. This assumes, of course, that we, the current generation, are storing up goods that will be of value to future ones. How should we allocate our goods among our descendants, loved ones, and far-off neighbors? The same balancing act needs to done among these competing goods. The preferential option for the poor—guaranteeing the dignity of all people—is one guiding principle. This commitment can offset, at least to some extent, the propensity of people to favor their own.

Sharing community extends beyond the walls of our homes and the gates of our churches—far beyond them. We can mutually improve well-being by investing together in public goods such as schools, parks, and roads. In a society in which we repeatedly hear the message, "It's your money; don't let the government take it," it is perhaps ironic that we may better realize our well-being by pooling our resources toward such public projects.

And sharing extends beyond our national borders. The ONE Campaign and sister movements in Britain, Ireland, and continental Europe have shown that a few million citizens can make a difference in combating extreme global poverty. Extending our moral community to the global level is not just a nice thing to do; it is a fundamental part of living out the Christian obligation to love one's neighbor.

Thus living faithfully in the global economy calls us to share at levels from the personal to the global. We invest ourselves in our own vocational choices and our spending, saving, and giving habits. We do so in the nature of the communities we join and help create. We do so in how we share with our neighbors, locally and globally, in generous giving and working for justice.

We do not need to use our gifts and talents in the ways that our consumer culture expects of us. We have the power to shape our own lives and our common future. Let there be no doubt about it, though: We face an uphill battle against the marketing forces in society to discern those desires that contribute not only to our happiness, however sentimental or fleeting, but to genuine well-being. This requires faith in the God who provides for our needs, even when we do not always know what those needs are. It calls us into community, even as it calls us to shape those communities toward developing our capabilities, building the common good, and caring for creation. It charges us to work for public policies that are consistent with a preferential option for the poor and other vulnerable people.

Do not let anyone tell you that living a relatively simple lifestyle is an easy practice of faith. It is one of the most difficult. Believing we can live free of the influence of the market economy is a dangerous thing. But it is even more perilous to embrace the messages of consumerism and the promises of abundant life that they offer. We need to forge the habits—and community connections—needed to engage critically in economic life every day: to decide what we require to live on, how we will spend our time and talents, and how we can expand the global community.

The Christian story is also a story of abundance, fulfillment, and justice. After the disciples passed baskets of food to the five thousand, all had eaten and were satisfied—and there was more left over than they had started with. Talking about "enough" in a world of too much disparity and deprivation requires a certain humility. It challenges us to reach out to our neighbors in need and to establish practices that will be sustainable for future generations.

So, *How much is enough?* We can draw some strands together by recasting this question in a number of ways. The astute reader has realized that I have posed more questions than provided answers in the book. This has been no accident: My teacher Tom McCollough taught me that the key to any ethical enterprise is not to offer pat answers but to pose the right questions. So, in closing, I offer a few guiding questions related to our central theme.

First, we must ask, *Enough of what?* Is the answer money? Baseball cards? Days off? Friends? Blessings? I have suggested that money is a means and not an end. Having the means to acquire basic goods and services is essential, and income can provide a rough measure of well-being. For instance, knowing that 1.4 billion people earn less than $1.25 a day is important information. It undermines any claims that our global economy stands on a morally or theologically acceptable foundation. But we should care more about capabilities—what people are able to do and be in their societies. How well are they educated? How many have access to decent health care? How able are they to participate in their political or cultural life? Especially in industrialized or developed societies, including the United States, income is not a reliable predictor of happiness or well-being. These other capabilities, especially seen together, are better indicators. Let us focus on attaining enough money and other sufficient resources so that people can develop their full potential. Let us value human capabilities themselves—whether it is the list I offered in Chapter Two or an alternative list. Indeed, the very exercise of joining with our friends and colleagues to discuss which aspects of well-being matter is itself an important practice related to shaping our values, participating in community, and discerning our desires.

A second question to ask is, *Enough for whom?* We must shift the question from, "Do I have enough?" to "Do we have enough?" This question applies at various levels, from sharing at home to sharing within God's household. I have invited readers to consider expanding our community, beyond a circle of family and loved ones, beyond our church and other local groups, and beyond the nation-state. I acknowledge that "global community" remains abstract. This is one of the key challenges in applying a Christian economic ethic, developed in terms of interpersonal relations, to an impersonal, global economy. So we must find ways to make the transnational personal. We must exercise the moral imagination. We must share our personal stories, if we have them, that connect us to actual people around the world—and "across the tracks" in our own communities. Indeed, in most every metropolitan area in America, we can find voices from Latin America, Europe, Africa, and Asia. The best way to get people to care about distant others is probably neither Adam Smith's strategy—have them imagine the victims of an earthquake—or Peter Singer's—make a moral argument based on equalizing marginal utilities. Instead, we should invite our local neighbors to tell us about, and share photos of, their brothers, mothers, cousins, and friends to whom they are connected.

Third, we must also ask, *Enough until when?* This is the issue of sustainable economic and ecological practices. Experts disagree radically on sustainable population levels, the rates of climate change, and the adequacy of food, water, and energy supplies. But we know the general direction that our behaviors need to go—and on the more complicated questions of ecology and economy, we have consensus on the trade-offs and areas needing further technological advances. There is consensus that U.S. economic habits are not replicable now across the world. Our national parks and international wildlife treasures are in distress now. And, on the economic front, we must worry now about the Social Security and Medicare crises that stand less than one generation forward. Living faithfully in the global economy calls us to be environmental stewards, from our personal practices of recycling and efficient energy usage to our philanthropic and political support for eco-friendly technologies and public policies.

Finally, it is valuable to ask, *Enough for what?* In theocentric perspective, the chief end of human beings is to glorify God and enjoy God forever. Living out that vision in the current moment means, among other things, to work for an economy and society in which all people, created in God's image, can enjoy and express their human dignity. Material goods are part of a faithful life, and they contribute to our well-being. God intends for each person to live life abundantly, but that is achieved through economic adequacy, not, as Jesus stated, in the abundance of our possessions (Luke 12:15b). Our economic goods combine with spiritual, cultural, political, and social-relational aspects of well-being. Pope Paul VI called the sum total of these "integral human development."[20] I have more often spoken in terms of well-being and human capabilities.

These questions (and related ones) help move us from an individualistic focus on maximizing our self-interest to fitting those interests into broader perspective. This does not mean, of course, that the everyday questions of how much to spend on clothing, how much to give to church or alma mater, or whether to take a day off will go away. Rather, they are framed with wider questions in mind about justice and a worldwide community. How do we address these questions, and consequently act, so that we tend to develop our own capabilities and the capabilities of others?

I hope that these efforts to connect the macro-level questions of theocentric values to the everyday practices of working, shopping, and sharing will help us live with integrity in the global economy. Achieving this goal is indeed a matter of our money. But beyond that, it is also a matter of our very selves, the vocational and consumer choices we make, and the grateful giving and work for justice that we do. It requires the faith that we will have enough material goods to live adequately and that there are enough resources, when they are shared, to fulfill the needs of all people in God's household.

Notes

PREFACE

1. Kara E. Powell, discussion, Association of Youth Ministry Educators annual meeting, October 19, 2008.

CHAPTER ONE: SURVIVING

1. U.S. Census Bureau, "Poverty Thresholds for 2008 by Size of Family and Number of Related Children Under 18 Years," www.census .gov/hhes/www/poverty/threshld/thresh08.html, accessed August 1, 2009.

2. U.S. Department of Labor, Bureau of Labor Statistics, "Changes in Men's and Women's Labor Force Participation Rates," www.bls.gov/opub/ted/2007/jan/wk2/art03.htm, accessed August 25, 2009; Juliet Schor, *The Overworked American: The Unexpected Decline of Leisure* (New York: Basic Books, 1992), pp. 24–34.

3. Due to the complications of comparing incomes across nations, there is no definitive world income distribution. One careful analysis is Branko Milanovic, *Worlds Apart: Measuring International and Global Inequality* (Princeton, NJ: Princeton University Press, 2005). Milanovic uses the global median income figure, after a purchasing-power

adjustment based on 1998 data, of $1,328 (p. 209, note 118). Milanovic found that the percentage of the world population living in "rich" countries—defined as those with an average income above Portugal's—was 16 percent (p. 131). The United States has a per-capita income that is twice that of Portugal's (when incomes are adjusted for purchasing power). Briefly stated, then, the United States is far up the scale among these rich countries comprising 16 percent of the world's population.

4. World Bank, "World Bank Updates Estimates for the Developing World," http://econ.worldbank.org/WBSITE/EXTERNAL/EXTDEC/EXTRESEARCH/0,,contentMDK:21882162~pagePK:64165401~piPK:64165026~theSitePK:469382,00.html (http://tinyurl.com/world-bank-est), accessed July 22, 2009. A recent FAO estimate is that 923 million people were undernourished in 2007, and that number was rising in 2008 and 2009. Food and Agriculture Organization of the United Nations, *The State of Food Insecurity in the World 2008* (Rome: FAO, 2008), p. 6, downloadable at www.fao.org/docrep/011/i0291e/i0291e00.htm, accessed August 25, 2009. World Health Organization and UNICEF, 2004. "Meeting the MDG Drinking Water and Sanitation Target: A Mid-Term Assessment of Progress—Country, Regional and Global Estimates on Water & Sanitation," 2004, http://wssinfo.org/pdf/JMP_04_tables.pdf, accessed August 25, 2009.

5. For extended discussions and a series of estimates concerning the magnitude of additional aid needed to achieve the Millennium Development Goals and meet all basic needs, see Jeffrey Sachs, *The End of Poverty: Economic Possibilities for Our Time* (New York: Penguin Books, 2005), pp. 288–308, and Jeffrey Sachs, *Common Wealth: Economics for a Crowded Planet* (New York: Penguin Press, 2008), pp. 238–246.

6. Lionel Robbins, *An Essay on the Nature and Significance of Economic Science* (London: Macmillan, 1954 [1932]), p. 16. Robbins defines economics as "the science which studies human behaviour as a relationship between ends and scarce means which have alternative uses."

7. Alfred Marshall, *Principles of Economics,* 8th ed. (London: Macmillan, 1920), "Introduction."

8. William Wordsworth, "The World Is Too Much with Us," www.poetryfoundation.org/archive/poem.html?id=174833, accessed August 1, 2009.

9. Julie Scelfo, "The Makeover Moment," *New York Times,* April 23, 2009, p. D1.

10. Stanley Fish, "Faith and Deficits," *New York Times,* March 1, 2009, http://fish.blogs.nytimes.com/2009/03/01/faith-and-deficits/, accessed July 23, 2009.

11. Rowan Williams, "Ethics, Economics, and Global Justice," speech, March 7, 2009, www.archbishopofcanterbury.org, accessed June 23, 2009.

12. Rebecca M. Blank, "A Christian Perspective on the Role of Government in a Market Economy," in *Global Neighbors: Christian Faith and Moral Obligation in Today's Economy,* edited by Douglas A. Hicks and Mark Valeri (Grand Rapids, MI: Eerdmans, 2008), pp. 224–247.

13. Max Weber, *The Protestant Ethic and the Spirit of Capitalism,* translated by Talcott Parsons (New York: Routledge, 1992 [1930, 1904/5]).

14. Deirdre McCloskey, "Avarice, Prudence, and the Bourgeois Virtues," in *Having: Property and Possession in Religious and Social Life,* edited by William Schweiker and Charles Mathewes (Grand Rapids, MI: Eerdmans, 2004), pp. 312–336, quote on p. 322.

15. McCloskey, "Avarice, Prudence, and the Bourgeois Virtues," p. 321.

16. George Will, "Eco-clerics vs. SUV Sinners," *Pittsburgh Tribune-Review,* November 28, 2002, http://pittsburghlive.com/x/pittsburghtrib/opinion/columnists/will/s_104669.html, accessed July 22, 2009.

17. Associated Press, "Pols Want New Name for Mets Home: Citi/Taxpayer Field," *USA Today,* November 25, 2008, www.usatoday.com/sports/baseball/nl/mets/2008-11-25-citi-field_N.htm, accessed August 1, 2009.

Chapter Two: Valuing

1. Kenneth R. Feinberg, *What Is Life Worth? The Unprecedented Effort to Compensate the Victims of 9/11* (New York: Public Affairs, 2005).

2. Kenneth Feinberg, "What Is the Value of a Human Life?" commentary, National Public Radio *Weekend Edition,* May 25, 2008, http://thisibelieve.org/essay/45426/, accessed August 1, 2009; see also "Statement of Kenneth R. Feinberg Concerning the Announcement and Dissemination of a Final Protocol for the Distribution of the Hokie Spirit Memorial Fund," August 15, 2007, www.vtnews.vt.edu/documents/statement_of_krf_8_15_07.pdf, accessed August 1, 2009.

3. This quip is attributed to Brad Templeton. See "Bill Gates Wealth Index [1998]," www.templetons.com/brad/billg.html, accessed August 1, 2009.

4. Jean-Jacques Rousseau, *On the Social Contract,* edited by Roger D. Masters, translated by Judith R. Masters (New York: St. Martin's Press, 1978 [1762]), IV.8, p. 129.

5. Charles E. Lindblom, *The Market System: What It Is, How It Works, and What to Make of It* (New Haven, CT: Yale University Press, 2001).

6. H. Richard Niebuhr, *Christ and Culture* (New York: Harper-Collins, 1951), pp. 237–241, quote from p. 241; "The Center of Value," in *Radical Monotheism and Western Culture* (New York: HarperCollins, 1970), pp. 100–113.

7. M. Craig Barnes, "Holy Ground: A Pastoral Call," *Christian Century,* May 19, 2009, pp. 10–11.

8. The most accessible introduction to the capabilities approach, as connected to economic and human development, is Amartya Sen, *Development as Freedom* (New York: Knopf, 1999). See also Douglas A. Hicks, "Gender, Discrimination, and Capability: Insights from Amartya Sen," *Journal of Religious Ethics* 30, no. 1 (Spring 2002), pp. 137–154.

9. See Martha Nussbaum, *Women and Human Development: The Capabilities Approach* (Cambridge, UK: Cambridge University Press, 2000), pp. 78–80.

10. Martha Nussbaum, "Compassion and Terror," *Daedalus,* Winter 2003, pp. 10–26.

11. I have pursued the relationship between the capabilities approach and a Christian economic ethics in Douglas A. Hicks, *Inequality and Christian Ethics* (Cambridge, UK: Cambridge University Press, 2000); Douglas A. Hicks, "Self-Interest, Deprivation, and Agency: Expanding the Capabilities Approach," *Journal of the Society of Christian Ethics* 25, no. 1 (Spring 2005), pp. 147–167; and in Hicks, "Gender, Discrimination, and Capability."

12. *The Westminster Shorter Catechism* [1647], in *The Evangelical Protestant Creeds, with Translations,* 4th edition, vol. 3 of *The Creeds of Christendom, with a History and Critical Notes,* edited by Philip Schaff (Grand Rapids, MI: Baker Book House, 1977 [1919]), pp. 676–704, www.ccel.org/ccel/schaff/creeds3.iv.xviii.html, accessed August 1, 2009.

13. Amartya Sen, *Development as Freedom* (New York: Knopf, 1999), Figure 2.1, p. 47; United Nations Development Programme, *Human Development Report 2007/2008: Fighting Climate Change: Human Solidarity in a Divided World* (New York: Palgrave Macmillan for the UNDP, 2007), Table 1, p. 229.

14. Amartya Sen, "More Than 100 Million Women Are Missing," *New York Review of Books* 37/20, December 20, 1990, a revised and expanded version of "Women's Survival as a Development Problem," *Bulletin of the American Academy of Arts and Sciences* 43 (November 1989). For a comprehensive, updated analysis of this issue and the scholarly

debate, see Stephan Klasen and Claudia Wink, "'Missing Women': Revisiting the Debate," in *Amartya Sen's Work and Ideas: A Gender Perspective*, edited by Bina Agarwal, Jane Humphries, and Ingrid Robeyns (London: Routledge, 2005), pp. 265–301.

15. Mayra Buvinić, "Women in Poverty: A New Global Underclass," *Foreign Policy,* Fall 1997.

16. Sam Roberts, "U.S. Births Hint at Bias for Boys in Some Asians," *New York Times,* June 15, 2009, www.nytimes.com/2009/06/15/nyregion/15babies.html, accessed August 24, 2009.

17. Hicks, "Gender, Discrimination, and Capability."

CHAPTER THREE: DISCERNING DESIRES

1. The Coca-Cola Company, "World of Coca-Cola," www.worldofcoca-cola.com, accessed July 23, 2009.

2. Annys Shin, "Removing Schools' Soda Is Sticky Point: Bottlers' Contracts Limit Cash-Strapped Districts," *Washington Post,* March 22, 2007, www.washingtonpost.com/wp-dyn/content/article/2007/03/21/AR2007032101966.html, accessed August 24, 2007.

3. "Coca-Cola and Farmers Fight Over Water Use," Online News Hour Extra, November 18, 2008, www.pbs.org/newshour/extra/video/blog/2008/11/coca-cola_and_farmers_fight_ov.html, accessed July 23, 2009.

4. Milton Friedman, "The Methodology of Positive Economics," in *Essays in Positive Economics* (Chicago: Chicago University Press, 1953), pp. 3–43.

5. Adam Smith, *An Inquiry into the Nature and Causes of the Wealth of Nations,* edited by R. H. Campbell, A. S. Skinner, and W. B. Todd, *Glasgow Edition of the Works and Correspondence of Adam Smith,* 2 vols. (New York: Oxford University Press, 1976), pp. 869–870; see also Amartya Sen, "Poor, Relatively Speaking," *Oxford Economic Papers* 35 (1983), pp. 153–169.

6. I have discussed these issues in detail in Douglas A. Hicks, "Inequality, Globalization, and Leadership: 'Keeping Up with the Joneses' across National Boundaries," *Annual of the Society of Christian Ethics* 21 (2001), pp. 63–80.

7. James Duesenberry, *Income, Saving, and the Theory of Consumer Behavior* (Cambridge, MA: Harvard University Press, 1962 [1949]), p. 27.

8. Richard A. Easterlin, "The Economics of Happiness," *Daedalus,* Spring 2004, pp. 26–33.

9. U.S. Department of Agriculture Agricultural Marketing Service, "Wholesale and Farmers Markets: Farmers Markets Growth: 1994–2008," www.ams.usda.gov/AMSv1.0/ams.fetchTemplateData.do ?template=TemplateS&navID=WholesaleandFarmersMarkets&leftNav=WholesaleandFarmersMarkets&page=WFMFarmersMarketGrowth&description=Farmers%20Market%20Growth&acct=frmrdirmkt (http://tinyurl.com/market-triple), accessed June 24, 2009.

10. U.S. Energy Information Administration, "Table E1. World Primary Energy," *International Energy Annual 2006* tables, www.eia .doe.gov/pub/international/iealf/tablee1.xls, accessed August 24, 2009.

11. Benjamin Barber, *Jihad Versus McWorld* (New York: Times Books, 1995), pp. 37–38.

12. United Nations Development Programme, *Human Development Report 1998* (New York: Oxford University Press), p. 2.

13. Karl Marx, "Contribution to the Critique of Hegel's *Philosophy of Right* [1844]," in *The Marx-Engels Reader*, second edition, edited by Robert C. Tucker (Princeton, NJ: Princeton University Press, 1978 [1972]), p. 54.

14. Daniel Gilbert, "What You Don't Know Makes You Nervous," *New York Times,* May 20, 2009, http://happydays.blogs.nytimes .com/2009/05/20/what-you-dont-know-makes-you-nervous/, accessed July 23, 2009.

CHAPTER FOUR: PROVIDING

1. John Calvin, *Institutes of the Christian Religion,* edited by John T. McNeill, translated by Ford Lewis Battles, Vol. 20 of *The Library of Christian Classics* (Philadelphia: Westminster Press, 1960 [1536, 1559]), Bk. 1, Ch. 17, Para. 7, p. 219.

2. Food and Agriculture Organization of the United Nations, *The State of Food Insecurity in the World 2008* (Rome: FAO, 2008), p. 6, downloadable at www.fao.org/docrep/011/i0291e/i0291e00.htm, accessed August 25, 2009.

3. Food and Agriculture Organization of the United Nations (FAO), *World Agriculture: Towards 2015/2030—Summary Report* (Rome: FAO, 2002), p. 9, downloadable at www.fao.org/docrep/004/Y3557E/ Y3557E00.htm, accessed August 25, 2009.

4. Claire E. Wolfteich offers a winsome account of Taizé's integration of prayer and community life in her book in the Practices of Faith Series: *Lord Have Mercy: Praying for Justice with Conviction and Humility* (San Francisco: Jossey-Bass, 2006).

5. Brother Roger Schutz, *Parable of Community: The Rule and Other Basic Texts of Taizé,* translated by Emily Chisholm and the Brothers (London: Mowbray, 1981), p. 39.

6. Angélique Janssens, "The Rise and Decline of the Male Breadwinner Family? An Overview of the Debate," *International Review of Social History* 42 (1997 Supplement), pp. 1–23, quote on p. 2.

7. A classic discussion within Marx's understanding of workers, wages, and the reserve army in the development of capitalism in his chapter 25, "The General Law of Capitalist Accumulation," in *Capital* [1867], volume 1, introduced by Ernest Mandel, translated by Ben Fowkes (New York: Vintage Books, 1977), pp. 762–870.

8. Leo XIII, "*Rerum Novarum:* Of New Things—The Condition of Labor," in *Catholic Social Thought: The Documentary Heritage,* edited by David J. O'Brien and Thomas A. Shannon (Maryknoll, NY: Orbis, 1992 [1891]), pp. 14–39.

9. John A. Ryan, "Distributive Justice," in *Economic Justice,* edited by Harlan Beckley (Louisville, KY: Westminster/John Knox Press, 1996 [1942]), p. 121.

10. Janssens, "The Rise and Decline of the Male Breadwinner Family?"

11. U.S. Department of Labor, Bureau of Labor Statistics, "Employment Status by Marital Status and Sex, 2005 Annual Averages," September 2006; www.bls.gov/cps/wlf-table4-2006.pdf, accessed July 31, 2009.

12. Andrea Goodell and Thomas J. Morrisey, "Mental Health Meltdown: Depression, Stress Rise as 264,000 Michigan Jobs Lost," *Holland Sentinel,* March 26, 2009, http://nl.newsbank.com/nl-search/we/Archives?p_action=print&p_docid=1272C70B3314FB08, accessed August 24, 2009.

13. Max Weber, *The Protestant Ethic and the Spirit of Capitalism,* translated by Talcott Parsons (New York: Routledge, 1992 [1930, 1904/5]).

14. Arlie Russell Hochschild, *The Second Shift: Working Parents and the Revolution at Home* (New York: Viking, 1989); Juliet Schor, *The Overworked American: The Unexpected Decline of Leisure* (New York: Basic Books, 1992).

15. John Locke, *Second Treatise of Government,* in *Two Treatises of Government,* edited by Peter Laslett (Cambridge, UK: Cambridge University Press, 1960), chap. 5, para. 27, pp. 287–288.

16. Locke, *Second Treatise of Government,* chap. 5, para. 27, pp. 287–288.

17. Locke, *Second Treatise of Government,* chap. 5, para. 33, p. 291.

1. For one classic series of descriptions and analyses, see chapter 10, "The Working Day," in Karl Marx, *Capital* [1867], volume 1, introduced by Ernest Mandel, translated by Ben Fowkes (New York: Vintage Books, 1977), pp. 340–416.

2. International Labour Organization (ILO), "KILM 6—Hours Worked," *Key Indicators of the Labour Market,* 5th edition (Geneva: ILO, 2007), www.ilo.org/public/english/employment/strat/kilm/download/kilm06.pdf, accessed August 24, 2009.

3. Frederick Winslow Taylor, *The Principles of Scientific Management* (New York: Norton, 1911).

4. Thomas J. Peters and Robert H. Waterman, *In Search of Excellence: Lessons from America's Best-Run Companies* (New York: Warner Books, 1982).

5. Joanne B. Ciulla, "Leadership and the Problem of Bogus Empowerment," in *Ethics: The Heart of Leadership,* edited by Joanne B. Ciulla (Westport, CT: Praeger, 1998), pp. 63–86.

6. Barbara Ehrenreich, *Nickel and Dimed: On (Not) Getting By in America* (New York: Metropolitan Books, 2001).

7. Adam Smith, *An Inquiry into the Nature and Causes of the Wealth of Nations,* edited by R. H. Campbell, A. S. Skinner, and W. B. Todd, *Glasgow Edition of the Works and Correspondence of Adam Smith,* 2 vols. (New York: Oxford University Press, 1976), V.i.f.50, p. 782.

8. Matthew B. Crawford, *Shop Class as Soulcraft: An Inquiry into the Value of Work* (New York: Penguin, 2009).

9. Sonali Gulati, *Nalini by Day, Nancy by Night,* n.d., www.sonalifilm.com/nalini.html.

⌐10. A leading book on the topic is Douglas J. Schuurman, *Vocation: Discerning Our Callings in Life* (Grand Rapids, MI: Eerdmans, 2004).⌐

11. Frederick Buechner, *Wishful Thinking: A Seeker's ABC* (San Francisco: HarperOne, 1973), p. 95.

12. John Calvin, quoted in Ronald H. Stone, "The Reformed Economic Ethics of John Calvin," in *Reformed Faith and Economics,* edited by Robert L. Stivers (Lanham, MD: University Press of America, 1989), p. 37.

13. Ernst Troeltsch, *Protestantism and Progress: A Historical Study of the Relation of Protestantism to the Modern World* (Boston: Beacon Press, 1958 [1912]), pp. 129–130.

14. Nicholas Wolterstorff, *Until Justice and Peace Embrace* (Grand Rapids, MI: Eerdmans, 1983).

1. Dorothy Bass offers a rich book-length reflection of Christian practices of living in time in *Receiving the Day: Christian Practices for Opening the Gift of Time* in the Practices of Faith Series (San Francisco: Jossey-Bass, 2001).

2. E. P. Thompson, "Time, Work-Discipline and Industrial Capitalism," *Past and Present* 38 (December 1967).

3. Benjamin Franklin, *Selections from Autobiography, Poor Richard's Almanac, Advice to a Young Tradesman, The Whistle, Necessary Hints to Those That Would Be Rich, Motion for Prayers, Selected Letters* (New York: Doubleday: 1898 [1748]).

4. Benjamin Barber, *Jihad Versus McWorld* (New York: Times Books, 1995).

5. Thomas L. Friedman, *The World Is Flat: A Brief History of the Twenty-First Century* (New York: Farrar, Straus and Giroux, 2005).

6. Juliet Schor, *The Overworked American: The Unexpected Decline of Leisure* (New York: Basic Books, 1992).

7. Sylvia Ann Hewlett, *When the Bough Breaks: The Cost of Neglecting Our Children* (New York: Harper Perennial, 1991).

8. Hal R. Varian, *Intermediate Microeconomics: A Modern Approach,* 2nd ed. (New York: Norton, 1990), p. 170.

9. This differential in wage rate and hence opportunity costs is relevant to the current distribution of income in the United States. "The fact that the quantity of labor supplied increases as the wage rate increases results in the distribution of income being more unequal than the distribution of hourly wages": Michael Parkin, *Microeconomics* (Reading, MA: Addison-Wesley, 1990), p. 484.

10. This results from the "substitution effect" by which consumer goods become relatively cheaper vis-à-vis leisure when wages go up; at some point in the rise of wages, the substitution effect might be overtaken by the "income effect," in which case people would begin to supply less labor in order to purchase more leisure.

11. Milton Friedman, "The Methodology of Positive Economics," in *Essays in Positive Economics* (Chicago: University of Chicago Press, 1953), pp. 3–43.

12. Gary Becker, Friedman's successor at Chicago and like Friedman, a Nobel laureate in economics, earned his notoriety for describing what he calls "the economic approach to human behavior," including "the economic approach to the allocation of time." See Gary Becker, *The Economic Approach to Human Behavior* (Chicago: University of Chicago Press, 1978).

13. Hewlett, *When the Bough Breaks,* pp. 294, 301.

14. Hewlett, *When the Bough Breaks,* p. 91.

15. An engaging analysis of modern multi-tasking and its perils is Maggie Jackson, *Distracted: The Erosion of Attention and the Coming Dark Age* (New York: Prometheus Books, 2008).

16. Gordon Hempton, *One Square Inch of Silence: One Man's Search for Natural Silence in a Noisy World* (New York: Free Press, 2009).

17. Michael Walzer, *Spheres of Justice: A Defense of Pluralism and Equality* (New York: Basic Books, 1983), p. 192.

18. Daniel K. Finn, *The Moral Ecology of Markets: Assessing Claims About Markets and Justice* (New York: Cambridge University Press, 2006).

19. "Wal-Mart Settles Worker's Religious Bias Suit," *St. Louis Post-Dispatch,* August 23, 1995; Owen Moritz, "Biz Shalt Not Force Work on Sabbath," *New York Daily News,* April 5, 2000.

20. Louis Llovio, "Ukrop's Loses No. 1 Spot to Food Lion in Sales Survey," *Richmond Times-Dispatch,* June 18, 2009, p. A1.

21. Jeff Van Duzer examines the ways in which faith-based companies find their respective niches in market inefficiencies in "Free Markets and the Reign of God: Identifying Potential Conflicts," in *Global Neighbors: Christian Faith and Moral Obligation in Today's Economy,* edited by Douglas A. Hicks and Mark Valeri (Grand Rapids, MI: Eerdmans, 2008), pp. 109–132.

22. Thomas Schelling, *Choice and Consequence: Perspectives of an Errant Economist* (Cambridge, MA: Harvard University Press, 1984).

23. Walzer, *Spheres of Justice,* p. 193, quoting Max Weber.

24. See Accreditation Council for Graduate Medical Education, "Information Related to the ACGME's Effort to Address Resident Duty Hours and Other Relevant Resource Materials," www.acgme. org/acWebsite/dutyhours/dh_index.asp, accessed August 25, 2009; Joan Lowy, "Lawmakers Seek to Fix Pilot Fatigue, Training," ABC News, June 11, 2009, http://abcnews.go.com/Business/wireStory?id=7813427, accessed August 25, 2009.

25. Robert Putnam, *Bowling Alone: The Collapse and Revival of American Community* (New York: Simon & Schuster, 2000), pp. 80–92.

CHAPTER SEVEN: EXPANDING THE COMMUNITY

1. Anwar al-Sadat, "Statement Before the Israeli Knesset," Jerusalem, November 29, 1977, quoted in Harold H. Saunders, *The Other Walls: The Arab-Israeli Peace Process in a Global Perspective,* revised ed. (Princeton, NJ: Princeton University Press, 1991), p. vi.

2. Quoted in Saunders, *The Other Walls,* p. xi.

3. Adam Smith, *The Theory of Moral Sentiments,* edited by D. D. Raphael and A. L. Macfie, *Glasgow Edition of the Works and Correspondence of Adam Smith* (New York: Oxford University Press, 1976), III.3.4, p. 136.

4. Adam Smith, *The Theory of Moral Sentiments* III.3.4, p. 136.

5. Martha C. Nussbaum, *For Love of Country: Debating the Limits of Patriotism* (Boston: Beacon Press, 1996); Martha Nussbaum, "Compassion and Terror," *Daedalus,* Winter 2003, pp. 10–26.

6. One thoughtful book on service trips is Don C. Richter, *Mission Trips That Matter: Embodied Faith for the Sake of the World* (Nashville, TN: Upper Room Books, 2008).

7. For a fuller discussion, see Douglas A. Hicks, "Inequality, Globalization, and Leadership: 'Keeping Up with the Joneses' Across National Boundaries," *Annual of the Society of Christian Ethics* 21 (2001), pp. 63–80.

8. Douglas A. Hicks, *Inequality and Christian Ethics* (Cambridge, UK: Cambridge University Press, 2000).

9. See Robert D. Putnam, "*E Pluribus Unum:* Diversity and Community in the Twenty-First Century (The 2006 Johan Skytte Prize Lecture)," *Scandinavian Political Studies* 30, no. 2 (2007), pp. 137–174.

10. Leonardo Boff, *Ecology and Liberation: A New Paradigm,* translated by John Cumming (Maryknoll, NY: Orbis, 1995 [1993]), pp. 93–108.

11. Dani Rodrik, *One Economics, Many Recipes: Globalization, Institutions, and Economic Growth* (Princeton, NJ: Princeton University Press, 2008). An earlier article is Sudhir Anand and Martin Ravallion, "Human Development in Poor Countries: On the Role of Private Incomes and Public Services," *Journal of Economic Perspectives* 7, no. 1 (1993), pp. 133–150.

12. Robert A. Pratt, *The Color of Their Skin: Education and Race in Richmond, Virginia 1954-89* (Charlottesville, VA: University Press of Virginia, 1992), pp. 15–16.

13. John Rawls, *A Theory of Justice* (Cambridge, MA: Belknap Press of Harvard University Press, 1971), pp. 83–90.

14. John Stuart Mill, *The Collected Works of John Stuart Mill, Volume III—The Principles of Political Economy with Some of Their Applications to Social Philosophy (Books III-V and Appendices),* edited by John M. Robson, Introduction by V. W. Bladen (Toronto: University of Toronto Press, 1965). Chapter XVII: Of International Trade, http://oll.libertyfund.org/title/243/7193, accessed July 22, 2009.

15. Bono, quoted in David Waters, "Bono Hopes You, Too, Will Care," *Memphis Commercial Appeal,* December 13, 2003, p. F1.

16. Michka Assayas, *Bono in Conversation with Michka Assayas* (New York: Riverhead Books/Penguin, 2005), pp. 80–81.

17. Assayas, *Bono in Conversation with Michka Assayas,* pp. 81–82.

18. U2, *Vertigo 2005//U2 Live from Chicago* (DVD) (Universal City, CA: Universal Music and Video Distribution, 2005).

19. Direct Action and Training Research Center, "RISC—Richmonders Involved in Strengthening our Communities," www.thedart center.org/RISC.html, accessed July 21, 2009; "Colaborando Juntos," www.colaborandojuntosva.com, accessed July 23, 2009.

20. "AlterNatives," www.alternativesonline.com/, accessed July 23, 2009; "Highland Support Project," www.highlandsupportproject. org/, accessed August 1, 2009.

Chapter Eight: Doing Justice

1. Similarly, the psalmist calls righteousness and justice the foundation of God's throne (Psalm 89:14; 97:2).

2. Adam Smith, *The Theory of Moral Sentiments,* edited by D. D. Raphael and A. L. Macfie, *Glasgow Edition of the Works and Correspondence of Adam Smith* (New York, Oxford University Press, 1976 [1790]), II.ii.3.4, p. 86.

3. Leo XIII, "*Rerum Novarum:* Of New Things—The Condition of Labor," in *Catholic Social Thought: The Documentary Heritage,* edited by David J. O'Brien and Thomas A. Shannon (Maryknoll, NY: Orbis, 1992 [1891]), pp. 14–39.

4. Benedict XVI, *Caritas in Veritate,* para. 6, www.vatican.va/holy _father/benedict_xvi/encyclicals/documents/hf_ben-xvi_enc_20090629 _caritas-in-veritate_en.html (http://tinyurl.com/caritas-text), accessed July 23, 2009.

5. Paul VI, "*Populorum Progressio:* On the Development of Peoples [1967]," in *Catholic Social Thought: The Documentary Heritage,* para. 3, pp. 240–262, quote from p. 240.

6. National Conference of Catholic Bishops, *Economic Justice for All: Pastoral Letter on Catholic Social Teaching and the U.S. Economy* (Washington, DC: United States Catholic Conference, 1986), para. 68, p. 35.

7. Marc Cooper, "No Sweat: Uniting Workers and Students, a New Movement Is Born," *The Nation,* June 7, 1999, pp. 11–15; see also United Students Against Sweatshops, "History and Formation of USAS," www.studentsagainstsweatshops.org/index.php?option=com _content&task=view&id=21&Itemid=88888915, accessed July 23, 2009.

8. Jon P. Gunnemann, "Capitalism and Commutative Justice," *Annual of the Society of Christian Ethics* (1985), pp. 101–122, quote on p. 104.

9. Ten Thousand Villages, "About Us," www.tenthousandvillages .com/php/about.uis/index.php, accessed July 22, 2009; SERRV, "Frequently Asked Questions," www.serrv.org/aboutus/faq.aspx, accessed July 22, 2009.

10. Nobel Foundation, "Autobiography: Amartya Sen," from *Les Prix Nobel: The Nobel Prizes 1998,* edited by Tore Frängsmyr [Nobel Foundation], Stockholm, 1999; http://nobelprize.org/nobel_prizes/economics/laureates/1998/sen-autobio.html, accessed July 22, 2009.

11. See Jeff Van Duzer, "Free Markets and the Reign of God: Identifying Potential Conflicts," in *Global Neighbors: Christian Faith and Moral Obligation in Today's Economy,* edited by Douglas A. Hicks and Mark Valeri (Grand Rapids, MI: Eerdmans, 2008), pp. 109–132.

12. For an extended discussion of the preferential option, see Douglas A. Hicks, *Inequality and Christian Ethics* (Cambridge, UK: Cambridge University Press, 2000), pp. 174–179.

13. Gustavo Gutiérrez, "Option for the Poor," translated by Robert R. Barr, in *Mysterium Liberationis: Fundamental Concepts in Liberation Theology,* edited by Ignacio Ellacuría, S.J., and Jon Sobrino, S.J., (Maryknoll, NY: Orbis, 1993), pp. 235–250; Leonardo Boff, *Ecology and Liberation: A New Paradigm,* translated by John Cumming (Maryknoll, NY: Orbis, 1995 [1993]); Ivone Gebara, "Option for the Poor as an Option for Poor Women," in *The Power of Naming: A Concilium Reader in Feminist Liberation Theology,* edited by Elisabeth Schüssler Fiorenza (Maryknoll, NY: Orbis, 1996), pp. 142–149.

14. John XXIII, "*Pacem in Terris:* Peace on Earth [1963]," in *Catholic Social Thought: The Documentary Heritage,* para. 56, p. 140.

15. Rebecca M. Blank, *It Takes a Nation: A New Agenda for Fighting Poverty* (New York: Russell Sage Foundation and Princeton University Press, 1997), pp. 205–206.

16. Rebecca M. Blank, "A Christian Perspective on the Role of Government in a Market Economy," in *Global Neighbors,* pp. 224–247, quote on p. 243.

17. Muhammad Yunus, with Alan Jolis, *Banker to the Poor: Micro-Lending and the Battle Against World Poverty* (New York: Public Affairs, 1999).

18. Microcredit Foundation of India (MFI), *Project Report* (Chennai, India: MFI, 2002).

19. MFI, *Project Report.*

20. "Loan #2: Abrahan Teran Gutierrez," July 16, 2009, http://cuscogracias.blogspot.com/, accessed August 25, 2009.

21. Kiva, www.kiva.org, accessed July 22, 2009.

22. Kristi Heim, "The Business of Giving: Matt Flannery Answers Your Questions About Kiva," March 5, 2009, http://blog.seattletimes.nwsource.com/philanthropy/2009/03/05/microfinance_in_seattle_21_org.html, accessed July 22, 2009.

23. Oikocredit, "History," www.oikocredit.org/site/en/doc.phtml?p=History3, accessed July 22, 2009.

24. Benedict XVI, *Caritas in Veritate,* para. 6.

Chapter Nine: Sharing

1. "Live Earth Is Promoting Green to Save the Planet—What Planet Are They On?" *Daily Mail,* July 7, 2007, www.dailymail.co.uk/pages/live/femail/article.html?in_article_id=466775&in_page_id=1879, accessed July 22, 2009.

2. David Smith, "Rockin' All Over the World (But Just Watch Your Carbon Footprint)," *Observer,* July 8, 2007, http://observer.guardian.co.uk/uk_news/story/0,,2121489,00.html, accessed August 1, 2009.

3. Ben Eisen, "Sustainable for a Year," *Inside Higher Ed,* July 10, 2009, www.insidehighered.com/news/2009/07/10/sustainability, accessed August 25, 2009.

4. Tamar Lewin, "For Colleges, Small Cuts Add Up to Big Savings," *New York Times,* June 19, 2009, www.nytimes.com/2009/06/19/education/19college.html?_r=1, accessed August 25, 2009; see also "Sustainability Initiatives," Davidson College, www3.davidson.edu/cms/x31822.xml, accessed August 25, 2009.

5. Philip Elmer-Dewitt, "Summit to Save the Earth: Rich vs. Poor," *Time* 139, no. 2 (1992), pp. 42–58.

6. Roseanne Tellez, "New Eco-Friendly Milk Jugs Draw Mixed Reviews," CBS2 Chicago, June 30, 2008, http://cbs2chicago.com/consumer/milk.gallon.container.2.760663.html, accessed July 22, 2009.

7. Peter Miller, "It Starts at Home," *National Geographic,* March 2009, http://ngm.nationalgeographic.com/2009/03/energy-conservation/miller-text.html, accessed July 16, 2009.

8. Victoria Burnett, "Spain's High-Speed Rail Offers Guideposts for U.S.," *New York Times,* May 29, 2009, www.nytimes.com/2009/05/30/business/energy-environment/30trains.html?scp=6&sq=victoria%20burnett&st=cse, accessed August 25, 2009.

9. Robert Frank, *Luxury Fever: Why Money Fails to Satisfy in an Era of Excess* (New York: Free Press, 1999).

10. Peter Singer, "Famine, Affluence, and Morality," *Philosophy and Public Affairs* 1, no. 1 (1972), pp. 229–243; Peter Singer, *One World: The Ethics of Globalization* (New Haven, CT: Yale University Press, 2002).

11. Peter Singer, "America's Shame: When Are We Going to Do Something About Global Poverty?" *Chronicle of Higher Education,* March 13, 2009, http://chronicle.com/free/v55/i27/27b00601.htm, accessed July 16, 2009. This article is adapted from Singer's argument in his book *The Life You Can Save: Acting Now to End World Poverty* (New York: Random House, 2009).

12. Eric Gregory, "Agape and Special Relations in a Global Economy: Theological Sources," in *Global Neighbors: Christian Faith and Moral Obligation in Today's Economy,* edited by Douglas A. Hicks and Mark Valeri (Grand Rapids, MI: Eerdmans, 2008), pp. 16–42.

13. The cited text is Exodus 16:18.

14. Amartya Sen, "Gender and Cooperative Conflicts," in *Persistent Inequalities,* edited by Irene Tinker (New York: Oxford University Press, 1990), pp. 123–149.

15. U.S. Census Bureau, "Historical Income Tables—People—Table P 36 Full-Time, Year-Round All Workers by Median Income and Sex: 1955 to 2007," www.census.gov/hhes/www/income/histinc/p36AR.html, accessed August 25, 2009.

16. John Maynard Keynes's masterwork is *The General Theory of Employment, Interest, and Money* (New York: Harcourt and Brace, 1936).

17. Bank of America, "Keep the Change," 2008, www.bankofamerica.com/promos/jump/ktc/index.cfm?&statecheck=VA, accessed July 20, 2009.

18. Thomas Berry, *The Dream of the Earth* (San Francisco: Sierra Club Books, 1988).

19. Bill Gates Sr., "Reinstate 'the Grateful Heirs Tax,'" *Seattle Post-Intelligencer,* April 1, 2005, www.seattlepi.com/opinion/218330_gatestax01.html, accessed June 20, 2009.

20. Paul VI, "*Populorum Progressio:* On the Development of Peoples [1967]," in *Catholic Social Thought: The Documentary Heritage,* edited by David J. O'Brien and Thomas A. Shannon (Maryknoll, NY: Orbis, 1992 [1967]), pp. 240–262, quote from para. 14, p. 243.

The Author

Douglas A. Hicks is associate professor of leadership studies and religion at the Jepson School of Leadership Studies of the University of Richmond. He holds an A.B. degree in economics from Davidson College, an M.Div. from Duke University, and a Ph.D. in religion, ethics, and economics from Harvard University, where he studied with the theologian Ronald F. Thiemann and the Nobel-winning economist Amartya Sen. An ordained minister in the Presbyterian Church (USA), Hicks has held visiting faculty positions at Union-PSCE in Richmond and at the Harvard Divinity School. He is the author of three earlier books: *Inequality and Christian Ethics* (2000), *Religion and the Workplace: Pluralism, Spirituality, Leadership* (2003), and *With God on All Sides: Leadership in a Devout and Diverse America* (2009). He also edited, with Mark Valeri, *Global Neighbors: Christian Faith and Moral Obligation in Today's Economy* (2008), and the three-volume reference collection, with J. Thomas Wren and Terry L. Price, *The International Library of Leadership* (2004). Hicks is married to Dr. Catherine Bagwell, an associate professor of psychology at the University of Richmond, and they have two children, Noah and Ada.

Index

Catholic social teachings, 139–140
Charitable giving: Christian call for, 169–172; Paul's principle for, 170–171; tithing practice for, 171, 172; utilitarianism framework for, 168–169; various means available for, 167–168. *See also* Inequalities
Child labor, 142
Child obesity, 37
Children: parental practices encouraging capabilities of, 32; "quality time" with, 102
Christianity: charitable giving practice of, 169–172; concept of stewardship in, 71; Sabbath dimension of life emphasized by, 104–105, 107–108; thrift practice associated with, 12–13; tithing practice of, 171, 172; vocation notion of, 90–95. *See also* Theocentrism
Church of the Brethren, 144
Citi Field (Queens), 15
Citigroup, 15
"Citi/Taxpayer Field" proposal, 15
Ciulla, Joanne, 83
Clinton, Bill, 149, 154
Coca-Cola: connection between healthy water and, 38; global influence of, 36–39
"Coca-Cola Experience" (Atlanta), 36
Colaborando Juntos ("Working Together"), 134
Community: challenging the inequalities within, 125–127; cross-cultural bargaining example of inequalities between, 116–118, 123–124; crossing borders of our, 115–121; demographic differences of U.S., 133–134; dignity of a "one world," 115–116; finding enough to share with, 179–182; imagining our neighbors and, 121–125; market exchange used to expand, 127–130; power of cross-cultural interaction of, 130–135; sharing practice within a, 158–159. *See also* Neighbors
Commutative justice: biblical standards on, 140–141; "connector" nonprofit organizations promoting, 49, 142–145; fair trade principles as, 144–145; global challenges related to practicing, 141–142; market-clearing (or equilibrium) wages and, 146; practicing ethical standards of market exchange, 141
Consumerism: bibliocentrism as expression of, 24–25; happiness studies on drivers of, 42–44; marketing messages encouraging, 46; pressure of runaway, 3–4; shaping perceived needs to increase, 39–42; work-

spend pressures of, 8. *See also* Goods; Marketing campaigns; Materialism
Continental Express flight crash (2009), 109
Corinthian church, 170
Costco, 165–166
Council of Economic Advisors, 149
Crawford, Matthew B., 87, 88
CuscoGracias, 154

D

Dave Matthews Band, 160
Davidson College, 7, 163–164
"Death tax," 178
Desires. *See* Wants
Developing countries: challenging inequalities of developed and, 125–127; cross-cultural bargaining example of inequality of developed and, 116–118, 123–124; market exchange as bridge building for, 127–130; pollution produced by, 161
Diego, 116–118, 123–124
"Dilbert" (cartoon), 78, 83
Distributive justice: description of, 140, 147; moral legitimacy of, 149–150; preferential option for the poor concept of, 147–150, 178. *See also* Sharing
Doctrine of moral equality, 18
Doing justice. *See* Justice
Duesenberry, James, 43, 126
Duke University, 24

E

Earned Income Tax Credit, 150
Earth deficit, 177–178
Eco House (Davidson College), 164
Eco-friendly consumption, 165–167
Eco-Spider Challenge (University of Richmond), 51
Econocentrism: contrast of theocentrism and, 23–24; definition of, 23
Economic downturn (2008): consequences of the, 1; making ends meet during the, 1–4; saving more and spending less response to, 9, 12; theodicy used to understand the, 9–13
Economic productivity: building "pockets of inefficiency" within, 111; as center of value in market, 22; connection between well-being and, 80–81; costs of environmental damage when calculating, 163–167; high cultural value placed on, 2; idol of efficiency and, 101–102; perfecting efficiency of, 81–85; time viewed in context of, 99–101. *See also* Employees; Laboring/labor; Money

Economic survival: globalizing our view of, 4–5; questions related to, 1–4

Economics: building fences or constraints around, 105–110; definition of, 6; etymology exercise on meaning of, 6; managing God's household view of, 7–8; "moral ecology" of, 106–110; practicing "enough," 7–8; time imagery tied to, 101–102

Egocentrism, 23

Ehrenreich, Barbara, 85

Elijah, 103

Émile, Brother, 112

Employees: alienation of, 86–88; call-center, 87–88; family leave allowed to, 109; gender wage gap, 173–174; market-clearing (or equilibrium) wages paid to, 146; Perfection Paint and Color Company experience with, 83–85; pressures of searching for work, 89–90; Taylorism management of, 82–83, 85; "Walking around" management of, 82. *See also* Economic productivity

Enough to share, 179–182

Enron Corporation, 15

Environmental issues: challenges of personal consumption related to, 165–167; earth deficit, 177–178; eco-friendly shopping versus pollution, 49–51; Kyoto Protocol, 162; pollution produced by developing nations, 161; sharing creation and related, 159–167; sustainability commitment as, 163–164; U.S. production of pollution, 50

Equality: doctrine of moral, 18; market economy application of, 19

Esau and Jacob, 89–90

F

Fair trade principles, 144–145

Faison communities (North Carolina), 119–120

Faith: doing justice as practice of, 155–156; providence doctrine on, 56; sharing as practice of, 157–158

The fall of humankind, 79–80

Family and Medical Leave Act (1993), 109

Farmers markets, 49

Federal Aviation Administration, 109

Feinberg, Kenneth, 17, 18

Female-to-male birth rate gap, 31–32

Female-to-male wage gap, 173–174

Finn, Daniel K., 106

Five thousand fed story, 58–60, 180

Flannery, Matt, 154

Ford, Henry, 86

Forman Christian College (Pakistan), 7

Frank, Robert, 167

Franklin, Benjamin, 98, 100

Free time concept, 106

Free trade movement, 128–129

Friday Night Lights (TV show), 40

Friedman, Milton, 101

Future generations: laboring as contributing to, 175–176; preferential option for the poor and sharing with, 178; sharing with, 175–178

G

Gandhi, Mahatma, 144

Gates, Bill, 19, 131, 178

Gates, Bill, Sr., 178

Gates, Melinda, 131

Gebara, Ivone, 147

Geico marketing campaign, 40

Gender differences: differential birth rates and, 31–32; male-to-female labor force gap, 68–69; male-to-female wage gap, 173–174

Genesis (rock band), 160

Gerald R. Ford School of Public Policy (University of Michigan), 149

Gethsemani Abbey (Kentucky), 105

Global household: description of, 6; faith-based view of managing, 7, 135; finding enough to share with, 179–182; making global neighbors for increasing, 130–135; power of cross-cultural interaction to expand, 130–135; sharing with future generations, 175–178; viewing economics as managing, 7–8. *See also* Household

Global inequalities: challenging community and, 125–127; cross-cultural bargaining example of, 116–118, 123–124; distributive justice to lessen, 140, 147–150; market exchange to reduce, 127–130; social justice to lessen, 140, 150–155

Global Village, 131

Global Water Challenge, 38

Globalizing economic: cross-cultural bargaining example of inequalities of, 116–118, 123–124; learning to survive the, 4–5

God: creation in the image of, 28–29; laboring relationship to creative activity of, 79–80; Levitical codes on communal justice, 140; placing ultimate value in, 22–23; preferential option for the poor by, 147–150, 178; providence doctrine as faith in, 56–76; theocentrism on centrality of, 23; vocation as calling by, 91–92. *See also* Jesus Christ

God's shalom, 7

Good Samaritan parable, 118–119, 120, 122, 131, 170

Goods: eco-friendly consumption of, 165–167; marketing campaigns pushing, 36–40, 53; moral activity of shopping for, 46–49; nonprofit organization niche markets for international, 49; sharing our, 167–172; theocentric view of accumulating, 52–53. *See also* Consumerism

Gore, Al, 159, 160

Gospel of Luke, 24

Grameen Bank of Bangladesh, 151, 154

Gratitude, 171

Great Depression, 69

Gregory, Eric, 169

Gulati, Sonali, 88

Gutiérrez, Gustavo, 147, 148

H

Habitat for Humanity, 7

Happiness: marketing campaigns using pursuit of, 36–37, 53; pursuit of human capabilities and not, 51–53; studies on link between consumerism and, 42–44; wants versus needs and, 39–42

Health insurance coverage, 109–110

Hebrew Bible. *See* Old Testament

Hempton, Gordon, 103, 104

Hicks, Ada, 32

Hicks, Noah, 32, 35

Higher education valuation, 20–21

Highland Support Project (Guatemala), 134

Hochschild, Arlie, 111

Hokie Spirit Memorial Fund, 18

Hoosier Dome (Indianapolis), 15

Hoschschild, Arlie, 70

Hospitality: organized concept of, 64; Sahara House (India) practice of, 60–62, 65; Taizé monastery's practice of, 63–65

Household: altruism of the, 172; "cooperative conflict" of relationships in, 173; impact of market-based valuing on roles in, 173–174; sharing with future generations, 175–178. *See also* Global household

Human activity "noise," 102–105

Human capabilities: community life as central, 159; description of, 27; examples of important, 27–28; needs in the context of, 42; parental practices encouraging children's, 32; pursuit of happiness versus, 51–53; theocentric perspective of, 28–29; value context of, 28

Human dignity: advertising exploiting, 40; of a "one world" community, 115–116

Human life: conflicts over values pervading, 21–24; doctrine of moral equality applied to, 18; September 11th "Special Master" formula of, 17–18, 32

I

Idolatry, 23

India: efforts to reduce sex selective abortions in, 31; Gandhi quote on villages of, 144; Microcredit Foundation of India, 151–153, 159; partition of Bangladesh from, 145

Industrial Revolution, 8

Inequalities: challenging community and global, 125–127; cross-cultural bargaining example of, 116–118, 123–124; health insurance and health care, 20; market exchange to reduce global, 127–130; money's role in exacerbating, 19; Paul's giving principle for economic, 170–171; social and moral issues of, 17–18. *See also* Charitable giving

ING marketing campaign, 40

Inheritance tax, 178

"Inside the Happiness Factory: A Documentary" (Coca-Cola Theater), 35–36

The Institutes of the Christian Religion (Calvin), 56

International Monetary Fund, 130

International service-mission trips, 124–125

Isaiah, 51

Israel-Egypt peace negotiations, 121

It Takes a Nation: A New Agenda for Fighting Poverty (Blank), 149

J

Jackley, Jessica, 154

Jay, 116–118, 123–124

Jennifer and Rick's story, 152–153

Jesus Christ: Good Samaritan parable told by, 118–119, 120, 122, 131, 170; on life and abundance of possessions, 30; on loving your neighbor, 118; on materialism, 45, 52; preferential option for the poor practiced by, 148; rich young ruler confronting, 169–170; on theocentric view of goods, 52–53. *See also* God

Jim Crow era, 26

John Paul II, Pope, 72

John XXIII, Pope, 149

Jonah, 46

Joseph of Egypt, 175–176, 178

Jubilee 2000 campaign, 72

Jubilee year, 71–72, 75

Judaism: Jubilee year of, 71–72, 75; Sabbath dimension of life emphasized by, 104–105, 107–108

Justice: biblical principles for, 137–138; Catholic and Protestant approaches to, 139; commutative, 140–146; distributive, 140, 147–150; faith practiced through doing, 155–156; as fundamental practice of global living, 137; local, national, and global levels of, 138; sharing component of doing, 172; social, 140, 150–155

K

"Keep the change" program (Bank of America), 177

"Keeping up with the Joneses," 43–44

"Kenya Water for Schools" program, 38

Keynes, John Maynard, 176

Keynesian macroeconomic policy, 175–176

Kierkegaard, Søren, 25

King, Martin Luther, Jr., 106, 132

Kiva, 154

Kyoto Protocol, 162

L

Laboring/labor: alienation of, 86–88; blue laws on mandatory closing of stories, 108; contributing to future generations, 175–176; "the corporate way" approach to, 77–78; discerning vocation, 90–95; free trade movement and, 128–129; God's creative activity relationship to, 79–80; Industrial Age and, 80–81; notion of limiting "billable hours," 108–109; Old Testament on, 79–80; perfecting efficiency of, 81–85; Perfection Paint and Color Company experience on, 83–85; pressures of searching for work, 89–90; Taylorism management of, 82–83, 85; tradeoff between leisure and, 98–99; varied emotional and social aspects of, 78–79; "Walking around" management of, 82. *See also* Economic productivity; Toiling

Lady (loaf kneader), 66

Learning valuation, 20–21

Leave It to Beaver (TV show), 67

Leisure: commercialized practices of, 111–112; finding ways to create non-market time and, 106–110; trade-off between labor and, 98–99; vacation form of, 105–106; wage-rate as increasing rate of, 100

Leo XIII, Pope, 67, 139

Levites, 171

Levitical codes, 140

Life and work balance, 3

Life expectancy: impact of income on, 29–30; "missing women" problem and, 30–32

Live 8 concerts, 132

Live Earth concerts, 159–161, 164

Loaf ward, 66

Locke, John, 73–74

Lucas Oil Stadium (Indianapolis), 15

Luther, Martin, 90, 92, 105

Lutheran World Relief, 144

M

Macedonians, 170

Madonna, 160

Make Poverty History, 130–131

Male breadwinner ideology, 66–68

Male-to-female birth rate gap, 31–32

Male-to-female wage gap, 173–174

Marco, 153–154

"Market day," 47–48

Market economy equality, 19

Market exchange: commutative justice and ethical conditions of, 140–146; cross-cultural bargaining example of inequalities in, 116–118, 123–124; expanding community through, 127–130; fair trade principles of, 144–145

Market-clearing (or equilibrium) wages, 146

Marketing campaigns: appealing to desires and promise of happiness, 53; Applebee's, 40; encouraging consumerism, 46; Geico insurance company, 40; global impact of Coca-Cola's, 36–39; ING, 40; Nike, 40; shaping perceived needs, 39–42. *See also* Consumerism; Shopping

Marshall, Alfred, 7

Martin Luther King Jr. holiday, 106

Marx, Karl, 67, 86

Materialism: centering life around value of money and, 2, 22; happiness studies on drivers of, 42–44; needs versus wants and, 39; negative aspects of, 44–46. *See also* Consumerism

McCloskey, Deirdre, 12

McCollough, Mary Lee, 24

McCollough, Thomas E., Jr., 24, 25, 180

"McWorld," 98

Mealtime prayer, 56–57

Medicare crisis, 181

Mennonite Central Committee, 144

Mia, Kader, 145–146

Thrift: as economic downturn (2008) response, 9; practice of Christian, 12–13; simplifying without exiting approach to, 13–14. *See also* Money

Time: economic view of, 99–101; economic-based imagery for, 101–102; finding ways to create nonmarket, 106–110; modern "spending" of, 97–98; relationship between money and, 97–99; as resource, 99

Tithing, 171, 172

Toiling, 80–81. *See also* Laboring/labor

Trinity College (Cambridge University), 8

Troeltsch, Ernst, 92

U

U2's 2005–06 Vertigo world tour, 131–132

Ukrop, Joe, 107

Ukrop, Robert S., 108

Ukrop's (grocery chain), 107–108

UN Food and Agriculture Organization, 4, 57

UNICEF, 4

United Nations, 5

United Nations Development Programme, 50, 130, 131

United Nations Millennium Development Campaign, 131, 133

United States: child obesity in the, 37; demographical differences of communities in the, 133–134; differential male/female birth rates in the, 32; economic issues facing the, 181; growing national debt of the, 176; labor and economic well-being in the, 80–81; life expectancy in the, 29; pollution rates in the, 50

University of Michigan, 142, 149

University of North Carolina at Chapel Hill, 142

University of Richmond, 48, 51

University of Wisconsin at Madison, 142

Urban, Keith, 160

U.S. Census Bureau's poverty threshold, 2–3

U.S. Department of Commerce, 149

USAS (United Students Against Sweatshops), 142–143

Utilitarianism, 168–169

V

Vacation industry, 111–112

Value/valuation: barriers to accurately measuring, 21; conflicts over human life, 21–24; economic productivity as center of market, 2, 22; God as ultimate center of, 22–23; of higher education and learning, 20–21; human capabilities in context of, 28; of human life, 17–18; impact on household roles and chores by, 173–174; living faithfully by shifting our, 33; September 11th "Special Master" formula of, 17–18, 32

Virginia Tech massacre (2007), 18

Vocare (to call), 90

Vocatio (calling), 90

Vocation: child rearing and working components of, 91; conscious reflection in theocentric view of, 93–95; definition and meaning of, 90–91; employment aspect of, 92–93; religious framing of, 91–92, 105

W

Wages: male-to-female gap in, 173–174; market-clearing (or equilibrium), 146

"Walking around" management, 82

Wall Street bailout (2008), 5

Walmart, 85, 107

Walzer, Michael, 19, 105–106

Wants: consumerism driven by, 42–44; marketing campaigns appealing to, 53; needs versus, 39; recreating practices tied to discerning, 112–113. *See also* Needs

Weber, Max, 12, 69

What Is Life Worth? (Feinberg), 18

Williams, Archbishop Rowan, 10, 11

Winfrey, Oprah, 154

Women: birth rate gap between men and, 31–32; wage gap suffered by, 173–174

Wordsworth, William, 8

Work-and-spend cycle, 3–4

Working women, 68–69

Workplace: call-center, 87–88; sociality and friendships at the, 110–111; Taylorism management of, 82–83, 85; "Walking around" management of, 82

World Bank, 4, 130

World Council of Churches, 140

World Health Organization, 4

"World of Coca-Cola" museum (Atlanta), 35–36

World Trade Organization, 130

World Vision, 154

Wright, Jonathan, 48

WWF (formerly World Wildlife Fund), 38

Y

Yunus, Muhammad, 151, 154